THIS IS MADNESS

*A critical look at psychiatry
and the future of mental
health services*

edited by

Craig Newnes, Guy Holmes
and Cailzie Dunn

PCCS BOOKS
Ross-on-Wye

First published in 1999

PCCS BOOKS
Llangarron
Ross-on-Wye
Herefordshire
HR9 6PT
UK
Tel +44 (0)1989 77 07 07
email enquiries@pccsbks.globalnet.co.uk

This is Madness
**A Critical Look at Psychiatry and the Future of Mental Health
Services**

British Library Cataloguing in Publication Data.
A catalogue record for this book is available from the British Library.

ISBN 1 898059 25 X

Cover design by Denis Postle.
Front cover photograph by kind permission of
Peter Lehmann (1990) *Der Chemische Knebel.*
Back cover photograph by Dr Vivien Lewis.
Printed by Redwood Books, Trowbridge, Wiltshire, UK.

CONTENTS

Part Three: Alternatives and alliances

Part Four: Beyond psychiatry

DEDICATION

To John Winter,
for his kindness, his generosity and his friendship.

ACKNOWLEDGEMENTS

THE EDITORS WOULD like to thank the contributors, all those who participated in the Thinking About Psychiatry course, members of Shelton Patients' Council, the management of Shropshire's Community and Mental Health Services NHS Trust, especially Terry Cripps, Dorothy Rowe for her kind help, Jonathan Calder for writing our press relesase, Suzy Colville, Helen Raisewell, Sue Davies, Isabel Goodwin, Eustace Johnson, Biza Stenfert Kroese and Pete and Maggie at PCCS Books for their unflagging enthusiasm. And our mums and dads.

INTRODUCTION

Be wary of any number with a nine in it.
Sid G, a man in a cafe, a man with no shares in a share-
owning democracy

IT IS MARCH 1999. I am sitting in my local cafe listening to an
impoverished man explain how to win next Saturday's rollover
lottery jackpot. 'Be wary of any number with a nine in it . . . look
out for the ones . . . twenty-one, thirty-one, eleven . . . one . . . they'll
all be coming up.' Glancing down at my newspaper, I notice an
article about the *Millennium Show at the Millennium Dome*: the
powerful, the rich, the famous and the beautiful are all planning to
see in the new millennium on the back of Sid's money.

In the same newspaper there is an article describing (yet
another) survey that links poverty and poor housing to physical
and mental health problems, and (yet another) report of the Labour
government's intention to keep to its pledges to set a minimum
wage that makes people poor and to rate-cap any Local Authority
that significantly increases its expenditure.

This is madness.

Help is on hand, however, because in our society there is a
system that claims to have treatments that can cure madness. It is
something that we find even more maddening than a lottery-
sponsored millennium dome. Occasionally known as the psy-
complex, more often referred to as the mental health system, in
this book we have simply called it psychiatry.

Information is power.
Michel F, a French psychologist and philosopher

John Sweeny, journalist of the year in 1998, said that good journalism enables the people without power to discover what the people with power know. One of the main aims of this book is to provide people who feel powerless when faced with the psychiatric system, be they psychiatric survivors, in-patients, friends, relatives or professionals within the system, with insights into what the psychiatric system is really like and ideas about what might constitute a better response to madness in our society. Armed with this information, it is hoped that people will be able to challenge, change or perhaps escape the psychiatric system. This might occur at various levels. One reader might be able to prevent electroconvulsive therapy (ECT) being given to a person who does not know about the consequences of electric shocks going through the brain. Another might become aware of and subsequently seek alternatives to 'treatments' as ways of living with, surviving or overcoming psychological distress. Perhaps another will be inspired to follow the examples of people like Pam Jenkinson and Brian Davey (see later chapters), who, when they saw the psychiatric system for what it is rather than what they imagined or hoped it to be, set up their own alternative means of providing help outside the mental health services.

Who knows what benefits information can bring?

If you know your history . . . then you would know where you coming from.
Bob M, a rastafarian, a songwriter, an inspiration

One of the challenges that this book lays down is a challenge to the idea that the psychiatric system is largely benign, and that there has been continual progress towards more humane and helpful ways of alleviating psychological distress. The chapters in this book, including the opening chapter by Craig Newnes on the history (or histories) of psychiatry, question such a view. The *stories* in these chapters offer insights into how the current system has come to be characterised by treatments that can harm rather than help, by 'experts' who seem to be on a different planet to the 'patients', by systems that sometimes crush people who are different, by categorising, monitoring, and removing people, and by coercion rather than care.

A balancing rather than a balanced view.
David C, a voice for many that have been silenced, and
chapter writer in this book

David Crepaz-Keay, whilst facilitating a workshop on medication
during the 'Thinking about Psychiatry' course (a course which inspired
the writing of this book), used this phrase to describe the aim of his
workshop. He meant that the literature, newspapers and psychiatric
system were full of people extolling the virtues of psychotropic
medication, and he was going to provide some balance to this by
solely concentrating on the negative aspects of medication. In a similar
way, this book aims to provide a balancing view to the notion that
psychiatry is benign and the best way of responding to madness.

The psychiatric system gives weight to expert opinion; this
book gives weight to the lived experience of people. Thus half of the
chapters are written by people who have been in the system. Peter
Campbell gives an historical overview of the user/psychiatric system
survivor movement. Others from this movement write about their
experiences and give a voice to the experiences of many others who
have survived, and sometimes not survived, their involvement with
psychiatric services (see chapters by Marese Hudson, Ron Coleman
and David Crepaz-Keay). Alongside these accounts, the chapters
from mental health workers and academics also attempt to balance
prevailing psychiatric opinion that both medicalises and
individualises psycho-social problems. Thus the bedrock of
psychiatry, diagnosis and the medical model, is critiqued by Mary
Boyle in terms of its lack of validity and usefulness as a means of
describing (let alone alleviating) the misery and pain of those
diagnosed as mentally ill. The idea that schizophrenia is an illness
and can be treated like other medical illnesses, a view constantly
repeated by psychiatrists, mental health workers, organisations
such as SANE, the newsmedia, politicians, as well as by many
people with the diagnosis and their relatives, is challenged by Mary
and, amongst others in this book, Ron Coleman and Lucy
Johnstone. People's immediate and more distal (e.g. social)
environment is given much greater weight as a counterbalance to
the emphasis in the 1990s on genes and biochemistry. Poverty,
abuse, and sexual and racial discrimination are given far greater
credence as factors in the creation of human distress (see chapters
by Jennie Williams, and Nimisha Patel and Iyabo Fatimilehin).
Alleviation of that distress requires changes in people's environment,
whether that be their family or home environment (see the chapter

by Lucy Johnstone), their work or educational environment (see chapters by Brian Davey and Tracey Austin), their community (see chapters by Valerie Noble and Rachel Winters) or the wider, social environment (see chapters by Jennie Williams, and Nimisha Patel and Iyabo Fatimilehin).

The need for alternatives to psychiatry is clear when one reads the chapters by Marese Hudson, David Crepaz-Keay and Katy Arscott (on hospitalisation, medication and electroconvulsive therapy respectively). Some of the alternatives described in this book include the exploration of meaning behind so-called symptoms of mental illness (see the chapters by Ron Coleman on hearing voices, and Peter Hulme and Lucy Johnstone on people with a diagnosis of schizophrenia), crisis houses run separately from mental health services and not staffed by mental health professionals (Pam Jenkinson's chapter), self help and user-led initiatives (Vivien Lindow's chapter), work within communities to reduce and ameliorate the causes of psychological distress and accessing meaningful work and education opportunities (chapters by Brian Davey and Tracey Austin).

Ron Coleman emphasises the need for alliances when tackling something as powerful as psychiatry. David Pilgrim and Lesley Waldron show how mental health professionals and users of services can work together, sharing and exchanging their expertise in attempts to improve and change the current system. This chapter, like many others in the book, provides a balancing view to the notion that 'mental health professionals know best'. The final chapter (by Craig Newnes and Guy Holmes) entertains the possibility of a future that is released from this hubris; a future where people's expertise relates more to what they have learned from their experiences and the personal skills that they have in helping people, rather than their professional status. It draws together all the conclusions from the preceding chapters in an attempt to map out a radical alternative to the current mental health system. Future responses to what we tend to call madness need not be so mad.

'Nothing that goes on in the psychiatric hospital is remotely normal'
Olive B, a psychiatric survivor and participant on the Thinking about Psychiatry course

In the past five years in Shropshire, two courses ('Thinking about Psychiatry' and 'Alternatives to Psychiatry') were organised by a mix of ex-users of psychiatric services and mental health professionals, and were attended by a mix of current and past users of psychiatric services, qualified professionals, people in training and interested others. The people who lectured and ran workshops on the courses are largely the chapter writers in this book. The bringing together of these people was intended to encourage and enable an open and frank debate, and to allow people to exchange their experiences and ideas in a way that rarely happens in the mental health system. It is hoped that on reading the book, whatever your background and whatever your views, you too will have found plenty to make you think.

CHAPTER 1

Histories of psychiatry

CRAIG NEWNES

History has had assigned to it the task of judging the past, of instructing the present for the benefit of the ages to come. To such lofty functions this work does not aspire. Its aim is merely to show how things actually were. (Ranke, 1952)

IMAGINE YOU ARE a parent with three children, you have recently lost a part-time job and your marriage is a loveless mixture of argument and unhappiness. You have a fair idea of why you feel so lousy in the mornings and why the future looks so bleak. In the middle of a consultation with your doctor about your youngest child's health you find yourself crying. Your doctor first suggests anti-depressants and later an appointment with a psychiatrist. You picture a gentle, concerned older man offering some comfort and clarification of your difficulties. When you arrive for your appointment your psychiatrist is not only late but younger than you expected and seems to be in a hurry. You are told that you have a brain biochemical imbalance and that you will need to take some tablets that will help you sleep, but if things don't improve then a rest may help. Soon after you refuse to eat or leave the house and you are admitted to the psychiatric ward of your local hospital. After a sleepless night in a dormitory shared with fifteen other people you are visited the next day by someone who identifies themselves as a member of a psychiatric advocacy group. She wants to know if you have any concerns about the way you have been dealt with so far and if all the unwanted effects of your medication have been fully explained to you. Later you meet a student nurse arriving to work for the first time on a psychiatric ward. She tells you that she started her training because of the need to earn a living and a vague notion of being helpful to people in distress. She has been taught that late twentieth century psychiatry is a powerful amalgam of psychosocial and medical interventions which lead inexorably to people getting better. This help is offered in the context of a multidisciplinary team where skilled professionals share their expertise in a concerted effort to help patients and their families. The ward is a curious mixture of disinterested and charming nursing staff, patients dulled by medication and other patients who are angry or grateful to find themselves there. Some staff seem very nice but their kindness stems from a natural humanity rather than from any systematic training. Consultant psychiatrists conduct ward rounds in a dizzying variety of ways, many patients seem to have little access to their consultants and certain members of the professional team, notably clinical psychologists, are simply absent. Indeed, most forms of therapy which the student's course has dutifully discussed are also absent, and the patients complain that their stay is dominated by a sense that staff are too busy to talk to them and that their drugs make daily life miserable. Some fear that if they step out of line they will be detained against their will.

Attempts to alleviate human misery and understand people are grounded in a cultural context shaped by major social movements, particularly science and religion: the 'mad or bad' debate. Within this overall societal context many formal histories of psychiatry merge. Any student of psychiatry is likely to come across some or all of these histories; each one needs to pass some key tests before being are acceptable to us, not least of which is whether the history can help make sense of our experience of mental health services. For patients and practitioners alike the search for meaning will be guided by the particular histories they are offered.

The essential problems for any historian attempting to fulfil Ranke's ideal of portraying things how they really were are that a great deal of historical data may be available but little of it reflects the daily experience of peoples' lives, accounts are difficult to verify and, in the case of psychiatry, the experience of the patient is largely absent. This chapter examines several ways of telling the history of psychiatry and concludes with an attempt to understand how psychiatry has come to a position whereby both the patient's and student nurse's experiences outlined above are common in contemporary mental health services.

Conflicting histories of psychiatry

Tosh (1984) suggests six main themes pursued by the historian: politics, ideas, language, economy, society, and mentalities: the history of psychiatry falls within the general ambit of social history. This history is usually presented as a chronology focussed on North American or European developments since the mid nineteenth century (see, for example, Berrios and Freeman, 1991; 1996; Berrios and Porter, 1995; Shorter, 1997).

In recent years, general histories of psychiatry have focussed on particular perspectives, most notably the perspective of gender, with major contributions from Showalter (1987), Ussher (1991) and Faith (1993). Allen (1986), however, remarks that the inclusion of her chapter in *The Power of Psychiatry* (Miller and Rose, 1986) on psychiatry's approach to women as a special issue is 'curious and misleading' as the 'female is not the "special" but the *normal* form of the psychiatric patient' (p. 85). She further notes that standard texts in psychiatry routinely refer to the patient as male even when acknowledging that the majority of patients have always been female. Although this female majority has been something of a given for students of mental health history, careful exploration of the data can still occasionally reveal a different picture. Busfield (1986) notes that the 1844 report of the Metropolitan Commission in Lunacy indicates that there were slightly more women than men in charitable institutions, but by the end of the century the proportions had been reversed. In general, however, women have received more invasive treatments more often than men, frequently for so called conditions which reflect nothing more than the woman's place in society. Late nineteenth century women were incarcerated as mad for wanting to marry the wrong man, or planning to leave home for a career; they were diagnosed as hysteric, and given a hysterectomy, for expressing rage in ways uncomfortable to their families. Hysterectomy was but one of a range of surgical procedures carried out on women considered mad. In 1866 Isaac Baker Brown pioneered the clitoridectomy as a treatment for female epilepsy and mania: in 1867 he was stripped of his Fellowship of the Obstetrical Society (Fennell, 1996).

The records of many women patients of early twentieth century asylums reveal a diagnosis of 'love affair' for those admitted after falling pregnant out of wedlock; in the 1920s women diagnosed with schizophrenia were again given hysterectomies; for much of the mid-twentieth century the experiences of women in psychiatric hospitals commonly included rape and assault by staff and other patients; in the 1960s huge numbers of distressed women were given barbiturates, in the 1970s, Valium and in the 1980s, Ativan; now, millions receive Prozac. A feminist historian might argue that this history is simply one aspect of the way in which women's bodies and minds have never been allowed to be their own. _historical_

Histories of treatment

Accounts and histories of particular physical treatments appear on a regular basis (e.g., Johnson, 1982; Swazey, 1974). Some have been scathingly critical. Valenstein (1986), for example, has shown that early claims of cure for patients undergoing frontal lobotomy were hugely exaggerated. He notes in particular that Moniz, awarded the Nobel Prize for medicine in 1949, was unable to demonstrate that any of his patients were enabled to live outside the hospital. Indeed, for the majority of patients the outcome was one of surgically induced apathy. Freeman and Watts had been responsible for a new surgical procedure in 1937, the severing of nerve connections between the frontal lobes and the remainder of the brain. This became the standard lobotomy until Freeman pioneered the transorbital lobotomy in 1945. In this modified procedure, an ice pick was inserted through the eye socket in order to sever nerve connections. Famously, in 1947 Freeman persuaded the relatives of an uncooperative patient to hold him down while he administered some bursts of Electro Convulsive Therapy (ECT). While the patient was unconscious Freeman performed a transorbital lobotomy; and all of this in a motel room. Between 1936 and 1951 over 18,000 lobotomies were performed in the US. The first leucotomies in England were performed by Golla, at Bristol's Burden Neurological Unit in December 1940 (Fennell, 1996). By 1954 over 12,000 leucotomies had been performed in England and Wales. The treatment gradually fell from favour as neuroleptic drugs, introduced in the early 1950s, were found to produce the same desired blunting effect on mood and motivation. A more sophisticated version of the procedure remains although it is rarely used and prospective patients must be given relatively extensive information about the risks, a process unheard of in the heyday of psychosurgery. The treatment is now one of last resort but in the 1950s was simply the most dramatic in a wide ranging battery of interventions carried out on 'empirical' grounds, i.e., in the hope that one would work. Fennell (1996) remarks that a patient at this time could begin with insulin coma, before receiving ECT; finally lobotomy was carried out, sometimes several times.

The history of the use of electricity on people in distress is an unsettling mixture of the comic and the barbaric. In antiquity electric eels were applied to slothful and melancholic individuals. Slaves wishing to escape their plight in nineteenth century America could find themselves with a diagnosis of drapetomania if they ran away too many times, the cure for which was electric shocks to their genitals. Strabeneck (1986) reports that an English physician, Allbutt, in 1872 passed electric currents through patients' heads as a cure for mania, melancholy and 'brain wasting'. By the 1914-18 war electrical experimentation was common in psychiatry. A particularly harrowing account of the application of electric shocks to the inside of the throats of shell shocked and mute soldiers can be found in Barker (1991). The idea that the induction of epileptic type seizures might cure schizophrenia led Cerletti and Bini, in 1938, to experiment with electric shocks to the head. Jones and Baldwin (1992) note that Cerletti failed to seek ethical approval for applying electric shocks to a vagrant referred to hospital for observation and diagnosed with schizophrenia. After the first shock, the patient called out, 'Not another one! It's deadly', but Cerletti and Bini continued and induced the desired convulsion. Cerletti immediately named the new procedure 'electroshock'. Since such humble, if alarming, beginnings, electroshock, renamed Electro Convulsive Therapy, has proliferated. It was first carried out in England by Walter and Golla in Bristol and was used increasingly at Bethlem from 1940 (Fennell, 1996). It has been used for a wide variety of diagnosed conditions and has been particularly recommended for elderly depressed people. It now has its own journal, *Convulsive Therapy*, and society, The Association for Convulsive Therapy (Breggin, 1991, informs us that Gary Aden, first president of this society's forerunner, The International Psychiatric Association for the Advancement of Electrotherapy, voluntarily gave up his medical license in 1989 after allegations of having sex with patients, beating and finally *branding* them with his initials. p 213). Meanwhile numerous studies have attempted, without success, to demonstrate its efficacy: any beneficial effects generally only last a month, evidence according to Breggin (1991) that ECT's negative *and* positive effects are due to brain damage. Concerns about its safety have been rebutted over the past sixty years by psychiatrists who claim that they would willingly undergo the treatment themselves.

Valenstein (1996) has remarked that many treatments like lobotomy and ECT have been described along the lines of heroic efforts being made by courageous pioneers working at the margins of discovery in alleviating human distress. Such accounts are unlikely to admit that doctors don't quite know what they are doing and that professionals are engaged in an experimental programme where the public are their unwitting guinea pigs. Any account which suggested that psychiatric treatments are experimental and unnecessary rather than systematic and crucial to the patient's well being would run the risk of revealing physicians and others as heroic only in the sense that they have been prepared to sacrifice others in the search for cure. Such an account would be far more likely to be written from a perspective suggesting that treatments sit within a context where economic imperatives are just as important as humane ones. Various recent histories of drug treatment (for example, Healy, 1997; 1998; and Fisher and Greenberg, 1998) and the drug industry (Braithwaite, 1984) often do more than hint at just such a perspective.

Drugs have been used to change mood and consciousness for thousands of years. The development of modern psychiatry is inextricably linked to drug-based attempts to change particular moods and behaviour deemed undesirable. Cannabis was regularly used by eighteenth century mad-doctors to suppress behaviour. The growth of the asylum and subsequent overcrowding saw a rise in conduct which asylum staff found unacceptable or inconvenient. The Victorian era already had a tradition of the use of opium and it was a natural progression to extend this usage to those proving difficult to handle in asylums: by 1870, morphine was the drug of choice for troublesome patients. The mid-nineteenth century saw extensive experimentation with ether, chloroform and the bromides of potassium and ammonium, the latter continuing until the 1930s, despite the danger of bromism (the sought-after sedation was often accompanied by bromide induced hallucinations and paranoia: Medewar, 1992). By the mid 1870s, chloral hydrate, an hypnotic, had replaced morphia at the centre of psychiatry's drug cornucopia. The less desirable effects of chloral ranged from nausea to death but it was used almost universally until the 1930s. Fennell (1996) suggests that the abolition of mechanical constraint in late nineteenth century psychiatric hospitals was achieved by the substitution of chemical restraint. The use of strychnine and hyoscyamine as powerful, if potentially lethal, sedatives was popular until the establishment of paraldehyde as a common way of suppressing unwanted behaviour. Its faintly nauseating characteristic smell remained a feature of psychiatric life until the

1960s. Nurses were warned when administering it to use glass syringes due to its destructive effect on plastic. All these drugs were introduced following the empirical principle: if it works, continue with the treatment, if it doesn't, change the dose or change the drug. All were primarily introduced in order to pacify unruly patients in crowded institutions. The two major psychotropic drugs of the twentieth century, chlorpromazine and lithium, were introduced for the same reason. It is only later that drug companies and individual researchers have attempted to justify their use by reference to theories of neurotransmitter deviation or brain biochemical imbalance as the cause of psychiatric disorder which necessitates drug treatment. In fact no research to date has demonstrated a brain biochemical abnormality in anyone diagnosed manic depressive or depressed and attempts to show that people with a diagnosis of schizophrenia have something wrong with their brains are doomed to failure as all research subjects have already been treated with neuroleptics, a group of drugs known to cause brain changes.

Delay and Deniker published the first report of the use of chlorpromazine (later sold under the name Largactil) in France in 1952, followed in Canada by Lehmann in 1954 (Breggin, 1991). Healy (1998) has used interviews with such pioneers to chart the development of psychopharmacology as a discipline. As he says in the preface to 'The Psychopharmacologists':

> In the case of the natural experiment that is psychopharmacology, those who were around at the birth of the new species are for the most part alive and can answer back. This is a challenge that neither the historian nor the scientist should shirk. (Healy, 1998 p. xiii)

De Chadarevian (1997) explores the pitfalls and advantages of using the interview as a way of establishing historical events, critically reminding us that memory is constantly changing in order to meet the perceived requirements of the present. The outcome is frequently a reconstruction of the past which puts the narrator in the best possible light or at least one which suits the purpose of the story teller. Early drug researchers, however, claimed no effect on hallucinations or delusions after the administration of neuroleptics but noted the chemically induced indifference and lack of mobility. These effects were highly desirable in the management of difficult individuals. Less desirable were the effects characteristic of tardive dyskinesia, a condition induced by chlorpromazine and related neuroleptic drugs. This condition is marked by involuntary mouth and limb movements, sweating, an odd gait and other signs which stigmatize the sufferer. Breggin (1991) estimates that up to ten million people a year in North America alone are now given neuroleptics (often called anti-psychotics in an attempt to disguise the real tranquillizing action of the drug). David Hill (1983) has estimated that sixty million neuroleptic recipients have drug-induced tardive dyskinesia.

Lithium was first hailed for its sedating properties before being marketed as a way of restoring the hypothetical brain biochemical imbalance in those with a diagnosis of manic depression or hypomania. It is striking that early, frank, accounts of the effects of morphine, chloral hydrate, chlorpromazine and lithium are very similar, emphasizing the sedative effects of these drugs and the consequent advantages to physicians charged with the care of unruly patients. There were, and remain, other advantages however, not least of which is the potential profit to pharmaceutical companies. Originally regarded as 'ethicals', in contrast to the manufacturers of fake potions and curatives, drug companies have become multi-national conglomerates generating thousands of jobs and vast profits. Their history is interwoven with that of the profession of psychiatry and its treatment orientation. They are not beyond the occasional sleight of hand: Healy (1991) for example, suggests that the development of certain psychiatric drugs is so costly, but their effects so similar, that drug companies are forced to invent conditions, for example panic disorder, for which particular drugs can then be marketed. These drugs have such similar properties to other drugs which are less expensive that they would simply fail in the open market without the suggestion that they can have a specific effect on certain psychiatric disorders.

The development of physical interventions in psychiatry has been matched by a proliferation of psychotherapeutic approaches. Szasz (1978) traces the development of therapy and counselling to Martin Luther's 'cure of souls'. While many late eighteenth century and early nineteenth century mad-doctors (Scull, 1993) had little to offer the insane over and above purging, restraining and variations on the humoral theme, some were offering what came to be known as moral treatment and others Mesmerism. Both forms of therapy were generally less invasive and destructive than the more traditional methods that medicine offered although Foucault has famously criticised moral treatment for its substitution of external with internal imprisonment (visible, external constraints like strait-jackets are replaced by invisible, but stronger, internal constraints like guilt). Modern psychotherapy can properly be traced back to Freud's explorations in psychoanalysis (see, Freedheim, 1992; Gauld, 1992). There is, however, no shortage of critics of psychotherapeutic practice, a kind of anti-psychotherapy movement, who have also used historical research to good effect (Masson, 1993; Szasz, 1978). The varieties of psychotherapy for people in distress have ranged from simply listening to people, through five times weekly psychoanalysis to sky diving and nude marathon encounter groups. Fashion and politics have played a major part in the development of therapies. The two World Wars saw massive expansion in the use of group therapies, partly because of the need to offer therapy to so many distressed people, notably shell shocked soldiers, and partly because military personnel were already familiar with working in groups, albeit for quite different ends. The usefulness or otherwise of psychotherapy was seriously challenged by the psychologist Eysenck in the 1950s but the proliferation of different therapies in the liberal 1960s made meaningful comparative reasearch immensely difficult. This problem continues to this day with over five hundred types of psychotherapy available and researchers notoriously distant from the real world of psychotherapeutic practice which, in the main, is hidden from view in one-to-one counselling sessions not accessible to the researcher's scrutiny. After over one hundred years of psychotherapeutic research it has been possible to agree that the main ingredient in successful psychotherapy is the relationship between therapist and client (known as the therapeutic alliance). Despite a matching proliferation in training schemes and accreditation bodies, however, it is impossible to *teach* therapists how to have good therapeutic alliances. Hence success rates remain constant across therapeutic methods and schools. It remains true that psychotherapy is seen as less harmful than invasive psychiatric procedures, one reason why talking therapies are heavily endorsed by the user movement.

Distress and disorder
Alongside histories of intervention and the professionalisation of helping are numerous accounts of disease and disorder, for example, delusions (Munro, 1999), psychiatric symptomatology (Berrios, 1996), melancholia (Jackson, 1986), eating disorder (Jacobs Brumberg, 1988), and neurosis (Drinka, 1984). Some commit the

historian's sin of retranslating the past in terms of the present: thus various states of mind and distress from a century or more ago are interpreted as *really* being forms of depression or schizophrenia. Critical accounts of the history of particular diagnostic entities (e.g., schizophrenia: Boyle, 1990; Hill, 1983) tend to be published less often than perspectives which support the disease model. Notably lacking from many accounts of these so-called disorders is any real acknowledgement that psychiatric conditions are categorizations and linguistic constructions rather than disease entities in the way say, influenza, is a real physical disorder with known aetiology and predictable course. Many histories of psychiatric disorder have the curious habit of mentioning Szasz or other major critics without grasping that a Szaszian view, if taken seriously, reveals fundamental flaws in the conceptual framework of psychiatric diagnosis and renders detailed discussion of differences in diagnosis or the criteria for certain supposed conditions irrelevant. This process is like including a section on atheism in a book on religious faith and expecting the reader to continue to tolerate the theist position having understood the atheistic argument. The whole diagnostic enterprise has come in for recent critical historical analysis (Kirk and Kutchins, 1992), where, far from being a scientific categorization of disorder, psychiatric diagnosis is revealed as an arbitrary procedure mostly determined by political and social processes to meet mostly social and economic ends. Diagnostic categories reflect the spirit of any given age and are as much a matter of fashion as science. Acidie, a condition featuring a combination of sloth and melancholy affected religious recluses in the seventh and eighth centuries. It was viewed as a sin because sufferers neglected prayer. Hysteria, neurasthenia, and masturbatory insanity were rife in the nineteenth century but had disappeared by the early 1900s. Psychopathy was first described in 1835 but was little diagnosed until the 1950s. Debates about its validity as a diagnostic category continue as some urge for the criminalisation of people whose essential 'disorder' is their potential for violence. Schizophrenia, invented by Bleuler in 1911, had several derivatives, but hebephrenia and paraphrenia are now rarely discussed. Debates in the 1950s and 1960s about the subtle distinctions between autism and child-hood schizophrenia have been replaced by argument over the existence of attention deficit disorder. Agoraphobia, commonly diagnosed in the 1970s, is now more often referred to as panic disorder, and the catch-all 'personality disorder' has become a short-hand for numerous behavioural and characterlogical traits that no-one understands. In the field of dementia distinctions between Pick's and Alzheimer's disease as *pre*-senile dementias has disappeared as Alzheimer's has become the preferred name for all dementias. Finally, homosexuality, a crime in the nineteenth century, was classed a disease in the middle of the twentieth and then voted out of the psychiatric classificatory system in the 1970s to be replaced by ego-dystonic homosexuality (unhappiness with a homosexual orientation).

Breggin has made the point that the idea of psychiatric disorder, for example depression, has to be sold to the public and prescribing physicians along with the supposed treatment. The increase in the diagnosis of attention deficit hyperactivity disorder (ADHD) in children is a case in point. Increasing numbers of children are diagnosed with a disorder the criteria for which include many examples of quite ordinary behaviour. The purpose of such diagnoses seems to be to legitimise certain actions which might include prescription of the drug Ritalin, instead of assessment for special schooling or examining the need to change the school.

Institutions and founding figures

For the modern student of mental health history, accounts of treatment and disorder are frequently linked to the histories of institutions and individual pioneers. In Britain, for example, Busfield (1986) notes that Bedlam began to specialise in the care of mad people during the fourteenth century (a riot about the state of the food quickly followed). Norwich established Bethel Hospital, an endowed institution for the insane in 1713. One of the earliest critics of the for-profit private madhouses was Daniel Defoe who thought they should 'be suppressed at once' (Defoe, 1728). The first lunatic asylum to be so-called was established in York in 1777. The York Retreat opened as a Quaker establishment in 1796. By the mid-1820s voluntary asylums had been established at Moorfields in London, Montrose in Scotland, Exeter, Lincoln, Manchester, Newcastle-upon-Tyne and Oxford. There were many more private institutions. Analyses of the economic benefits of coercive psychiatry can be found in accounts of the profits to be made by private mad-houses in the 'lunacy trade' (Parry-Jones, 1976). Asylums quickly grew in number and size: by 1800 Bethlem had more than doubled its resident inmates. The Lunatics Act enabled counties to erect asylums for pauper and criminal lunatics. County asylums were soon opened in Nottingham, Bedford, Norfolk and Lancaster. Busfield notes that the average asylum housed 100 inmates. Acts of 1842 and 1845 made the erection of county and borough asylums mandatory. A further series of Acts of Parliament gradually transferred the organization of these institutions into the hands of the medical profession. Simultaneously the profession of psychiatry established a foothold as the expert body in matters of the mind (the Royal Medico-Psychological Association, founded in 1841 became the Royal College of Psychiatrists in 1971; its history is well documented in Berrios and Freeman, 1991). The history of the psychiatric profession is as much about jostlings for power and status as scientific endeavour (Hervey, 1985). The successful attempt to take over the asylums was later to be repeated in claims to be the natural leaders of multidisciplinary teams and the most knowledgeable judges of those who could and could not take responsibility for their own actions and might require detention under section of the Mental Health Act. This policy might be seen to have back-fired as modern psychiatrists face an overwhelming demand to not only help people in distress but also to protect society from people who claim to have no control over their actions due to disordered personalities.

By 1900 there were 77 county and borough asylums in Britain. Accounts of many of these institutions are now to be find in published texts as well as in local archives (e.g., Allderidge, 1985; Digby, 1985; Hall, 1991; Morris, 1998). The social and political context for the development of psychiatric institutions has also been the subject of critical appraisal, crucially in the case of British psychiatry in relating developments to the formation and legal framework of the National Health Service (Hodgkinson, 1967).

Critical accounts of the rise of the asylum are not difficult to find, most famously from the sociological perspective (Goffman, 1961) and critiques in terms of power (Foucault, 1967). Partly as a result of Foucault's work, for example, the York Retreat and Pinel's work at the Bicêtre, widely viewed as the gold standard of enlightened moral therapy, have come under serious scrutiny:

> *The asylum of the age of positivism, which is Pinel's glory to have founded, is not a free realm of observation, diagnosis and therapeutics: it is a juridical space where one is accused, judged and condemned, and from which one is never released except by the version of this trial in psychological depth - that is, by remorse.* (Foucault, 1967)

Further, Digby (1985) notes that during the latter part of the nineteenth century the York Retreat made extensive use of sedative chloral and bromides despite an impression that the simple values of the Quaker life were all that were necessary for a return to health.

William Tuke, founder of the Retreat at York is but one in a pantheon of founding figures of psychiatry, many of whom have had their ideas introduced into the mainstream of contemporary life. Their histories have been told in biography (e.g., Jacobs 1992; Grosskurth, 1988; Scull, 1985; Turner, 1988;), autobiography (e.g., Jung, 1963), correspondence, film, plays and novels. They are often linked to treatment innovations or the institutions they dominated. Historians associate non-restraint with Connelly, superintendent at the Middlesex County Asylum from 1839 to 1852 (Scull, 1985). Freud and psychoanalysis, Cerletti and electro-shock, Rogers and counselling, Kraepelin and the diagnostic system are all natural associations. There is no shortage of material. A student of Freudian history, for example, rapidly discovers a huge archive of works, correspondence and related material. Paskauskas (1993) lists 111 works by Freud, Jacobs (1992) cites ten biographies, Freud's correspondence alone in Peskauskas (1993), Masson (1985) and McGuire (1974) totals some 1330 communications. Hughes (1997) is as concerned with the destruction of historical artifacts and data as their bulk and complexity. The traditional complaint that there is simply too much material for the historian to consider is balanced by a concern that material will be destroyed for political ends, of which one is to limit the kind of history that can be written.

Such histories perform a key function within any profession, gently indoctrinating the new professional into a view of the past as slow, but determined progress toward today's state of the art knowledge. This can be especially problematic for psychologists and related professions who may often feel that all this progress avails them nought in understanding their own human predicaments let alone those of their patients. At such times the profound yet unattainable wisdom and apparent clinical success of pioneers of psychoanalysis or psychiatry can feel more of a burden than an inspiration. Confusion is then heaped on confusion when the novice discovers that Freud himself had no greater success with patients than a junior doctor might, and for all his mighty theorising, his own life and loves were not without considerable distress over which he had little control.

The user voice

First hand accounts of the experiences of people who have been psychiatric in-patients (e.g. Laing and McQuarrie, 1989) have been dismissed as fabrication or distortion. Some reveal that discontent and anger with coerced treatment are by no means new experiences (see Beveridge 1993). It is less common to read accounts of good experiences of asylum dwelling. The few that are produced appear without critical comment (e.g. Bullock, 1992) and frequently praise elements of asylum life, notably the chance to talk with fellow inmates, above treatments or contact with medical and other professional staff who are seen as kindly but too busy to help (Goodwin et al., 1999).

There is no doubt that the voice of the patient is more frequently being heard in both fictional (Smith, 1936; West, 1918) and auto-biographical (e.g., Kaysen, 1993; Millet, 1991; Plath, 1963; White, 1979) accounts of psychiatric treatment. Some (Bullock, 1992; Smith and Swann, 1993) give positive stories of the benefits of particular treatment, but for every detailing of the benefits of psychiatric or psychological help there now appear individual and collected accounts of feeling harmed by the mental health system and brief accounts of the new history of the patient self help movement (Chamberlin, 1990; Campbell, this volume) formed in reaction to the perceived inadequacies and iniquities of professionally run mental health services. Even anti-psychiatry now has a substantial historical literature. While barely rating a dismissive entry in some major reviews and attacked in others, this influential movement now commands the attention of academic scholars interested in its pioneers and its internal struggles. Kotowicz (1997), for example, makes the point that divisions within the antipsychiatric movement came from ideologies as far apart as those distancing traditional psychiatry from anti-psychiatry.

Using history

The way we tell the histories of psychiatric events, practices and ideas changes over time. The comforting accounts of scientific and medical progress, told predominantly by members of the mental heath professions themselves, have gradually been replaced by more searching accounts from historians and sociologists (Pilgrim, 1990). In rebuttal, practitioners themselves have turned historian with new accounts of treatment innovations or the practices of colleagues and competitors. Where reputations were once enhanced by historical analysis, the trend, especially since Foucault, has been to examine practice, theory and the work of founding figures with a deeply sceptical eye. The gaze (Foucault, 1963) has turned against the clinic. The outcome has been accounts of fraud (e.g., Cyril Burt, a psychologist who invented data to show that intelligence was inherited), abuse (e.g., Masson reveals that Bruno Bettleheim, far from being a benign father figure to his young patients was a feared autocrat), and hiding foreknowledge of the devastating effects of some treatments which have nonetheless been promulgated (see, for example, Breggin, 1991, on the development of Thorazine). Such accounts have brought condemnation down on these modern critics. They have also produced further research, rebuttal and historical revision. For every recent attack on the past there has been, and will continue to be an historically based rewrite showing psychiatry in a better light. For every new deification of an inspirational figure there will be research to demonstrate the subject's feet of clay. These histories become part of the wider battleground for ascendancy between and within professions in substantiating the claims of one vested interest group or other. Many, indeed most, will not be read by either patients or busy practitioners. Further, those histories which confirm our world view are more likely to be accepted then those which challenge it, especially those, such as the work of Szasz or Breggin which might fundamentally question the tenets and evidence on which an entire mental health career has been based. Revelations about Jung's 'collaboration' with the Nazis (Masson, 1993) or Burt's invented data, or the psychologist Cattell's frank espousal of eugenic beliefs can be profoundly unsettling to psychotherapists and psychologists who have based their own careers, in good faith, on the work of these early pioneers. Attacks, rebuttals and revisions through historical analysis arise as much from a quest for personal meaning as they do from a desire to learn the truth. Indeed, the truth can barely ever be within our grasp. Ordinary events (which make up the overwhelming bulk of psychiatric experience) are only very rarely recorded: the smell on the ward, the tact with which a particular psychiatrist conducts ward rounds, the colour of the walls, the taste of the food, and so on. The truth about treatment is equally hard to discern: the dose of medication may be recorded, but not the attitude of the person giving it (nor even their qualifications: Morris, 1998, informs us that staff at Shelton Hospital were selected for their ability at football and cricket); the number of electric shocks may be recorded but not the therapeutic outcome or the extent of the person's resultant memory loss or disorientation. Ranke's ambition for the historian cannot be achieved. In the absence of comprehensive accounts we must make do with part histories written in a competing fashion. These histories can tell us that psychiatry has been no more than a series of experiments on the mad for the sake of drug company profit and glorification of certain practitioners or they can reveal genuine, thoughtful, professionals doing their best to alleviate human misery.

How can such a plethora of accounts be used to help the patient and student nurse make sense of their first experience of psychiatry? Indeed, could they be used at all? Both the patient and student nurse are anxious and in need of some comfort; little of this will be found in reading more searching accounts of psychiatry. Psychiatry's history reveals its multiple nature: as a healing and scientific enterprise, as a companion to the pharmaceutical industry, as a maker and breaker of reputations, as a state control mechanism, as a means of employment for countless professionals and allied trades, and as a vast human experiment. What both the patient and the student nurse encounter on the ward has been shaped by all these factors. Indeed, psychiatry has been shaped as much by legislation and professional self interest as by inspiration and written and revised as much from a spirit of self preservation as any need to find the truth (quite literally in many cases: patient notes, for example are written with half an eye on litigation while numerous management discussions are prefixed with the words 'not for minuting', thus hamstringing Risse's, 1987, claim that the dynamics of administrative decision making can be discerned by careful reading of the minutes of management meetings).

Psychiatry has a history of overvaluing the empirical approach (see if it works, and if it does, repeat it), an overvaluing of chemical solutions to internal and external difficulties and disputes about what is best for people. Thus, the patient is first offered antidepressants by the general practitioner because the doctor believes that crying is a sign that people are at the end of their tether and may need something to help them through. It is a short-term solution to difficulties which might actually require changes in the patient's life. The doctor believes that a psychiatrist might know more about the nature of unhappiness but the psychiatrist's training has emphasised only one supposed cause of distress, wayward brain biochemistry. The ward is crowded because the difficulties of the patients cannot be resolved by quick-acting medical interventions and people stay for much longer than a 'rest' might suggest. The solution to this overcrowding and its consequent additional pressures on patients is even more medication. The unwanted effects of this medication, although apparent for all to see, are frequently not recognised as training has emphasised the positive benefits of drugs but not their negative effects. Non-drug therapies are conspicuous by their absence because any staff trained to offer them are too busy monitoring patients and closely observing those seen to be at risk of hurting themselves or others. It might make sense to the student nurse that some patients fear being held against their will if the student knows that compulsory detention has long been one of the roles of psychiatry, but acting in a caring capacity is made much more difficult when you are seen as the gaoler rather than the nurse. The patient might get momentary relief from knowing that theories of brain biochemical imbalance are common currency in mental health systems but these theories discount the patient's own ideas about what might be wrong and position the patient as a victim of chemical aberration. Any subsequent interview with a different professional or fellow patient will all too likely throw up a different, equally plausible opinion concerning the causes of the patient's distress. The patient will quickly find that the rhetoric of controversy surrounding certain treatments actually can be applied to *all* interventions, from leucotomy to counselling. An historical reading can easily confirm that this controversy has dogged our attempts to help, control and change others from the outset.

Above all, psychiatry is a human endeavour full of the pitfalls, envy, competition, collaboration, desperation, greed and narcissim which accompany all such endeavour. Newcomers to the field will find that two thousand years of effort have not led to an agreement on the best ways to help people, nor even on how to discern which histories of that endeavour are more reliable. The newcomer will also find that the modern mental health service has not noticeably managed to attract or develop staff less prone to the many varieties of human distress than anyone else, despite developing countless ideas and practice on how such distress can be prevented or cured. If the newcomers are optimists they will look around and conclude that some good work is being done by some ordinary people doing their best. If they are overwhelmed by a disjunction of expectation and experience they might think that the whole enterprise will struggle to help people at all. History can readily support either position.

References

Allderidge, P. (1985) Bedlam: fact or fantasy? In: Bynum, Porter and Shepherd (eds.) *The Anatomy of Madness Vol. II: Institutions and Society.* London: Tavistock

Allen, H. (1986) Psychiatry and the construction of the feminine. In: Miller and Rose (eds.) *The Power of Psychiatry.* Cambridge: Polity Press

Barker, P. (1991) *Regeneration.* Harmondsworth: Penguin

Berrios, G. E. (1996) *The History of Mental Symptoms: Descriptive psychopathology since the nineteenth century.* Cambridge: Cambridge University Press

Berrios, G. E. and Freeman, H. (1996) *One Hundred and Fifty Years of British Psychiatry. Vol. II.* London: Athlone Press

Berrios, G. E. and Porter, R. (1995) *A History of Clinical Psychiatry.* London: Athlone Press

Berrios, G. E. and Freeman, H. (1991) *One Hundred and Fifty Years of British Psychiatry. Vol. I.* London: Athlone Press

Beveridge, A. (1993) 'If you want to demoralise a man in every way, put him in a madhouse'. In: de Goie and Vijslaar (eds) *Proceedings: Ist European Congress on the History of Psychiatry and Mental Health Care.* Rotterdam: Erasmus

Boyle, M. (1990) *Schizophrenia. A Scientific Delusion?* London: Routledge

Braithwaite, J. (1984) *Corporate Crime in the Pharmaceutical Industry.* London: Routledge and Keegan Paul

Breggin, P. R. (1991) *Toxic Psychiatry.* New York: St. Martin's Press

Bullock, A. (1992) Escape to a sanctuary. *Changes: An International Journal of Psychology and Psychotherapy 10, 2,* 123-125

Busfield, J. (1986) *Managing Madness: Changing ideas and practice.* London: Unwin Hyman

Bynum, W.F., Porter, R., and Shepherd, M. (1988) *The Anatomy of Madness Vol. III: The asylum and its psychiatry.* London: Routledge

Chamberlin, J. (1990) The ex-patients' movement: where we've been and where we're going. In: Cohen (ed.) *Challenging the therapeutic state: critical perspectives on psychiatry and the mental health system. Special issue of The Journal of Mind and Behavior 11, 3* and *4*

de Chadarevian, S. (1997) Using interviews to write the history of science. In: Soderquist (ed.) *The Historiography of Contemporary Science and Technology.* Amsterdam: Harwood Academic Publishers

Defoe, D. (1728) Augusta Triumphans In: R. Hunter and I. Macalpine (eds.). (1963) *Three Hundred Years of Psychiatry: 1535-1860.* London: Oxford University Press

Digby, A. (1985) Moral treatment at the retreat, 1796-1846. In: Bynum, Porter and Shepherd (eds.) *The Anatomy of Madness Vol. II: Institutions and Society.* London: Tavistock

Drinka, G. F. (1984) *The Birth of Neurosis: Myth, malady and the Victorians.* New York: Touchstone

Faith, K. (1993) *Unruly Women: The politics of confinement and resistance.*

Vancouver: Press Gang Publishers

Fennell, P. (1996) *Treatment Without Consent: Law, psychiatry and the treatment of mentally disordered people since 1845* London: Routledge

Fisher, S. and Greenberg (1997) (eds.) *From Placebo to Panacea: Putting psychiatric drugs to the test.* New York: John Wiley and Sons

Foucault, M. (1963) *The Birth of the Clinic (trans)* New York: Pantheon

Foucault, M. (1965) *Madness and Civilisation: A history of insanity in the age of reason.* (trans) New York: Pantheon

Franz, A. G., and Selesnick, S.T. (1967) *The History of Psychiatry: An evaluation of psychiatric thought and practice from prehistoric times to the present.* London: George Allen & Unwin

Freidheim, D. K. (1992) *History of Psychotherapy: A century of change.* Washington: American Psychological Association

Gauld, A. (1992) *A History of Hypnotism.* Cambridge: Cambridge University Press

Goffman, E. (1961) *Asylums.* Harmondsworth: Penguin

Goodwin, I., Holmes, G., Newnes, C., and Waltho, D. (1999) A qualitative analysis of the views of in-patient mental health service users. *Journal of Mental Health, 8, 1,* 43-52

Grosskurth, P. (1987) *Melanie Klein, Her World and Her Work.* Cambridge Ma: Harvard University Press

Hall, P. (1991) The history of Powick hospital. In: Hall and Brockington (eds.) *The Closure of Mental Hospitals.* London: Gaskell/RCP

Healy, D. (1991) The ethics of psychopharmacology. *Changes: An International Journal of Psychology and Psychotherapy 9, 4,* 234-47

Healy, D. (1997) *The Anti-Depressant Era.* Cambridge, MA, Harvard University Press

Healy, D. (1998) *The Psychopharmacologists II.* London: Chapman and Hall

Hervey, N. (1985) A slavish bowing down: the Lunacy Commission and the psychiatric profession *1845-60.* In: Bynum, Porter and Shepherd (eds) *The Anatomy of Madness Vol II: Institutions and society.* London: Tavistock

Hill, D. (1983) *The Politics of Schizophrenia.* London: University Press of America

Hodgkinson, R.G. (1967) *The Origins of the National Health Service: The medical services of the new poor law, 1834-1871.* London: The Wellcome Historical Medical Library

Hughes, J. (1997) Whigs, prigs and politics: Problems in the historiography of contemporary science. In: Soderquist (ed) *The Historiography of Contemporary Science and Technology.* Amsterdam: Harwood Academic Publishers

Jackson, S. W. (1986) *Melancholia and Depression from Hippocratic Times to Modern Times.* New Haven: Yale University Press

Jacobs, M. (1992) *Sigmund Freud.* London: Sage

Jacobs Brumberg, J. (1988) *Fasting Girls: The emergence of anorexia nervosa as a modern disease.* Cambridge, Ma: Harvard University Press

Johnson, F.N. (1982) *A History of Lithium Therapy.* Basigstoke: Macmillan Press

Jones, Y., and Baldwin, S. (1992) ECT: shock, lies and psychiatry. *Changes: An International Journal of Psychology and Psychotherapy, 10, 2,* 126-35

Jung, C.G. (1963) *Memories, Dreams and Reflections.* London: Collins

Kaysen, S. (1993) *gi.rl, interrupted.* London: Virago

Kirk, S.A., and Kutchins, H. (1992) *The Selling of DSM: The rhetoric of science in psychiatry.* New York: Aldine

Kotowicz, (1997) *R. D. Laing and the Paths of Antipsychiatry.* London: Routledge

Laing, J., and McQuarrie, J. (1989) *Fifty Years in the System.* London: Corgi Books

Masson, J. M. (1985) (Ed.) *The Complete Letters of Sigmund Freud to Wilhelm Fleiss, 1887-1904.* Cambridge, Mass.: Belknap Harvard

Masson, J. (1993) *Against Therapy.* London: Harper Collins

McGuire, W. (1974) *The Freud Jung Letters.* London: Routledge

Medawar, C. (1992) *Power and Dependence: Social audit on the safety of medicines.* London: Social Audit Ltd.

Millett, K. (1991) *The Loony Bin Trip.* London: Virago

Morris, R. (1998) *Shelton: Past and present.* Shrewsbury: Shropshire's Community and Mental Health Services NHS Trust

Munro, A. (1999) *Delusional Disorder: Paranoia and related illnesses.* Cambridge: Cambridge University Press

Parry-Jones W. Ll. (1972) *The Trade in Lunacy: A study of private madhouses in England in the eighteenth and nineteenth centuries.* London: Routledge

Paskauskas, R. A. (1993) (Ed.) *The Complete Correspondence of Sigmund Freud and Ernest Jones 1908-1939.* London: Harvard University Press

Pilgrim, D. (1990) Competing histories of madness. In R. Bentall (ed.) *Reconstructing Schizophrenia.* London: Routledge

Plath, S. (1963) *The Bell Jar.* London: Heineman

Ranke, L. Von, (1952) Histories of the Latin and German nations from 1494–1514. In: G.P. Gooch (ed.) *History and Historians in the Nineteenth Century.* 2nd edition London: Longman

Risse, G.B. (1987) Hospital history: new sources and methods. In: R. Porter and A. Wear (eds.) *Problems and Methods in the History of Medicine.* London: Croom Helm

Scull, A. (1985) A Victorian alienist: John Conolly, FRCP, DCL (1794–1866) In: Bynum, Porter and Shepherd (eds) *The Anatomy of Madness Vol I: People and ideas,* London:Tavistock

Scull, A (1993) *The Most Solitary of Afflictions: Madness and Society in Britain, 1700–1900.* London: Yale University Press

Shorter, E. (1997) *A History of Psychiatry: From the era of the asylum to the age of Prozac.* Chichester: John Wiley and Sons

Showalter, E. (1987) *The Female Malady: Momen, madness and English culture 1830–1980.* London: Virago

Smith, D. And Swann, A. (1993) In praise of the asylum – the writings of two nineteenth century Glasgow patients. In: de Goie and Vijslaar (eds) *Proceedings: 1st European Congress on the History of Psychiatry and Mental Health Care.* Rotterdam: Erasmus

Smith, S. (1936) *Novel on Yellow Paper.* London: Jonathan Cape

Stone, M. (1998) *Healing the Mind: A history of psychiatry from antiquity to the present.* London: Pimlico

Strabaneck, P. (1986) Convulsive therapy: a critical review of its origins and value. *Irish Medical Journal, 79 (6),* 157–65

Swazey, (1974) *Chlorpromazine.* Boston: MIT Press

Szasz, T. (1978) *The Myth of Psychotherapy: Mental healing as religion, rhetoric and repression.* Syracuse: Syracuse University Press

Tosh, J. (1991) *The Pursuit of History: Aims, methods and new directions in the study of modern history.* London: Longman

Ussher, J. (1991) *Women's Madness: Misogyny or mental illness?* Hemel Hempstead: Harvester Wheatsheaf

Valenstein, E.S. (1986) *Great and Desparate Cures. The rise and decline of psychosurgeyry and other radical cures for mental illness.* New York: Basic Books

West, R. (1918) *The Return of the Soldier.* London: Nisbet

White, A. (1979) *Beyond the Glass.* London: Virago

CHAPTER 2

Social inequalities and mental health

JENNIE WILLIAMS

THE AIM OF this chapter is to add weight to growing demands for social inequalities to be taken seriously within mental health services, and to make explicit that until this happens mental health services will continue to be unsafe, ineffective, oppressive and wasteful of human and financial resources. In the process of exploring these issues I will use the definition of social inequality that Gilli Watson and I used in our earlier work:

> *Social inequality exists when an ascribed characteristic such as sex, race, ethnicity, class, and disability determines access to socially valued resources. These resources include access to money, status and power, especially the power to define societal rules, rights and privileges.* (Williams and Watson, 1988 p. 292)

I will begin by emphasising some of the important characteristics of social inequality, on the grounds that the concept is still unfamiliar and often misunderstood in the field of mental health. A more detailed consideration of these, and related issues, can be found elsewhere (e.g. Thompson, 1998; Weber, 1998). We should not forget that dimensions of social inequality, including gender, race, class, age and sexuality, are hierarchies of domination that limit and restrict some people while privileging others. They mediate power relationships which serve one group at the expense of another; fundamental conflicts of interests lie at their core. Consequently many of the manifest differences between inequitable social groups are not simply due to different lifestyle preferences or cultural beliefs, values and practices, but are intimately related to the existence of inequality. The basis of these differences is not always easy to detect because inequalities are perpetuated by ideologies – diversionary explanations – which mask conflict and injustice between social groups. This phenomenon is very evident in psychiatry where there is a long tradition of explaining relationships between gender, race and mental health without reference to the existence of structural inequalities in our society (Fernando, 1995; Fernando et al.,1998; Ussher, 1991). I would also suggest that we remember that social inequalities not only structure society, but also are deeply embedded in our personal identities. Therefore, we should not be surprised when we find them difficult to speak about, and hard to change.

Background

The literature on social inequalities and mental health exists as a loose aggregate of work without formal status within psychiatry. An historical overview of its development reveals that it has been driven by the emergence into the political arena of groups representing the interests of women, people from black and minority ethnic groups, gays and lesbians, and more recently service users. The force behind the development of the field is personal experience of injustice in society and within mental health services. Impetus has not come from the social institutions that have responsibility for mental health services. Although individuals working in the caring professions and services, the Department of Health, and academia, have contributed to the field, most of these individuals appear to work from an outsider within perspective.

As I have noted elsewhere (Williams, 1996b) there are a number of important implications arising from the dynamics of the development of knowledge in this field. First, we know most about the mental health implications of social inequalities for people belonging to oppressed social groups who have a strong collective voice. Conversely, much less is known about the mental health implications of social inequalities for people belonging to oppressed social groups whose collective voice is non-existent, weak or emergent. This includes people with psychiatric diagnoses, people with learning disabilities, children, young people from marginalised social groups, and old people. Paradoxically, little is also known about the mental health implications of social inequalities for people belonging to privileged social groups, especially white men, where there is limited collective interest in identifying structural advantage as a problem. Second, the political forces shaping the development of the literature have tended to give priority to single dimensions of oppression defined by gender, race, sexuality or use of mental health services. Though this may be politically functional it has resulted in a mental health literature that is fragmented and limited in usefulness to those who work with clients whose distress is linked to the confluence of multiple major dimensions of inequality. Finally, the origins of the knowledge in this field make it very easy for it to be ignored, trivialised and minimised by mainstream services. This has seriously limited its impact on service provision, development and training.

Social inequalities and mental health: implications for women
The critical question here, as Brown (1992) and others (e.g. Baker-Miller 1976; Williams et al., 1993) have argued, is whether behaviours defined as symptoms and disorders are best understood as creative responses to difficult personal and social histories, rooted in a person's experience of oppression(s). The literature I shall now summarise suggests that the answer to this question is an unequivocal 'yes': it leaves little doubt that social inequalities – including those based on gender, race and class – are a root cause of the despair, distress, and confusion that is named 'mental illness'. This work has directed attention to the effects of social inequalities on mental health, and to studying the factors, events and processes that mediate these relationships. It will be reviewed here with primary reference to the axis of gender, partly reflecting my own competence in the field of women's mental health, but mainly because gender has particular significance for mental health due to its centrality in family life (Williams, 1984; Williams and Watson, 1988). Of necessity this review will be illustrative rather than exhaustive.

Physical violence
As noted in the recent report from the Women's Aid Federation (1998), physical violence can be a means of expressing and maintaining dominance in family and community settings:

> . . . *those men who do abuse still believe, at some level, that they have the right to control the members of their household and to expect domestic and sexual services from their partners or wives, believing that it is acceptable to use intimidation, threats, abuse and violence to achieve these things.* (Women's Aid Federation of England,1998 p.1)

The scale of violence against women and children is of considerable concern to the international health and development community: this is evident in the reports and initiatives of organizations and bodies such as the World Health Organisation, the World Bank and the United Nations (see Heise, 1996). Domestic violence is largely committed against women by male partners, and is reported to be suffered by between one in four and one in ten women in the populations sampled (Mirrlees-Black, 1995; Smith, 1989). Being pregnant does not appear to protect women against violence, and for some women it may be associated with an onset or increase of violence. Studies find one in six (Macfarlane et al, 1995) to one in nine (Cokkinides and Coker, 1998) pregnant women experience violence from male partners.

There is now an extensive body of evidence documenting the mental health outcomes of domestic violence experienced in childhood and as an adult: the links between battery and long-term mental health difficulties are now well established (Goodman et al, 1997). Findings also indicate that abuse during pregnancy is associated with poorer physical and mental health outcomes for women (Petersen et al, 1997; Ratner, 1998), and one study found violence was the single most important cause of suicide and attempted suicide, particularly among black and pregnant women (Stark and Flitcraft, 1995).

That domestic violence is an issue for mental health services is so obvious it seems barely worth stating. However, there is very little to suggest that it is taken seriously within most service contexts. For example, it is still exceptional to find multi-disciplinary work between statutory services and women's refuges that is concerned with the well being of women and not just children. It also remains unusual to find mental health workers who have been trained to consider the possibility that violence is an etiological factor in a client's distress, although sensitive assessment tools are available (Gondolf, 1998). There is little concern in assessing the risk to women of violence by others, despite the considerable professional and public interest in risk assessment, and even though good practice in safety planning has been developed and could be easily utilised (Gondolf, 1998):

> As women who go into the mental health services, many of us have been abused as children, some of us have been sexually abused. You find very often that they don't want to do anything about it, they are not interested. Some of us are married to alcoholics or people who have got

their own problems that put those problems back on us.
One of my dearest friends – her husband beat her, abused
her, she was the one that went into the bin. (Conlan, 1992)

Childhood sexual abuse

From the extensive body of research on child sexual abuse we learn that between one in three and one in ten girl children are sexually abused in childhood (Goodman et al., 1997). Perpetrators of childhood sexual abuse are predominantly male: the sexual abuse of children and women mainly involves the serious exploitation of power available to men in our society. Research also finds that one in four women have experienced rape or attempted rape in adult life, and that victimisation is a powerful predictor of psychiatric treatment (Davidson et al.,1996). Findings from a range of studies (for a review see Williams and Watson, 1996) suggest that at least 50% of women using hospital and community based mental health services have histories of sexual and physical trauma. Amongst women using secure mental health services having a history of sexual abuse is sufficiently common to be normal in that context (Adshead, 1994; Warner, 1996):

I am familiar with the histories of many women living in Ashworth, they have all experienced disrupted family lives. Their security has been shattered at an early age by the intrusive acts of powerful others, including physical, emotional and, most notably, sexual abuse (often in the context of generational abuse). The subsequent devastating sequelæ include a very poor or non-existent sense of self, shattered trust, non-existent or poorly defined boundaries between self and others underlying a tendency under stress to regress to psychotic like states, consequent very low self-esteem and the experience at times of overwhelming guilt, anger, hopelessness and despair leading to all forms of self abuse including para-suicidal behaviour. There is a common existential experience shared by the women of not being heard and rarely believed, of feeling chronically frightened and overwhelmingly powerless (except in outbursts of impotent rage against property, self or others). (Potier, 1993)

Such histories of abuse often remain unheard within the mental health services: many women have spent decades in services without being given a safe opportunity to talk about their experiences. Lack of relevant training means that workers may not be alert to the etiological role of abuse in mental health difficulties, or know what to do with knowledge of a woman's history of abuse. As Watson et al (1996) note, the significance of abuse is often minimised and trivialised, and women held responsible for its occurrence. It is understandably difficult to focus on the impact of abuse on a woman's mental health in a context where the established discourse may name the problem as 'borderline personality disorder', 'psychosis', and 'post-natal depression', and then ties these labels closely with familiar albeit ineffectual and punitive – treatment responses (Rosewater, 1985; Williams, et al., 1998). Given these difficulties it is unsurprising that with few exceptions (e.g. Watson et al., 1996) most of the development in service provision for women survivors of abuse and violence has been in the independent and voluntary sector.

Poverty
Relationships between poverty and gender are often ignored or trivialised in research and policy (Buck, 1997). As Payne (1991) notes, there has been a reluctance to take social inequalities, such as gender, race, disability and age, seriously in the study of poverty, and consequently the literature is modest. Nonetheless, existing evidence indicates that poverty amongst women is strongly associated with being a single parent, being divorced, being old, and being Black or a member of an ethnic minority group (Bayne Smith and McBarnette, 1996; Payne, 1991). It is noteworthy that levels of psychological distress are commonly found to be higher in these groups.

That poverty can cause mental health difficulties is an unsurprising and well-established research finding (Belle 1990; Bruce et al., 1991). However, it remains quite uncommon for this robust finding to inform the functioning of mainstream mental health services (Pacitti and Dimmick, 1996). Concern about poverty is rarely evident in core service activities e.g. assessments, interventions, service developments, and inter-agency working. Indeed the majority of people using residential mental health services are currently expected to exist on a disposable weekly income of £12.60. How can people be expected to meet their basic needs let alone sustain their self-respect at this level of income? Such a paradox would be very unlikely to persist if there was widespread appreciation of the role of poverty in distress.

Family life
Gender inequality throughout society supports, and is supported by, persistent gender inequalities in family life. Like other social institutions family life persists in forms that serve the interests of men often at women's expense (Dallos and Dallos, 1997; Dryden, 1999). This does not preclude the possibility that some families have a shared commitment to values of equality and fairness, nor that many women work very hard to ensure they get the very best possible deal for themselves in this context (Williams and Watson, 1988). Nonetheless, the evidence summarised above reminds us that serious abuses of male power take place in families. Inequality within family life also supports precedence being given to men's needs over those of women. Hence, it is perhaps unsurprising that marriage is generally found to be comparatively more beneficial to the psychological well-being of men than women (McRae and Brody, 1989).

The association between psychological distress and motherhood is well-documented (Brown and Harris, 1978; Pound and Abel, 1996). An inequalities perspective reminds us that the stressful aspects of motherhood can be attributed to a combination of factors linked to women's position in families and the wider society. First, motherhood is associated with a rapid increase in short and long-term responsibilities, which rarely sit easily alongside responsibilities and aspirations associated with paid work. Second, many women do not experience becoming a mother as empowering. Becoming a mother is commonly associated with increased dependency on others, and reduced access to valued sources of power and resources in society. There is minimal preparation for the task of parenting, few rituals, and little time to support transition to being a mother. Families are more isolated than in the past, and there is reduced structural support for family bonds, and less close community supervision of behavior in the family. Finally, caring is women's work and as such is de-valued in our society; most women experience being blamed more often than rewarded for their efforts to care for children and vulnerable family members. Caring for children and dependent relatives carries high costs when associated with isolation, low social value and a lack of resources.

A further strand of research indicates that women with histories of trauma and abuse may encounter additional difficulties when becoming a mother. Studies have found an association between childhood sexual abuse and increased risk of unintended pregnancies and abortions (Wyatt, Guthrie and Notgrass, 1992), and physical and mental health problems during pregnancy and childbirth (Jacobs, 1992; Buist and Barnett, 1995). There are indications that childhood sexual abuse may affect the mental health of women who are mothers because cues in the mothering role can recall abusive events (Buist and Barnett, 1995), and because the secrecy, shame and self-blame often associated with sexual abuse may make it more difficult for women to view themselves as competent mothers (Cohen, 1995).

Multiple oppression
Gender has particular significance for the mental health of women, but the lives of many women are also shaped by lifetime experiences of racism, classism, homophobia and ageism. It is therefore important to take account of the work exploring the mental health implications for women of racism (Bayne Smith 1996; Cook and Watt, 1992; Holland, 1995; Ismail 1996; see also Patel and Fatimilehin in this book); classism (Bayne Smith 1996; Brown and Harris, 1978); homophobia (Bridget and Lucille, 1996; Brown, 1996; Herek and Berril, 1990); and ageism (Nadien et al, 1996; Padgett et al, 1998). There has also been a welcome shift of attention towards women with severe mental health problems (Harris and Landis, 1997; Mowbray et al, 1998), and growing efforts to meet the mental health needs of women with learning disabilities (Baum and Burns, in press).

The risk of being
It is not only trauma, exploitation and discrimination that mediate the relationship between inequalities and women's mental health. There have now been many studies (e.g. Beckwith, 1993; Broverman et al., 1970) which consistently demonstrate that women's feelings, thoughts and behaviors are more likely to be defined as madness than those of men. Being female is a risk factor for being labeled mad. This is sometimes interpreted as an illustration of the phenomenon that anything differing from the male standard is commonly deemed to be deviant and inferior. However, it is probably best interpreted within the broader context of psychiatry's troubled relationship with women. Historical analyses (e.g. Busfield 1996a; Fernando et al., 1998; Ussher 1991; see also Newnes in this book) make it quite clear that psychiatry has a particular enthusiasm for labeling the experiences and behaviour of oppressed people as psychiatrically disturbed or distressed. Psychiatry supports the status quo by invalidating and managing individuals' struggles to survive the consequences of social injustice. In so doing individuals

are denied access to a language that would enable them either to make sense of, or speak out about, their experiences of oppression. Furthermore, as mental health service users readily testify, once you have been labeled as having a mental health problem, it is especially difficult to have your views, opinions and experiences taken seriously (Lindow, 1991).

Social inequalities and mental health: implications for men

There has been a strong lobby from women to substantiate and work clinically with the widely held belief 'that the political is the personal' (Watson and Williams, 1992). There has been no comparable lobby from men to link the existence of social inequalities with their psychological well-being. Recently I asked a group of mental health workers in training to explain this phenomenon - a strategy I use to reduce the chances I will be held personally responsible for the limited literature in this field. A white psychiatrist replied 'because we don't think we have a problem'. I would add that even if men think that masculinity and the social and economic dominance of men might be a problem, they receive very little encouragement from each other to explore the implications. As studies in the field of intergroup behaviour clearly demonstrate (e.g. Marques et al., 1998), members of dominant social groups who break ranks are more likely to be punished than rewarded for their efforts by in-group members, though they can help achieve justice for oppressed social groups. This is very different from the situation of people from oppressed social groups who may greatly benefit from the support of in-group members when naming and challenging problems rooted in oppression (Collins, 1998).

Although the literature on men's mental health is comparatively slight, nonetheless it permits us to trace some important links between social inequalities and men's mental health. Miller and Bell (1996) and other writers (e.g. Baker-Miller, 1976; Collins, 1998; Thomas, 1996) convincingly argue that the privileged male role imposes expectations about masculinity that may have a serious detrimental effect on the mental health of men and the women and children in their families. They argue that one of the most pernicious consequences for men of masculinity are the injunctions placed upon emotional entitlement. Successful male socialization requires men to be silent and strong, leaving individuals little scope to acknowledge and deal constructively with feelings of vulnerability or powerlessness. Instead men are offered safety through dominance and control of the external world, and survival sanctioned means of violence. As Miller and Bell (1996)

> *ne end product of male socialization is alienation from meaningful intimacy, and objectification of all those who are are not me.* (p.320)

Masculinity persists in this form because internal and external constraints make it difficult for men to speak about its costs. It is also functional for countries to have a viable number of people in the population who are willing and able to go to war (Busfield, 1996b). Masculinity also persists in this form because there are advantages associated with male dominance: men have better access to socially valued resources, including money, status and power. White, middle-class, heterosexual men may well gain some satisfaction from having fulfilled the male script and from being one of the 'real men' i.e. one of 'those who have power in the economic realm, where ownership, authority, competitiveness, and mental – not physical – labor are valued' (Weber, 1998, p.26). However, this is unlikely to be the case for men who are poor, unemployed, from Black and minority ethnic groups, who are gay: men who need to reconcile the gap between the expectation of dominance and their experience of powerlessness:

> *Cultural expectations of male and female roles may mean that the frustrations, hopelessness and loss of self-esteem associated with unemployment are felt more keenly by the male partner of an unemployed couple, even if both are seeking work. Again, such feelings are not compatible with good mental health.* (Acheson, 1998 p.106)

Neither the rewards nor the costs of male dominance are evenly distributed throughout society. We know that many men, as children and adults, experience bullying, brutality, sexual abuse and violence within the home and their communities – traumas that are consistently under-reported because they shouldn't have happened, or shouldn't matter if the person was a real man (Freeman and Fallot, 1997; Miller and Bell, 1996).

Social inequalities and mental health: summary
Thirty years ago there was very little research evidence, or published work, making connections between inequalities in society and the

psychological well-being of individuals. This is no longer the case. There is now an extensive literature in this field, and even though it has not reached the stage of being either well integrated or comprehensive it supports two important conclusions. First, there can be no doubt that social inequalities are a major determinant of the mental health of people who belong to oppressed social groups. Second, there is now convincing evidence that social inequalities are a major determinant of the mental health of people who belong to privileged social groups. It is not being claimed that social 'inequalities are the only significant etiological factors in the distress, despair and disturbance called mental illness, but that they are evidently of considerable importance. The impact of these findings on mental health services will now be considered.

Social inequalities and mental health services

The capacity of mainstream mental health services to simultaneously claim to be evidence based whilst ignoring the research literature on social inequalities and mental health is remarkable. There are service providers and trainers who both draw upon and contribute to work on social inequalities and mental health, but what I learn from talking to people managing, providing and using services is that these individuals are exceptions. A clearer lead from the Department of Health might begin to make a difference, and we might take some encouragement from the publication of the report 'Inequalities in Health' (Acheson, 1998). Though the coverage of mental health issues in this report is rather limited, it does indicate a greater willingness from central government to name social inequalities as a health issue.

Inequalities within mental health services
The Acheson report (1998) reminds us that 'Equity was a founding principle of the NHS and is central to Government policy' (p.111), and identifies one of the key elements of equity as 'ensuring that health care services serving disadvantaged populations are not of poorer quality or less accessible' (p.111). Regretfully this principle does not appear to have shaped many statutory mental health services. Inequalities in the wider society are clearly embedded within services and determine the quality, and safety, of care provided to different social groups.

People from oppressed social groups are more likely to receive forcible treatment, treatment with drugs and ECT. This includes women (Williams and Watson, 1996), particularly older women

(Nadien, 1996), and people from Black and minority ethnic groups (Boast and Chesterman, 1995; Glazer et al, 1994). Grave concerns about these interventions continue to be voiced by the service user movement and their allies (Campbell et al., 1998: Arscott, this volume: Crepaz-Keay, this volume). There is also evidence that access to the more valued talking treatments is affected by race, ethnicity and social class (Wade, 1993). Older people, people with learning disabilities and those with serious mental health problems are likely to encounter particular difficulties accessing these services regardless of their need.

Safety
Although service user complaints about psychiatric services have a long history (see Campbell, 1996, and later in this book), it is only during this decade that the possibility of widespread abuse in this setting has become a source of public concern (e.g. Crossmaker, 1991; Wood and Copperman, 1996). Although there has been no study in the UK to establish the incidence and prevalence of abuse in mental health services, available evidence suggests that those people who are disadvantaged, mistreated and discriminated against within the wider society are also at risk within mental health services. For example, the 1996 survey of acute psychiatric wards in England and Wales (Warner and Ford, 1998), found little indication that campaigns to improve the safety of women in these contexts were making an impact. 94% (N=291) of the units offering care to women were mixed-sex, and 57% of staff in these units reported that women patients were sexually harassed. Studies, findings of public inquiries, and reports from service users also indicate that mental health services are especially unsafe for people from Black and minority ethnic groups (e.g. Browne 1995), lesbian and gay people (Brown, 1996; Haslam, 1998), and older people (Aitken and Griffin, 1996). In summary, being a member of a disadvantaged social group, or groups, appears to be associated with the increased probability of receiving physical treatments, and a reduced probability of receiving safe and effective psychosocial care.

It has already been noted that much of the training, education and socialisation available to mental health workers undermines their capacity to recognise the role of power inequalities in causing psychological distress. As I have argued elsewhere (Williams and Keating, in press) this also impacts on their ability to identify and name institutional and interpersonal abuse within mental health services. Most mental health workers do not have access to a discourse that allows them to name the abuses of power that are commonplace in their client's histories, or the ways that clients are re-victimised within services. Such thoughts and conversations have no legitimacy in these settings, and because of this mental health workers are denied the possibility of providing safe and effective care to clients.

Service development from a social inequalities perspective
Although service developments addressing social inequalities and mental health do exist within mainstream provision, they have mainly flourished within the independent and voluntary sector. These services do not always have the necessary resources to document their efforts and achievements. However, published work is steadily growing and constitutes a valuable resource (e.g. Abel et al., 1996; Good Practices in Mental Health, 1993; McFarlane and Wiist, 1997; Perkins et al., 1996; Williams et al., 1993; Williams 1996a).

Dynamics of resistance and change
From the work presented here it is evident that mainstream mental health services are very reluctant to name social inequalities as an issue for mental health. This is given substance by comments from those who have taken these matters seriously. Here Phyllis Chesler reviews her past twenty-five years work in the field of women and mental health:

> . . . *my analyses of how diagnostic labels were used to stigmatize women and of why more women than men were involved in 'careers' as psychiatric patients, was either ignored, treated as a sensation, or sharply criticized, by those in position of power within the mental-health professions.* (Chesler, 1994 p.299)

This is an account of what happened when the needs of women using forensic mental health services were surveyed:

> *One of the other things we did with management support, was carry out a needs survey of what women wanted. We talked to all the women and wrote to all the primary nurses, and then presented the findings in a report to management. Their response was 'This is not a needs*

survey, it's just a list of what women want'. It was ridiculed.
'What's this? You can't have this!'. (Helen Liebling in
Williams et al, 1998 p.366)

The difficulties encountered by these and other advocates for change
are understandable. Identifying social inequalities as a problem is
usually discouraged by those social groups that benefit from this
arrangement. Promoting equality inevitably involves entering into
conflict with the dominant social arrangements that help to maintain
existing power relations. Identifying social inequalities as a cause
of mental health problems undermines one of the prime social
functions of mental health services, which is to name as 'mental
illness' understandable, and often creative, responses to
oppression(s). It undermines the power base of the mental health
professions and is typically experienced as disempowering by mental
health workers who lack the training and support they need to use
this knowledge to empower service users.

Achieving Change
One of the important social functions of mental health services has
been to hide and manage the psychological distress created by the
existence of social inequalities within our society. Discrimination
and revictimisation of people within mental health services have
thrived in this context, and have been perpetuated and disguised
by the inequalities of power between those who use and those who
provide services. As long as services continue to fulfil this function
it will be extremely difficult to provide safe and effective services to
people in distress. The continuation of this situation is also not in
the interests of those who provide mental health services, the
overwhelming majority of whom want to make a useful contribution
to the lives of others. At this juncture, what are the possibilities for
change?

One strategy is to work for the transformation of mental health
training, so that the knowledge base of mental health workers is
shifted away from theories and practices which marginalise and
trivialise the impact of social inequalities on the lives of services
users. The knowledge we need to achieve this task has a number of
obvious sources. First, people with first-hand experience of using
mental health services. Second, the well-established and extensive
research literature on social inequalities and mental health. Third,
the mental health projects in the UK and elsewhere committed to
the provision of services shaped by principles of equality and to

addressing the damage caused by social inequalities. Finally, everyone working within mental health services will have personal knowledge of power and powerlessness, and of the personal and social responses to abuses of power, including those that have relevance for mental health. This personal knowledge needs to be valued and used. Achieving this change will not be easy, but at least we are now in the position of being able to draw attention to the irony of services claiming to be evidence based whilst consistently ignoring the extensive literature concerned with social inequalities. Furthermore, learning about implications of social inequalities does not have to be experienced as disempowering, at a time when there are many ways we can learn about its translation into practice. Achieving this change will need support from the Department of Health, national training bodies and organisations, coupled with a strategic approach from services to ensure these changes are supported through training and supervision, and the broader organisational culture. The possibility of securing this commitment is enhanced by the present government's interest in equality and social exclusion, and by the availability of good quality evidence for making the case. We can also take encouragement from the growing credibility of work in the broader field of inequality and health (e.g. Wilkinson, 1996).

Whilst working to transform the knowledge base of mental health services, we also need to address its current limitations. First, we need to develop an inclusive literature that accommodates all people who are damaged by the existence of social inequalities – not just those who are have achieved a strong collective voice, or attracted powerful advocates. This includes men: social inequalities are a major determinant of the mental health of men, and the significance of this should not be diminished by the fact that social inequalities also underlie the damage that men inflict upon each other, and the women and children in their lives. Second, the literature needs integration: work has typically been initiated and developed along single dimensions, such as gender, race, sexuality, class, and age. Within all these literatures there is recognition of the complexity of oppression, and the search for more elaborated analyses (e.g. Keating, 1998; Krawitz and Watson, 1997; Weber, 1998). It is time, therefore, for people working in these different domains to create opportunities to work together on these issues.

Conclusion
Mental health workers need to accept the implications of the research on inequalities and mental health, and refuse to provide care based on causal models which ignore the effects of abuse, discrimination and disadvantage. Instead of hiding the human costs of inequalities in our society, mental health workers could make them known and work alongside service users to transform mental health services (e.g. Sayce, 1996; Williams and Lindley, 1996). Substantial change is unlikely to be achieved in mental health services until there is widespread appreciation that structural inequalities are a major cause of psychological distress and disturbance, and that this has implications for all members of society.

References
Abel, K., Buszewicz, M., Davison, S., Johnson, S., and Staples, E. (1996) *Planning Community Mental Health Services for Women*. London: Routledge

Acheson, S. D. (1998) *Independent Inquiry into Inequalities in Health: Report*. London: HMSO

Adshead, G. (1994) Damage: Trauma and violence in a sample of women referred to a forensic service. *Behavioral Sciences and the Law, 12(3)*, 235–49

Aitken, L. and Griffin, G. (Eds.) (1996) *Gender Issues in Elder Abuse*. London: Sage

Baker-Miller, J. (1976) *Towards a New Psychology of Women*. Harmondsworth: Penguin

Baum, S., and Burns, J. (Eds) (In press). Waiting to be Asked – Women with Learning Disibilities. *Clinical Psychology Forum* (Special Issue)

Bayne Smith, M. E. (1996) *Race, Gender, and Health*. London: Sage.

Belle, D. (1990) Poverty and women's mental health. *American Psychologist, 45(3)*, 385–89

Beckwith, J. B. (1993) Gender stereotypes and mental health revisited. *Social Behavior and Personality, 21(1)*, 85–8

Boast, N., and Chesterman, P. (1995) Black people and secure psychiatric facilities: Patterns of processing and the role of stereotypes. *British Journal of Criminology, 35(2)*, 218–35

Bridget, J., and Lucille, S. (1996) Lesbian Youth Support Information Services (LYSIS): Developing a distance support agency for young lesbians. *Journal of Community and Applied Social Psychology, 6(5)*, 355–64

Broverman, I., Broverman, D. M., Clarkson, I. E., Rosenkrantz, P. S., and Vogel, S. R. (1970) Sex role stereotypes and clinical judgements of mental health. *Journal of Consulting and Clinical Psychology*, 34, 1-7

Brown, G. W., and Harris, T. (1978) *Social Origins of Depression*. London: Tavistock Publications

Brown, L. S. (1992) A feminist critique of the personality disorders. In L. S. Brown and M. Ballou (Eds.), *Personality and Psychopathology: Feminist Reappraisals*. (pp. 206–28). New York: Guilford.

Brown, L. S. (1996) Preventing heterosexism and bias in psychotherapy and counseling. In E. D. Rothblum and L. A. Bond (Eds.), *Preventing Heteorsexism and Homophobia* . London: Sage

Browne, D. (1995) Sectioning: the black experience. In S. Fernando (Ed.), *Mental Health in a Multi-ethnic Society* . London: Routledge

Bruce, M. L., Takeuchi, D. T., and Leaf, P. J. (1991) Poverty and psychiatric status: Longitudinal evidence from the New Haven Epidemiologic Catchment Area Study. *Archives of General Psychiatry, 48(5),* 470–74

Buck, M. (1997) The Price of Poverty: Mental Health and Gender. *Critical Social Policy, 17,* 79-97

Buist, A. and Barnett, B. (1995). Childhood sexual abuse: A risk factor for postpartum depression? *Australian and New Zealand Journal of Psychiatry, 29(4),* 604–8

Busfield, J. (1996a) *Men, Women and Madness: Understanding gender and mental disorder*. London: Macmillan

Busfield, J. (1996b). Trauma and powerlessness: war and sexual violence. In J. Busfield *Men, Women and Madness: Understanding gender and mental disorder* (pp. 209–29). London: Macmillan

Campbell, P. (1996) The history of the user movement in the United Kingdom. In T. Heller, J. Reynolds, R. Gomm, R. Muston, and S. Pattison (Eds.), *Mental Health Matters: A reader* . Milton Keynes: Macmillan/The Open University

Campbell, P., Cobb, A. and Darton, K. (1998) *Psychiatric Drugs: Users' Experiences and Current Policy and Practice*. London: Mind Publications

Chesler, P. (1994) Heroism is our only alternative. Special Feature: Women and Madness : A reappraisal. *Feminism and Psychology, 4(2),* 298–305

Cohen, T. (1995) Motherhood among incest survivors. *Child Abuse and Neglect, 19(12),* 1423–9

Cokkinides, V. E. and Coker, A. L. (1998) Experiencing physical violence during pregnancy: Prevalence and correlates. *Family and Community Health, 20(4),* 19–37

Collins, L. H. (1998) Illustrating feminist theory: power and psychopathology. *Psychology of Women Quarterly, 22(1),* 97–112

Conlan, E. M. (1992) *What we know*. Paper presented at the British Psychological Society (Psychology of Women Section Conference) 'Developing Mental Health Services for Women: Feminist Principles into Practice', Lancaster

Cook, J. and Watt, S. (1992) Racism, women and poverty. In C. Glendinning and J. Millar (Eds.), *Women and Poverty in Britain: the 1990s*. London:

Harvester

Crossmaker, M. (1991) Behind locked doors – institutional sexual abuse. *Sexuality and Disability, 9(3)*, 201–19

Dallos, S. and Dallos, R. (1997) *Couples, Sex and Power: The politics of desire*. Buckingham: Open University

Davidson, J. R. T., Hughes, D. C., George, L. K. and Blazer, D. G. (1996) The association of sexual assault and attempted suicide within the community. *Archives of General Psychiatry, 53(6)*, 550–5

Dryden, D. (1999) *Being Married: Doing gender*. London: Routledge

Fernando, S. (1995) Social realities and mental health. In S. Fernando (Ed) *Mental Health in a Multi-ethnic Society: A multi-disciplinary handbook*. (pp. 11–35) London: Routledge

Fernando, S., Ndegwa, D. and Wilson, M. (1998) *Forensic Psychiatry, Race and Culture*. London: Routledge

Freeman, D. W. and Fallot, R. D. (1997) Trauma and trauma recovery for dually diagnosed male survivors. In M. Harris and C. L. Landis (Eds.), *Sexual Abuse in the Lives of Women Diagnosed with Serious Mental Illness*. London: Harwood Academic

Glazer, W. M., Morgenstern, H. and Doucette, J. (1994) Race and tardive dyskinesia among outpatients at a CMHC. *Hospital and Community Psychiatry, 45(1)*, 38–42

Gondolf, E. W. (1998) Procedures for assessing woman battering. In E. W. Gondolf (Ed.), *Assessing Woman Battering in Mental Health Services* (pp. 65-92). London: Sage

Good Practices in Mental Health. (1993) *An Information Pack of Mental Health Services for Women in the United Kingdom* . London: Good Practices in Mental Health, 380–84 Harrow Road, London W9 2HU

Goodman, L. A., Johnson, M., Dutton, M. A., and Harris, M. (1997) Prevalence and Impact of Sexual and Physical Abuse. In M. Harris and C. L. Landis (Eds.), *Sexual Abuse in the Lives of Women Diagnosed with Serious Mental Illness* . London: Harwood Academic

Harris, M., and Landis, L. L. (Eds.) (1997) *Sexual Abuse in the Lives of Women Diagnosed with Serious Mental Illness*. London: Harwood Academic

Haslam, K. (1998) Mad to be gay. *Mental Health Care, 1(7)*, 222

Heise, L. L. (1996) Violence against women: global organizing for change. In J. L. Edleson and Z. C. Eisikovits (Eds.), *Future Interventions with Battered Women and their Families* (pp. 7-33). London: Sage

Herek, G. M. and Berrill, K. T. (1990) Anti-gay violence and mental health: Setting an agenda for research. Special Issue: Violence against lesbians and gay men: Issues for research, practice, and policy. *Journal of Interpersonal Violence, 5(3)*, 414–23

Holland, S. (1995) Interaction in women's mental health and neighbour-hood development. In S. Fernando (Ed.), *Mental Health in a Multi-ethnic Society*. London: Routledge

Ismail, K. (1996) Planning services for black women. In K. Abel, M.

Buszewicz, S. Davison, S. Johnson, and E. Staples (Eds.), *Planning Community Mental Health Services for Women*. London: Routledge

Jacobs, J. L. (1992) Child Sexual Abuse Victimization and Later Sequelae during Pregnancy and Childbirth. *Journal of Child Sexual Abuse, 1(1),* 103–12

Keating, F. (1998) *Towards a Draft Framework for A Multi-Dimensional Approach to Oppression.* London: Central Council for Education and Training in Social Work

Krawitz, R. and Watson, C. (1997) Gender, race and poverty: Bringing the sociopolitical into psychotherapy. *Australian and New Zealand Journal of Psychiatry, 31(4),* 474–9

Lindow, V. (1991) Experts, lies and stereotypes. *The Health Service Journal* (August 29)

Marques, J. M., Paez, D. and Abrams, D. (1998) Social identity and intragroup differentiation as subjective social control. In S. Worchel, J. F. Morales, and et-al. (Eds.), *Social identity: International perspectives.* (pp. 124-141). London: Sage

McFarlane, J., Parker, B. and Soeken, K. (1995) Abuse during pregnancy: Frequency, severity, perpetrator, and risk factors of homicide. *Public Health Nursing, 12(5),* 284–9

McFarlane, J. and Wiist, W. (1997) Preventing abuse to pregnant women: Implementation of a 'mentor mother' advocacy model. *Journal of Community Health Nursing, 14(4),* 237–49

McRae, J. A. and Brody, C. J. (1989) The differential importance of marital experiences for the well-being of women and men: A research note. *Social Science Research, 18(3),* 237–48

Miller, J. and Bell, C. (1996) Mapping men's mental health. *Journal of Community and Applied Social Psychology, 6(5),* 317–27

Mirlees-Black, C. (1995) Estimating the extent of domestic violence: findings from the 1992 British Crime Survey. *Research Bulletin, 37,* 1–9

Mowbray, C. T., Oyserman, D., Saunders, D. and Rueda-Riedle, A. (1998) Women with severe mental disorders: issues and service needs. In B. Lubotsky Levin, A. K. Blanch, and A. Jennings (Eds.), *Women's Mental Health Services: Public Health Perspective* (pp. 175–200) London: Sage

Nadien, M. (1996) Aging women: issues of mental health and maltreatment. In J. A. Sechzer and S. M. Pfafflin, E. L. Denmark, A. Griffin and S. S. Blumenthal (Eds.), *Women and Mental Health.* New York: New York Academy of Sciences

Pacitti, R. and Dimmick, J. (1996) Poverty and mental health: Underclaiming of welfare benefits. *Journal of Community and Applied Social Psychology, 6(5),* 395–402

Padgett, D. K., Burns, B. J. and Grau, L. A. (1998) Risk factors and resilience: mental health needs and service use of older women. In B. Lubotsky Levin, A. K. Blanch and A. Jennings (Eds.), *Women's*

Mental Health Services: Public Health Perspective (pp. 390–413)

Parker, B., McFarlane, J., Soeken, K., Torres, S. et al. (1993) Physical and emotional abuse in pregnancy: A comparison of adult and teenage women. *Nursing Research, 42(3)*, 173–8

Payne, S. (1991) *Women, Health and Poverty: An introduction.* London: Harvester Wheatsheaf

Perkins, R., Nadirshaw, Z., Copperman, J. and Andrews, C. (1996) *Women in Context: Good Practice in Mental Health Services for Women.* London: Good Practices in Mental Health

Petersen, R., Gazmararian, J. A., Spitz, A. M., Rowley, D. L., Goodwin, M. M., Saltzman, L. E. and Marks, J. S. (1997) Violence and adverse pregnancy outcomes: A review of the literature and directions for future research. *American Journal of Preventive Medicine, 13(5)*, 366–73

Potier, M. (1993) Giving evidence: women's lives in Ashworth maximum security psychiatric hospital. *Feminism and Psychology, 3(3)*, 335–47

Pound, A. and Abel, K. (1996) Motherhood and mental illness. In K. Abel, M. Buszewicz, S. Davidson, S. Johnson and E. Staples (Eds.), *Planning Community Mental Health Services for Women.* London: Routledge

Ratner, P. A. (1998) Modeling acts of aggression and dominance as wife abuse and exploring their adverse health effects. *Journal of Marriage and the Family, 60(2)*, 453–65

Rosewater, L. B. (1985) Schizophrenic, borderline, or battered? In L. B. Rosewater and L. E. A. Walker (Eds.), *Handbook of Feminist Therapy: Women's issues in psychotherapy.* New York: Springer

Sayce, L. (1996) Campaigning for change. In K. Abel, M. Busezwicz, S. Davison, S. Johnson, and E. Staples (Eds.), *Planning Community Mental Health Services for Women.* London: Routledge

Smith, L. J. F. (1989) *Domestic Violence: An overview of the literature.* A Home Office Research and Planning Report. London: HMSO

Stark, E. and Flitcraft, A. (1995) Killing the Beast Within: Woman battering and female suicidality. *International Journal of Health Services, 25(1)*, 43–64

Thomas, P. (1996) Big boys don't cry? Mental health and the politics of gender. *Journal of Mental Health, 5(2)*, 107–10

Thompson, N. (1998) *Promoting Equality: Challenging discrimination and oppression in the human services.* Basingstoke: MacMillan

Ussher, J. M. (1991) *Women's Madness: Misogyny or mental illness?* Amherst, MA: University of Massachusetts Press

Wade, J. C. (1993) Institutional racism: An analysis of the mental health system. *American Journal of Orthopsychiatry, 63(4)*, 536–44

Warner, S. (1996) Visibly special? Women, child sexual abuse and special hospitals. In C. Hemingway (Ed.), *Special Women? The Experience of Women in the Special Hospital System.* Aldershot: Avebury

Warner, L. and Ford, R. (1998) Conditions for women in in-patient psychiatric units: the Mental Health Act Commission 1996 national visit. *Mental Health Care, 11(7),* 225–8

Watson, G. and Williams, J. (1992) Feminist practice in therapy. In J. Ussher and P. Nicolson. (Eds.), *Gender Issues in Clinical Psychology* (pp. 212–36). London: Routledge

Watson, G., Scott, C.,and Ragalsky, S. (1996) Refusing to be marginalized: groupwork in mental health services for women survivors of childhood sexual abuse. *Journal of Community and Applied Social Psychology, 6(5),* 341–54

Weber, L. (1998) A conceptual framework for understanding race, class, gender, and sexuality. *Psychology of Women Quarterly, 22(1),* 13–32

Wilkinson, R. G. (1996) *Unhealthy Societies: The afflictions of inequality.* London: Routledge

Williams, J. and Watson, G. (1988) Sexual inequality, family life and family therapy. In E. Street and W. Dryden (Eds.), *Family Therapy in Britain.* Milton Keynes: Open University Press

Williams, J. A. (1984) Gender and intergroup behaviour: towards an integration. *British Journal of Social Psychology 23,* 311–16

Williams, J., Watson, G., Smith, H., Copperman, J. and Wood, D. (1993) *Purchasing Effective Mental Health Service for Women: A framework for action.* London: MIND publications/Tizard Centre, University of Kent at Canterbury

Williams, J. (Ed) (1996a) Social inequalities and mental health: developing services and developing knowledge. *Journal of Community and Applied Social Psychology (Special Issue), 6(5),* 311–16

Williams, J. (Ed) (1996b) Social inequalities and mental health: implications for service provision. *Journal of Community and Applied Social Psychology, 6 (Special Issue)*

Williams, J. and Watson, G. (1996) Mental health services that empower women. In T. Heller, J. Reynold, R. Gomm, R. Muston, and S. Pattison (Eds.), *Mental Health Matters: A reader* (pp. 242–51). London: Macmillan/Open University.

Williams, J. and Lindley, P. (1996) Working with mental health service users to change mental health services. *Journal of Community and Applied Social Psychology, 6(1),* 1–14

Williams, J., Liebling, H., Lovelock, C., Chipchase, H. and Herbert, Y. (1998) Working with women in special hospitals. *Feminism and Psychology, 8(3),* 357–69

Williams, J., and Keating, F. (In press) The abuse of adults in psychiatric settings. In N. Stanley, J. Manthorpe and B. Penhale (Eds.), *Letting in the Light: Studies in institutional abuse.* London: Routledge

Women's Aid Federation of England. (1998) *Families Without Fear: Women's aid agenda for action on domestic violence: Recommendations for a National Strategy.* Bristol: Women's Aid, PO Box 391, Bristol BS99 7WS

Wood, D. and Copperman, J. (1996) Sexual harassment and assault in psychiatric services. In R. Perkins, Z. Nadirshaw, J. Copperman and C. Andrews (Eds.), *Women in Context: Good practice in mental health services for women* (pp. 128–37). London: Good Practices in Mental Health

Wyatt, G. E., Guthrie, D. and Notgrass, C. M. (1992) Differential effects of women's child sexual abuse and subsequent sexual revictimization. Special Section: Adult survivors of childhood sexual abuse. *Journal of Consulting and Clinical Psychology, 60(2),* 167–73

CHAPTER 3

Racism and mental health

NIMISHA PATEL AND IYABO A. FATIMILEHIN

THIS CHAPTER HIGHLIGHTS the various ways in which Black and minority ethnic people continue to experience discrimination in Britain. It attempts to explore the material, social and psychological consequences of racism and the complex interrelationships between these factors. The reality of institutional racism within the mental health system is recognised as a major source of concern, particularly given the benign guise of the mental health system as an institution supposedly aimed at health restoration. The chapter concludes by offering some guiding pes and examples of services which could be utilised in developing an equitable, sensitive and socially responsible mental health service that might begin to adequately serve Black and minority ethnic communities in Britain.

Racism in Britain

The presence of Black people in Britain dates back to Roman times when Black soldiers in the Roman army occupied parts of Britain and Black African slaves were brought here by the Romans. However, most of the current population of Black people arrived in the post-war migrations of the 1950s and 1960s (Fryer, 1984) when they were invited by the British government to help re-build the 'mother country'. Many came to Britain with the promise and hope of a better quality of life. However, hostility and discrimination constituted the stark reality of their life in Britain. They found that their qualifications were disregarded, and they were given menial and low-paid jobs which could not be filled by the indigenous population, including jobs within health and public transport. Whilst the experiences of people from minority ethnic groups have differed, individual and institutional racism has impinged on all areas of their lives. Evidence of this can be found in employment, education, levels of racial harassment, health and the criminal justice system.

Employment
The Race Relations Act (1976) was intended to provide Black and minority ethnic people with some protection from racial discrimination, especially in terms of employment. However, the evidence from surveys that have been carried out since the Act suggests that racial discrimination has continued to have a profound and varied effect on people from minority ethnic groups. Braham et al (1992) found that at least one third of private employers discriminated against Asian and African-Caribbean applicants. Recent studies by the Policy Studies Institute (Modood, 1997) indicated that 90% of economically active White people thought that employers refuse people jobs for racial/religious reasons. Interestingly, only 60–75% of most of the minority groups believed such discrimination existed. In the same study, 20% of minority ethnic groups reported having experienced racial discrimination when applying for jobs. A quarter of those who believed they had been discriminated against in a job application believed that it was for both racial and religious reasons.

The Policy Studies Institute survey showed how the percentage of economically active people without work varies between ethnic groups (Modood, 1997). In their survey, 15% of White men under retirement age were unemployed compared with 9% of Chinese men, 14% of African Asians, 19% of Indians, 31% of Caribbeans, 38% of Pakistanis, and 42% of Bangladeshis. For women, the rates were: Whites (9%), Chinese (6%), African Asians (12%), Indians (12%), Caribbeans (18%), Pakistanis (39%), Bangladeshis (40%). White men who left full-time education at the age of 16 had an unemployment rate of 13% at the ages of 20–24; the rate among ethnic minorities was 43%. At each educational qualification level, the rate of unemployment for Pakistani/Bangladeshi and Caribbean men was much higher than that for White and Indian/African Asian men. Sixty one per cent of Caribbean men under 35 with no qualifications were unemployed. These higher unemployment rates could not be explained by occupation or geography. The survey's findings on the types of employment undertaken by different ethnic groups was also illuminating. Except for African Asians and Caribbean women, minorities are over-represented in manual work.

Caribbeans at 14% had the lowest representation in the top category of professionals, managers and employers, while nearly half of the Chinese men were in this category. All the minorities were distinctly less likely than White men to be employers and managers of large establishments. However, South Asians and Chinese are well-represented in professional and managerial categories because of the contribution of self-employment (Modood et al 1997). Another survey in 1995/1996 showed that men and women of African and Caribbean descent were still significantly more likely (26% and 46% respectively) than White men and women (18% and 31%) to be employed in the public sector (CRE, 1997a). Forty years following post war migration, the majority of Black and minority ethnic people are still employed predominantly within the confines of public sector, non-managerial positions or are self-employed. This begs the question of the extent to which patterns of employment for Black and minority ethnic people reflect systematic social exclusion in the social structures of a so-called multi-ethnic society.

Education
A pattern of social exclusion is also evident in the educational system. Bourne et al (1994) reported that in secondary schools in Nottingham, Reading, Bristol and Brent, African-Caribbean students were up to six times more likely to be suspended from school than their White peers. A Commission for Racial Equality inquiry into school suspensions in Birmingham found that African Caribbean pupils were four times more likely to be suspended from school for a given level of disruptive behaviour (CRE, 1984). In a further enquiry on school exclusions in Birmingham, the CRE reported that in 1995/96, 27% of all excluded pupils were African Caribbean, 49% were White and 14% were Asian. African Caribbeans formed 8% of the total school population, whereas Whites form 58% and Asians form 29% (Osler, 1997).

Bourne et al (1994) suggested that one reason for the high levels of exclusion of Black children is that they are often seen as having intractable behavioural problems due to their culture or upbringing. Sonuga-Barke et al. (1993) showed that where a White child and a Black child had similar activity levels in the classroom, the teacher was more likely to label the Black child as 'hyperactive'. The problem is located within the individual and their culture:

> *The exclusion of the black child . . . is once again being regarded as another element in the social pathology of*

*the black family, rather than as an indicator of a differently
structured racism that works against the poorest sections
of the black community in particular.'* (Sivanandan, 1994)

Lower academic achievement in Black and minority ethnic pupils
can also be seen as further evidence of discrimination. A recent
OFSTED report summarised the patterns of academic achievement
in all stages of education (Gillborn & Gipps, 1996). It highlighted a
consistent pattern of lower average attainments of Bangladeshi and
Pakistani pupils in the early stages of education. It also pointed to
the finding that African Caribbean pupils' average achievements
are significantly lower than other groups in many LEAs and that
the achievements of African Caribbean young men are a particular
cause for concern. Furthermore, the report showed how the
academic achievements of pupils from each ethnic group is
consistently linked with socio-economic status.

Black and minority ethnic young people have also faced racial
discrimination with regard to access to universities. White applicants
are more likely than minority ethnic applicants to be accepted by
the 'old' universities, and African Caribbean and African applicants
are accepted least often (Gillborn & Gipps, 1996). In addition, in
1988, a major national report called 'Learning in Terror' highlighted
the pervasiveness of racist incidents in educational institutions.
Only 47 of the 115 educational institutions surveyed had published
or were preparing guidelines to combat racial harassment (CRE,
1988).

Health
Inequalities in health have been the subject of considerable research
and debate since the publication of the Black Report in 1980 (e.g.
Illsley & Svensson, 1990; Davey Smith et. al., 1990; Macintyre,
1997). The Black Report (Townsend et al, 1988) was significant in
highlighting many health inequalities, including inequalities
experienced by minority ethnic people. For example, all immigrants
were reported as having higher mortality rates than average for
tuberculosis and accidents. There were also higher incidence rates
for diabetes, liver cancer and maternal conditions.

More recently, in 1993, the Department of Health produced a
guide for the National Health Service titled 'The Health of the Nation:
Ethnicity and Health'. The report indicated that in England and
Wales, mortality due to stroke was 76% higher in Caribbean men
and 110% higher in Caribbean women (about double the national

average). In addition, African Caribbean people and Asian people had a higher than average propensity for hypertension, and mortality from hypertensive disease was four times greater than the national average in Caribbean men and seven times greater in Caribbean women. Suicide rates for women from the Indian subcontinent were reported as being higher than the national average, and greatest among Asian girls aged 15–24 (double the national levels).

Inequalities in health can occur both as a result of economic hardship and as a consequence of racial discrimination which in itself can impact on one's opportunities in life and quality of life. Inequalities in mental health can also be attributed to similar factors and these issues, some of which are explored later on in this chapter, have been a major source of concern for researchers and practitioners alike.

Racial violence and harassment

Overt individual racism has characterised the relationships between minority ethnic groups and White groups for centuries. The history of slavery and colonisation is testament to this, and throughout this century there have been attacks on Black people, especially in the dock areas of Britain. In every era, these attacks have been bolstered by racist political and ideological doctrines which both legitimise and instigate racial discrimination.

The CRE defines racial harassment as 'verbal or physical violence towards individuals or groups on grounds of their colour, race, nationality, or ethnic or national origin, where the victims believe the aggression was racially motivated and/or there is evidence of racial motivation' (CRE, 1997b). The British Crime Survey reported that there were 130,000 racially motivated incidents in 1991, including 52,800 threats, 26,000 acts of vandalism, and 32,250 assaults (CRE, 1997b). Of these incidents, 89,000 were directed against Asians and 41,000 against people from the Black (Caribbean, African and 'other') groups. There is a significant under-reporting of racial incidents. For example, in 1991, the police recorded less than 8,000 incidents. The numbers recorded are rising (e.g. by 3% in 1995/1996), not necessarily because of an increase in the number of incidents but more likely because of an increase in reporting, and an increase in the number being recorded as racial incidents by the police.

Findings from the British Crime Survey suggest that Pakistanis are the most vulnerable to racially motivated crimes and threats, and that Asians as a group are more likely to be 'very worried' about being the victims of racial attacks – 38% compared with 29% of Black (Caribbean, African, other) people and 7% of White people (CRE, 1997b). Repeated victimisation was fairly common with 74% of Pakistanis, 61% of African Caribbeans and 53% of Indians reporting that the incidents were part of a series. Racially motivated crimes against Pakistanis were committed overwhelmingly (98%) by White offenders. Men were responsible for 80% of all racially motivated offences. In over three-quarters of racially motivated incidents, the offender(s) was a stranger. For Pakistanis this figure rose to 95% (CRE, 1997b).

Over the last couple of years the murder of Stephen Lawrence and the attempts by his parents to bring his murderers to justice have brought the issue of racial violence to the forefront of public consciousness. Sadly, this is not an isolated incident. The Runnymede Trust estimated that between 1970 and 1989, 74 people died as a result of attacks which were either known to be racially motivated because of evidence at subsequent trials, or widely believed to be so within the Black community (Gordon, 1990). Between 1991 and 1994, fifteen people died in Britain as a result of what are believed to be racially motivated attacks (Modood et al, 1997).

Criminal justice
The relationship between young Black people and the police has been extremely poor, and is symbolic of the endemic racial discrimination in the criminal justice system. The riots in inner city areas during the early part of the 1980s were only one manifestation of the degree of mistrust and suspicion that exists between the police and young Black people. Surveys have shown that 22% of people stopped and searched by the police in 1994/95 were from minority ethnic groups (CRE, 1997c). Moreover, almost 60% of young African Caribbean men in inner cities in England said they had been stopped or questioned by the police in the previous 12 months compared with just over 40% of young White men (Shaw, 1994). Forty two per cent of African Caribbeans with a car had been stopped by the police compared with 8% of White people with a car. A CRE study of seven police forces found that after controlling for relevant factors such as seriousness of offence and previous record, 64% of African Caribbeans who had been arrested were referred for prosecution compared with 42% of Asians and 36% of Whites (CRE, 1992).

Once prosecuted, official statistics have shown that African

Caribbean men and women are more likely to receive a custodial sentence than their White counterparts for similar offences (NACRO, 1990). African-Caribbean men and women are considerably over-represented in British prisons. In September 1989, African Caribbean men and women made up 10.6% and 20.6% of the prison population respectively, even though they only comprise 1–2% of the general population. The proportion of young Black men going into custody is twice as high as the proportion of young White men, this means that nearly one in 10 of the young men in the Black community will have been imprisoned by his 21st birthday. The average prison sentences for Black and Asian offenders were substantially longer than those for White people convicted of similar offences (CRE, 1997d).

The inquiry into the murder of Stephen Lawrence (Macpherson, 1999) has brought acknowledgement from the British government, for the first time, that institutional racism exists in the police force. The Macpherson report stated that the police investigation into the murder of Stephen Lawrence was flawed by institutional racism, as well as by professional incompetence and failures of leadership. The report made 70 recommendations which covered *inter alia* areas such as police powers, accountability, reporting and recording racist incidents, family liaison, prosecution of racist crimes, recruitment and retention of Black and minority ethnic police officers, training in racism awareness and valuing cultural diversity, and prevention and education. The report has been hailed as a watershed in the history of race relations in Britain, but its impact on the experiences of Black and minority ethnic people in the criminal justice system remains to be seen.

Although we have discussed these factors separately, indices of disadvantage are often linked so that, for example, poor educational attainment can lead to lower socio-economic status which can impact on one's health and one's opportunities for employment. A vicious circle can occur for Black and minority ethnic people when attempts to break out of the cycle of disadvantage are thwarted by institutional racism. Verbal and physical racial harassment and violence add insult to injury, even for those Black and minority ethnic people who enjoy the privileges of a higher socio-economic status.

The Impact of Racism
The significance of the extent of inequalities based on race in Britain and of all forms of racism can be ascertained only by exploring the

consequences for Black and minority ethnic people. The consequences extend beyond the individual alone and permeate people's daily lives and interactions within whole communities. Thus, the impact of racism is not merely psychological, but social and material.

Material consequences
Given the evidence on racial disadvantage in employment, the material consequences of racial inequalities are self-evident. The lack of opportunities, related financial hardships and material deprivation can all have profound implications for the structure, functions, and stability of families. Berthoud (1997) reports that many of the minority ethnic families surveyed in their study were sending money to other members of their family, a pattern commonly found with migrants from South Asia and the Caribbean. Economic responsibilities for one's own or extended family may mean that financial hardship has repercussions beyond the individual to whole families and communities. One's personal experience of discrimination can thus be experienced as more than a personal sense of failure, rejection and inadequacy; it can evoke a profound sense of injustice, guilt and helplessness at being unable to fulfil familial duties and loyalties.

Disadvantage contributing to unemployment, financial hardship and material deprivation may also severely undermine the supportive functions of existing networks. It is likely that where whole communities experience economic deprivation their capacity to provide emotional and economic support is significantly reduced, perhaps leading to social isolation within the community and exclusion from the wider society.

Social consequences
Material deprivation can be linked to the notion of social power (Orford, 1998) and people's experience of powerlessness in effecting change in their material and social context. Institutional racism can have the effect of continually subjugating minority ethnic people, reducing their social, economic and political power and marginalising whole communities. Minority ethnic people are seen and treated as 'other' in a process whereby they are deemed to be different from the majority ethnic, White people – the norm against which difference is ascertained and deviancy is measured. This process is both a result of racist constructions and a precursor to further racism at both individual and institutional levels.

Historically, Eurocentric constructions of Black and minority ethnic people have perpetuated racial prejudice and legitimised injustices from slavery and colonisation to inequalities in employment, housing, and education, as well as coercive practices in the mental health system. Minority ethnic people have been consistently homogenised in literature, in policy-making and even in national surveys. Until recently, many social and psychological studies did not adequately address the issue of heterogeneity within particular ethnic groups, let alone within the 'minority ethnic population' in Britain.

Fernando (1991) argues that 'the power within racism ensures that the application of race thinking invokes assumptions of inferiority-superiority, justifying exploitation and the allocation of individuals, their cultures, etc. to positions on a hierarchy' (p27). This construction of hierarchies and the homogenisation of minority ethnic people creates fertile ground for racism to flourish. However, some minority ethnic people create a common identity in response to racism and as a collective political statement. For example, the term 'Black' is often used as a self-description to denote the experience of oppression based on ethnicity, colour, or culture. In more recent times, there has been the emergence of new self-definitions such as 'Black British' and 'British Asian', perhaps in an effort to assert diversity in the heritages and experiences of minority ethnic people in Britain.

Any sense of belongingness and apparent unity within Black and minority ethnic groups may betray related experiences of continued uncertainty, lack of opportunity, helplessness, outrage at racial injustices and fear. Mistrust of each other, mistrust of one's neighbours, one's colleagues and one's peers is perhaps inevitable in a hostile environment when one is routinely subjected to subtle and overt institutional and individual racism. Thomas (1992) argues that racism has a detrimental effect on social relationships, both in relationships between Black and White people and between Black people themselves. Black people may come to have lower expectations of and aspirations for themselves, their family members and those from their communities. Mistrust, frustrations and resentment may be fuelled by those members of one's community who are seen as having somehow betrayed their communities, for example by seeking to behave or to be 'White'; by denying that racism exists and advocating a benevolent view of a British society as being based on meritocracy; or by minimising one's 'Blackness' or one's particular ethnic heritage.

The experience of social hypervigilance is not uncommon. There is the constant vigilance and alertness to the hostilities and dangers of living in a racist society, the continual caution with which institutions are viewed, and the perpetual threat of racial harassment and racist violence towards members of one's family and community. Racism's tentacles penetrate the sanctity of families and whole communities, further undermining their capacity to provide social support and to exercise social power in effecting social action that may lead to some change.

The impact of racism on families is perhaps most noticeable in the consequences for parents. Fatimilehin and Coleman (1999) state that parents have the task of making 'their children feel valued in a world that continually devalues Black children's experiences and contributions, and at best places them in the position of 'other' or exotic; at worst labels them as deviant (social exclusions) and dangerous (incarceration)'. Where parents themselves feel devalued, marginalised, discriminated against, powerless, subjugated and afraid, one wonders how children can develop a robust and positive sense of their ethnic identity which would enable them to cope with and combat racism without fearing or experiencing similar consequences as those experienced by their parents and those in their community.

Minority ethnic groups can become the repositories for the projections of the White majority groups. Negative and distasteful aspects of one's own histories and biases may feel untenable and be projected on to minority ethnic people. It is as if racism is both a cause and a result of historical and present-day inequalities, serving the function of enabling White majority ethnic groups to maintain a positive group identity, at the cost of other groups. As such, racism becomes a web of inequalities, injustices and an ideology which permeates every aspect of social living, involving all members of society, including minority ethnic people and majority ethnic White people.

Why is it then that racism becomes a problem that requires description, analysis and explanation by the very people who have suffered it? As Pence (1982) points out, the history of racism is a White history. However, the social, political and academic marginalisation of the issues of racism has tended to absolve non-minority ethnic people of the responsibility to examine their contributions to social injustice and to instigate change. Thus, an analysis of the social implications of racism needs also to come from those whose histories and privileges have made racism possible and ensured its maintenance to date.

Psychological consequences
The psychological consequences of racism tend to be far-reaching, affecting children, adolescents, adults and older people, and whole communities. However, in exploring the psychological consequences of racism there is a danger of privatising that which is essentially public and political. Whilst racism can have devastating consequences for the individual this has to be seen in the context of social consequences and the socio-political forces which perpetuate racial inequalities. Orford (1998) argues for an approach which places individuals within their social contexts and which does not psychologise "the materiality of social power" (Hagan and Smail, 1997).

Arguably, psychological models which are inherently individual in focus have limited validity in relation to socio-political processes such as racism, particularly when the aim is to reduce the impact of such processes to intra-psychic phenomena which can be examined by scrutinising the inner world of individuals, rather than their social contexts. In discussing psychological responses to interpersonal violence, Mezey (1997) suggests that the diagnostic formulation of 'post traumatic stress disorder' has limited relevance to racial discrimination and violence. She indicates that such violence gives 'rise to more complex, diffuse and long-term disturbance than simple PTSD' (p179). Similarly, Bowling (1993) suggests that racial victimisation cannot be construed as discrete episodes but as constantly evolving social processes which are diffuse, contextually bound and profoundly dislocating for victims. Both authors attempt to challenge traditional psychological approaches which locate the problems within the individual. However, the language used depicts the problem as having pathological consequences for the individual, who is construed as a victim, and thus reinforces the focus on the individual.

The impact of institutional and individual racism is difficult to measure or assess accurately because of its cumulative nature. Root (1992) suggests that cumulative racism can result in a decreased sense of optimism, displaced anger and a turn towards individualism for survival of the spirit. The experiences of rage and anger are not uncommon reactions to racism and Wilson (1981) argued that victimisation and exploitation can be seen as the cause of many of the problems faced by minority ethnic people.

Tajfel (1978) has suggested that those who have experienced racism may experience conflicts between self-realisation and the restrictions imposed by the realities of membership of a minority group. The sense of limited control over external, social realities may compound the experience of helplessness and powerlessness which Fernando (1984) believes may lead to depression. The social reality of racism may also lead to lowered expectations for oneself and of the availability of opportunities in all societal institutions. Racism can also deny the Black person individual characteristics which could be seen as normal (characteristics which White people are held to possess), and negative characteristics based on historical distortions may be ascribed to Black people (Thomas, 1992). Black and minority ethnic people themselves may be socialised to accept racism as part of their everyday life, including accepting negative constructions held of them. Internalised racism inevitably involves an acceptance and belief in the inferiority of Black and minority ethnic people and it may result in prejudices towards others from minority ethnic backgrounds.

The objectification and dehumanisation of Black and minority ethnic people which perpetuate racism holds particular significance for Black women. Root (1996) asserts that women of colour hold dual roles and identities as women and as Black people, both of which have ascribed secondary status constituting a 'double jeopardy'. She suggests that 'by placing women of colour at the bottom of the ladder of power, they become potential targets for the anger of all those subordinate to White men: White women and men of colour' (p371). Interpersonal violence towards Black women, including rape, domestic violence and sexual abuse are seen as evidence of such insidious effects of social hierarchies and discrimination based on ethnicity and gender (Root, 1996).

Hine (1989) suggests that Black women may actively hide the extent of their experiences of persecution, which Root (1996) asserts has a silencing effect on the women who use their silence as a defence against their oppressors. It is the silencing of those who suffer racism that facilitates the use of oppressive psychological explanations and tools for intervention. Professional and academic voices fill the silence, speaking on behalf of those who suffer from racism in society, in the institutions of mental health and in the consulting room itself. The following section explores some of the ways in which racism has manifested itself in the mental health system.

Racism and the mental health system
The lack of reference to the experiences of Black and minority ethnic people in psychological literature, models and practices within the

mental health system is an indication of the positioning of Black and minority ethnic people in this system. The very construct of mental health is in itself Eurocentric and systems based on such constructs have inherent biases which beg questions regarding their validity for Black and minority ethnic people. Sue et al. (1996) argue that a major stumbling block to moving beyond Eurocentricism is the reluctance of mental health professionals to acknowledge the varying manifestations of racism in the mental health field, including in their own racist attitudes and practices.

One common misconception is the notion that racism is more evident in psychiatric practice than elsewhere in the mental health system. Clinical Psychology, counselling and other psychological health professionals are as responsible as psychiatrists in the perpetuation of various forms of racism. Yet, psychiatry is the eternal demon and a container for the untenable realities of abusive practices within psychology, realities which are rarely acknowledged in training, in practice or in psychological literature. There are many ways in which racism is manifested in the mental health field, both overtly and covertly and as individual and as institutional racism.

Ridley (1995) proposes a behavioural model of racism which encompasses both institutional and individual racism and which can be overt or covert and intentional or unintentional. He suggests that overt racism is always intentional and may manifest itself, for example, in a therapist who believes that minority ethnic people are inferior and on this basis refuses to see them as clients. His example of covert racism is where a senior psychologist allocates a minority ethnic client to a trainee because of personal discomfort, whilst justifying it on the grounds of a heavy workload. Individual racism within the mental health system is often difficult to monitor as it tends to be covert and ethnic monitoring systems often do not provide sufficiently detailed data to ascertain the practices of individual clinicians. Indeed, Dovidio and Gaertner (1986) argue that there is increasing evidence that more subtle forms of racism have replaced blatant discrimination, perhaps pointing to a need for greater scrutiny of our existing systems and practices.

The overwhelming bias towards the use of traditional, Western models of psychological health and psychological and psychiatric practice is a testimony to one of the most blatant, yet often covert, forms of racism in the mental health system. The blanket imposition and application of inherently biased models to minority ethnic people can be described as secondary colonisation. Said (1993) cites the French writer Leroy-Beaulieu as espousing the view that 'the goal of colonisation is to place a new society in the best conditions for prosperity and growth' (p 129). In what more fertile ground could Eurocentric psychological technologies be placed than in the institutions of mental health where power relations and inequalities are most evident? The 'prosperity and growth' as a goal of colonisation could undoubtedly refer to the proliferation of Western psychological discourses, furnished in the language of pathology and applied to minority ethnic people whose experiences and difficulties may stem from social inequalities, not simply internal, psychic conflicts. Fernando (1991) also gives a cogent account of the manifestation of racism in the models utilised by psychiatry and psychology.

Ridley (1995) argues that many psychological models could be described as deficit models which are based on the premise that minority ethnic people have predetermined deficiencies and which can be used to explain their psychopathology (see Darwin, 1959; Stanton, 1960; Jensen, 1969; Rushton, 1988). The medical model is based on an assumed analogy between psychological difficulties and physical problems (Turner and Cumming, 1967). As such, formulations and interventions are aimed at altering the assumed illness by use of psychotropic medication or talking therapies. There are several difficulties with the application of models based on the medical model. In particular, there is a tendency to over pathologise using intrapsychic or organic explanations without consideration of external factors such as racism interacting with a person's emotional, spiritual, physical and material well-being. Sue et al (1996) suggest that clients who perceive their difficulty as residing in socio-cultural variables, such as oppression, may find the assumptions embedded within intrapsychic psychological approaches antagonistic to their own world views.

The overriding focus on pathology also prevents a balanced analysis of the strengths and resources that minority people may hold. Ponterotto and Casas (1991) call for psychological research to study positive attributes and characteristics of minority ethnic people that have helped them cope with stresses. Some authors have identified cultural strengths in African American families, such as supportive extended relatives, religious worldviews, Black pride and culture and training in surviving societal racism, which they argue should be cultivated in therapy (Stevenson and Renard, 1993).

Another major difficulty with the use of models based on the medical model is the discriminatory way in which practices based on these models have been applied to minority ethnic people. In reviewing the extent of discrimination in psychiatric diagnoses and treatment Fernando (1995) summarises the main findings as follows: Black and minority ethnic people are more often diagnosed as 'schizophrenic'; more often compulsorily detained under the Mental Health Act; more often admitted as 'offender patients'; more often held by police under section 136 of the Mental Health Act; more often transferred to locked wards; more often given high doses of medication; more often sent to psychiatrists by courts and more often not referred for psychological therapies. Whilst the reasons for the above findings may be varied and interrelated in a complex matrix, the question one needs to consider is to what extent overt and covert, intentional or unintentional racism is responsible for the inequitable treatment of Black and minority ethnic people in the mental health system.

Access to mental health services is another area where discrimination is central. Most mental health services have a tendency to be inaccessible to Black and minority ethnic people by virtue of their organisation, their choice of treatments or interventions offered, and their application of Eurocentric models. The absence of a clear, detailed and thorough policy of equal opportunity which considers not just recruitment of personnel but also access to appropriate services for Black and minority ethnic people is a common form of overt (though perhaps unintentional) racism in mental health services. The lack of interpreting services or the explicit reluctance to work with interpreters in psychological practice is another form of overt and intentional individual and institutional racism. Within psychological practice, the unquestioned use of Eurocentric assessment tools and tests which have not been validated for minority ethnic peoples in Britain is another example of discriminatory practice which serves to depict Black and minority ethnic people as deficient and deviant as determined in relation to Eurocentric norms. Likewise, the rigid adherence to existing models and clinical and research methods which are based on epistemological assumptions not shared by people from a range of minority ethnic backgrounds is an example of academic and clinical racism.

Even in the midst of a powerful user movement in mental health, Black and minority ethnic people are struggling to be heard and represented (Sassoon and Lindow, 1995). These authors propose that some of the obstacles for Black and minority ethnic users include the high levels of oppression that they are subjected to as users, including excessively high doses of medication, lack of clear communication with service providers and fear of being sectioned. The disempowered are further disempowered both in the mental health system and in the groups which struggle to implement collective action to facilitate change in the mental health system.

Any attempt at reconstructing a mental health service which is empowering and non-discriminatory would need to consider the many ways in which racism continues to be manifested in the present system.

A vision of a mental health system for black and minority ethnic people

Existing mental health services would need to be changed radically in order to begin to meet the requirements of Black and minority ethnic peoples. These changes are not merely structural, but require a radical re-thinking of the processes that have become integral to mental health service provision in the Western world. The development of anti-discriminatory services will involve major changes in the training and employment of health service staff, as well as a critical evaluation of existing policies, legislation, and monitoring systems.

Empowerment

The concept of empowerment has to become central so that people from Black and minority ethnic backgrounds feel that they do not need to give up all responsibility for their lives and health once they come into contact with services. Rogers et al (1997) identified five components of empowerment amongst users of mental health services. These were self-efficacy – self-esteem, power-powerlessness, community activism, righteous anger, and optimism-control over the future. In their study, self-efficacy – self-esteem and a sense of control over the future were the strongest and most consistent factors. Power was important in terms of access to financial resources. Righteous anger and community activism were important in terms of harnessing anger into action. Rogers et al (1997) found that empowerment was positively related to quality of life, income, and community activism and inversely related to the use of mental health services. This research supports the notion that mental health services must work in *partnership* with organisations within the community which have an interest in advocating for members of their community and are aware of the issues which impinge on their lives. Furthermore, a collaborative approach requires a firm commitment to being led primarily by clients' needs as defined by themselves.

People must be empowered to make choices about the services that would meet their needs. The issues of *advocacy* and *user involvement* need to be addressed. People from Black and minority ethnic backgrounds are under-represented in the user movement, and find that their voices are not heard within the mental health system. Services need to consider the ways in which they can involve Black and minority ethnic people in a meaningful way in service development. Services should also be *accountable* to the people whom they involve, so that those people are not just involved in the planning of services, but also have a right to *monitor and evaluate* the implementation and delivery of any new initiatives. These procedures should include methods and measures for determining the degree of satisfaction with the service.

A major concern for many Black and minority ethnic families is the stigma that is associated with mental health services, and the impact that this will have on their status in their communities. This means that some families will not approach services until they have reached a crisis point, and their difficulties are so severe that only tertiary services can be offered. Mental health services need to be offered in a non-stigmatising way so that people will feel able to use them. This means the development of *preventative, community-based* services which allow the users to retain control of and involvement in processes such as the writing of records and reports and the making of referrals. Preventative services need to *focus on family and cultural strengths* and the strengths of existing natural support systems rather than just on the deficits of the individual. The *location* of services is also important in the reduction of stigma, and services should be based in buildings which are already frequented by members of the community for other reasons (e.g. community centres and health centres).

Holistic services

The term holistic is derived from the theory that the fundamental principle of the universe is the creation of wholes (The Chambers Dictionary, 1993). Within mental health services, it is important that the whole of the person and their contexts are addressed so that issues of physical health, spirituality, housing, finances, employment, family issues, education, etc are taken into account and seen as legitimate areas of inquiry and action. In most mental health services, these issues are regarded as a corollary rather than being seen as central to the preservation of good mental health. An innovative inner city mental health project which aimed to address the needs of African Caribbean and Asian people through the provision of services which attended to social and socio-economic issues has been described by Watters (1996). Services should be provided with the person and their family in mind, rather than fragmented into services for children or adults. Holistic services also need to consider the whole community and not just the particular family unit. The individual and family are part of a whole community, and the issues that impinge on that community also impinge on the individual and family. Interventions addressing the whole community need to become part of mental health service provision. Holistic services would need to embrace recent developments in community psychology without colonising communities with Western psychological technologies, delivered by largely White middle class professionals.

Alternative models
The dominant models used for designing and implementing mental health services are Eurocentric in nature despite the fact that users of these services are not mono-ethnic in their backgrounds. Providers of mental health services are predominantly from White middle class backgrounds and their norms and values are embedded into the fabric of the institutions in which they work. The norms and values of Black and minority ethnic people may differ markedly from those espoused in the mental health system, resulting in a disjunction between the cultural values of the user and those of the service provider. For services to become appropriate to the requirements of Black and minority ethnic communities, culturally appropriate and anti-discriminatory models of service delivery must be implemented. Psychological models which draw on African and Asian Psychology are already in existence, and there are services which have attempted to take non-Western cultural values into account. Ipamo (an alternative mental health service for Black people) and NAFSYAT(an intercultural therapy centre) in Britain, and The Family Centre in New Zealand (Waldegrave, 1990) are noteworthy examples.

Separate versus integrated services
The failure of mainstream services to address the needs of various Black and minority ethnic communities in Britain has led to some members of the communities to take matters into their own hands and provide their own services for their own communities. This is

evident in many areas such as education where minority ethnic communities have developed supplementary educational activities which fill the gaps left by mainstream education. Examples include the Saturday Schools developed in many African Caribbean communities to provide additional academic support as well as an understanding of Black culture and history. Similarly, Koranic schools have been developed in Muslim communities to provide Muslim children with a sound grounding in Islam. Other examples where Black and minority ethnic people have created their own services include housing (e.g. Black housing associations) and Black mental health projects. Arguments in favour of these developments include the increase in self-efficacy for the community and the development of appropriate services which are not imbued with racism. The benefits are for both the users and providers of these services as there is no need to negotiate every aspect of the service that differs from the mainstream provision. However, a major disadvantage is the fact that these services are usually very small and vulnerable to the whims of funding agencies. In addition, it can be argued that Black and minority ethnic people are tax payers and full members of British society, and so are entitled to have their needs met to the same extent as the White population. Therefore, our argument would be that whilst separate services should be supported fully because of the significant benefits that accrue to their users, this does not mean that mainstream services should be allowed to neglect their duty to provide Black and minority ethnic communities with appropriate services. The provision of these services cannot be separated from the issue of *employing Black and minority ethnic staff* in mainstream services. Traditionally, Black staff in the mental health services have been employed as cleaners, caretakers, nurses, and administrative assistants and have not secured positions which involve them in decision making or service planning. The NHS Executive Mental Health Task Force (1994) note that Black staff are able to integrate their experience as Black people with their expertise as Black workers to help address issues of racism and to incorporate a Black perspective in service delivery.

Racism

Many people from Black and minority ethnic communities are concerned that by accessing services they leave themselves open to experiences of racism when they are at their most vulnerable. They are mindful that the response of services may mean the use of medication or coercive treatments, or that their concerns may simply be ignored or blamed on their cultural or racial heritage. For families, the futures of their children need to be taken into account, and whether contact with mental health services will be an added burden that the child has to bear. Services need to address this issue as a matter of urgency. Many services have (but do not implement) an Equal Opportunities Policy and there is often no systematic monitoring of its efficacy. All staff need to be trained in Equal Opportunities, and in the manifestations of racial discrimination. In addition, all mental health services need to ensure that they have adequate ethnic monitoring procedures which can identify the numbers of people from the local community who are accessing the service, as well as the numbers of Black and minority ethnic people who are employed within the service. Ethnic monitoring should also be mandatory in identifying and rectifying discriminatory practices.

Conclusions

The extent of individual and institutional racism in Britain should not be underestimated when identifying ways of developing equitable, sensitive and socially responsible mental health services which can adequately serve Black and minority ethnic people. The persistent, unquestioned use of Eurocentric theories, practices and models of service delivery should not be allowed to continue in a way which disadvantages and subjugates Black and minority ethnic people. There is a danger that mental health services will simply be tinkered with whilst individual, psychological models and interventions will continue to be employed in a way which reinforces the notion that the origins and locations of mental health problems are within the Black and minority ethnic people themselves, rather than in the structures of society. Racism is arguably implicated in much of the material, social and emotional difficulties experienced by Black and minority ethnic people and as such the challenge facing our mental health system is how to meaningfully identify and challenge structural inequalities based on race and how to develop services which actively seek to empower those whom we profess to serve.

References

Berthoud, R. (1997) Income and Standards of Living. In T. Modood, R. Berthoud, J. Lakey, J. Nazroo, P. Smith, S. Virdee and S. Beishon (Eds.), *Ethnic minorities in Britain: Diversity and disadvantage.* London: Policy Studies Institute

Bourne, J., Bridges, L. and Searle, C. (1994). *Outcast England: How Schools Exclude Black Children.* London: Institute of Race Relations

Bowling (1993) Racial harassment and the process of the victimisation. *British Journal of Criminology, 33,* 231–50

Braham, S., Rattansi, A. and Skellington, R. (Eds.) (1992). *Racism and Antiracism: Inequality, opportunities and policies.* London: Open University and Sage

Chambers. (1993) *The Chambers Dictionary.* Edinburgh: Chambers Harrap Publishers Ltd.

Commission for Racial Equaltiy. (1984) *Birmingham Local Authority and Schools. Referral and Suspension of Pupils: a report of a formal in vestigation.* London: CRE

Commission for Racial Equality. (1988) *Learning in Terror: a survey of racial harassment in schools and colleges.* London: CRE

Commission for Racial Equality. (1992) *Cautions versus prosecutions.* London: CRE

Commission for Racial Equality. (1997a) *CRE Factsheet: Employment and unemployment.* London: CRE

Commission for Racial Equality. (1997b) *CRE Factsheet: Racial attacks and harassment.* London: CRE

Commission for Racial Equality. (1997c) *CRE Factsheet: Policing and Race in England and Wales.* London: CRE

Commission for Racial Equality. (1997d) *CRE Factsheet: Criminal justice in England and Wales.* London: CRE

Darwin, C. (1959) *On the origin of species by means of natural selection.* London: J. Murray

Davey Smith, G., Bartley, M. and Blane, D. (1990). The Black Report on Socioeconomic inequalities in health, 10 years on. *British Medical Journal, 301,* 373–7

Department of Health. (1993) *The Health of the Nation. Ethnicity and Health. A Guide for the NHS.* London: HMSO

Dovidio, J. and Gaertner, S. (Eds.) (1986) *Prejudice, discrimination and racism.* Orlando, Florida: Academic Press

Fatimilehin, I. and Coleman, P. (1999) 'You've got to have a Chinese Chef to cook Chinese food!' Issues of power and control in mental health service use. *Journal of Community and Applied Social Psychology,* 9, 101–17

Fernando, S. (1984) Racism as a cause of depression. *International Journal of Social Psychiatry, 30,* 40–9

Fernando, S. (1991) *Mental Health, Race and Culture.* London: MacMillan and MIND

Fernando, S. (1995) Social realities and mental heath. In S. Fernando (Ed.), *Mental Health in a Multiethnic Society: a multidisciplinary handbook.* London: Routledge

Fryer, P. (1984) *Staying Power. The History of Black People in Britain.* London: Pluto

Gillborn, D. and Gipps, C. (1996) *Recent Research on the Achievements of Ethnic Minority Pupils. OFSTED Reviews of Research.* London: HMSO

Gordon, P. (1990) *Racial Violence and Harassment* London: Runnymede Trust

Hagan, T. and Smail, D. (1997) Power-mapping II: Practical application: the example of child sexual abuse. *Journal of Community and Applied Social Psychology, 4,* 269–85

Hine, D. (1989) Rape and the inner lives of Black women in the Middle West: Preliminary thoughts on the culture of dissemblance. *Signs, 14,* 912–20

Illsley, R. and Svensson, P. (Eds.) (1990) Health inequalities in Europe. *Social Science and Medicine,* Special Issue, *27*

Jensen, A. (1969) How much can we boost IQ and scholastic achievement? *Harvard Educational Review, 39,* 1, 1–123

Macintyre, S. (1997) The Black Report and beyond. What are the issues? *Social Science and Medicine, 44*(6), 723–45

Macpherson, W. (1999) *The Stephen Lawrence Inquiry.* London: HMSO

Mezey, G. (1997) Psychological responses to interpersonal violence. In D. Black, M. Newman, J. Harris-Hendriks and G. Mezey (Eds.), *Psychological Trauma: a developmental approach.* London: Royal College of Psychiatrists

Modood, T. (1997) Employment. In T. Modood, R. Berthoud, J. Lakey, J. Nazroo, P. Smith, S. Virdee and S. Beishon (Eds.), *Ethnic minorities in Britain: Diversity and Disadvantage.* London: Policy Studies Institute

Modood, T., Berthoud, R., Lakey, J., Nazroo, J., Smith, P., Virdee, S. and Beishon, S. (Eds.) (1997) *Ethnic minorities in Britain: Diversity and Disadvantage.* London: Policy Studies Institute

NACRO.(1990) *Black People Mental Health and The Courts.* Unpublished Report

NHS Executive Mental Health Task Force (1994) *Black Mental Health – A Dialogue for Change.* London: HMSO

Orford, J. (1998) Have we a theory of community psychology? *Clinical Psychology Forum, 122,* December, 6–10

Osler, A. (1997) *Exclusion from School and Racial Equality.* London: CRE

Pence, E. (1982) Racism – a White issue. In G. Hull, P. Bell-Scott and B. Smith (Eds.), *All the women are White, all the Blacks are men, but some of us are brave.* New York: Feminist Press

Ponterotto, J. and Casas, J. (1991) *Handbook of racial/ethnic minority counseling research.* Springfield, IL: Thomas

Ridley, C. (1995) *Overcoming unintentional racism in counseling and therapy.* California: Sage

Rogers, S. E., Chamberlin, J., Ellison, M. L., and Crean, T. (1997) A consumer-constructed scale to measure empowerment among users of mental health services. *Psychiatric Services 48*(8), 1042–47

Root, M. (1992) Reconstructing the impact of trauma on personality. In

L. Brown and M. Ballou (Eds.), *Personality and Psychopathology*. New York: Guildford

Root, M. (1996) Women of color and traumatic stress in 'domestic captivity': gender and race as disempowering statuses. In A. Marsella, M. Friedman, E. Gerrity and R. Scurfield (Eds.), *Ethnocultural aspects of post traumatic stress disorder: issues, research and clinical applications*. Washington: American Psychological Association

Rushton, J. (1988) Race differences in behaviour: A review and evolutionary analysis. *Journal of Personality and Individual Differences, 9,* 1009–24

Said, E. (1993) *Culture and Imperialism*. London: Vintage

Sassoon, M. and Lindow, V. (1995). Consulting and empowering Black mental health system users. In S. Fernando (Ed.), *Mental health in a multiethnic society: a multidisciplinary handbook*. London: Routledge

Shaw, C. (1994) *Changing Lives 3*. London: Policy Studies Institute

Sivanandan, A. (1994) Introduction. In J. Bourne, L. Bridges, and C. Searle. (Eds.) *Outcast England: How schools exclude Black children*. London: Institute of Race Relations

Sonuga-Barke, E. J. S., Minocha, K., Taylor, E.A. and Sandberg, S. (1993) Inter-ethnic bias in teachers' ratings of childhood hyperactivity. *British Journal of Developmental Psychology 11,* 187–200

Stanton, W. (1960) *The leopard's spots: Scientific attitudes toward race in America, 1815–1859*. Chicago: University of Chicago Press

Stevenson, H. and Renard, G. (1993) Trusting Ole' Wise Owls: Therapeutic use of cultural strengths in African American families. *Professional Psychology: Research and Practice, 24,* 4, 433–42

Sue, D., Ivey, A., and Pedersen, P. (1996) *A Theory of multicultural counseling and therapy*. Pacific Grove: Brooks/Cole

Tajfel, H. (1978) *The social psychology of minorities*, MRG Report No. 38. London: Minority Rights Group

Thomas, L. (1992) Psychotherapy in the context of race and culture: an inter-cultural therapeutic approach. In S. Fernando (Ed.), *Mental Health in a multiethnic society, a multi disciplinary handbook*. London: Routledge

Townsend, P., Davidson, N. and Whitehead, M. (1988) *Inequalities in Health: The Black Report and The Health Divide*. London: Penguin Books

Turner, R. and Cumming, J. (1967) Theoretical malaise and community mental health. In E. Cowen, E. Gardner and M. Zax (Eds.), *Emergent approaches to mental health problems*. New York: Appleton-Century-Crofts

Waldegrave, C. (1990) Just Therapy. *Dulwich Centre Newsletter 1*

Watters, C. (1996) Inequalities in Mental Health: the Inner City Mental Health Project *Journal of Community and Applied Social Psychology, 6,* 383–94

Wilson, A. (1981) *Black people and the Health Service*. Brent Community Health Council, April

CHAPTER 4

Diagnosis

MARY BOYLE

THE PRACTICE OF diagnosis is central to psychiatry for two major reasons. First, it apparently identifies individual mental disorders, in the same way as diagnosis in medicine identifies particular physical disorders. This apparent equivalence in the activities of psychiatry and medicine is important in supporting psychiatry's claim to be a branch of medicine, to be engaged in similar activities. Diagnosis is central, secondly, because it is based on classification, on the ordering of 'like with like' and it is frequently claimed that classification is central to science. Indeed, Michael Shepherd has claimed that 'to discard classification . . . is to discard scientific thinking' (1976: 3). Psychiatric diagnosis is therefore implicitly linked with science, so that whatever the admitted shortcomings of the present system, it is implied that it is a step in the right direction and that no fundamental examination is needed. One result of this taking-for-granted of diagnosis is that controversy over diagnostic systems and concepts often takes the form of discussions of diagnostic reliability, of disagreements about the criteria for a particular category, while the diagnostic system itself, and the process by which it is formed, remain unchallenged. But it is precisely because diagnosis is presented as a 'natural' part of psychiatric practice, and because it forms the basis for so many other practices, notably involving research and intervention, that it needs to be subjected to critical scrutiny. My aim in this chapter is to examine the diagnostic process and to ask whether its central role in attempts to understand and respond to psychological distress and disturbing behaviour can be justified.

What is meant by 'making a diagnosis'?

Any attempt to examine the diagnostic process immediately encounters the problem of language. Both lay people and professionals tend to talk about diagnosis in ways which offer few clues about what is actually going on, or what assumptions are being made, e.g. 'finding out what is wrong with someone' or 'they've discovered she's got multiple sclerosis'. Before I try to clarify what is actually being said here, two preliminary points need to be made. First, psychiatric diagnosis gains its professional and social legitimacy by presenting itself as equivalent to medical diagnosis. This is achieved, not least, by using the language of medicine to talk about behaviour and psychological experience. It is therefore important to understand the process of medical diagnosis in order to examine how far psychiatric diagnosis follows the same procedures and whether these procedures are actually appropriate in understanding people's behaviour and experience. The second point is that an understanding of diagnosis and the problems of psychiatric diagnosis are inseparable from an understanding of medical research in general. I shall therefore move back a few steps from diagnosis and briefly discuss the aims and conduct of medical research.

Medical research as pattern identification

The basic task of medical research, indeed of any scientific research, is to identify patterns or relationships amongst phenomena which at first glance might appear to be unrelated. The most basic phenomena of medical research are the complaints people make about their bodily state: fatigue, persistent thirst, constipation, nausea, pain, giddiness, blurred vision, hotness, etc. Such complaints are known as symptoms and they have three important characteristics. First, they are subjective in the sense that they rely on personal report. Even if some complaints may be objectively checked, the subjective element remains and may not completely match an objective measure. Second, symptoms are very common; indeed, most of us will have experienced some of the symptoms listed at one time or another. Third, symptoms are overdetermined, i.e. they may have many antecedents. It is for these reasons that trying to identify patterns from symptoms alone is an extremely hazardous business, because symptoms may often co-occur by chance. One of the reasons why medicine made so little progress before the nineteenth century was that its access to phenomena beyond the symptom level was so restricted.

The second level of medical phenomena, and much more important from the researchers' point of view, are signs. Unlike symptoms, signs are not dependent on personal report, but may be externally and reliably available to many people, for example, measures of blood sugar, white-cell count, and so on. Signs are also less common than symptoms: fewer people have raised blood sugar than feel thirsty. Finally, signs generally have fewer antecedents than symptoms. A final level of phenomena is a source indicator which, as the name implies, is a phenomenon which unambiguously indicates its antecedent. There are, however, very few such indicators available to medical researchers who are therefore highly dependent on signs in their task of identifying patterns amongst bodily phenomena.

It is the reliable association of a sign or signs with particular clusters of symptoms, where the sign is assumed to be an antecedent of the symptoms (e.g. the association of sugar in the urine with complaints of persistent thirst, fatigue and weight loss) which allows medical researchers to have some confidence that they have identified a *meaningful* grouping of phenomena and not simply a chance co-occurrence. When such a grouping has been identified, then researchers usually infer a concept (e.g. Down's syndrome; multiple sclerosis; rheumatoid arthritis) which acts as an heuristic for further research; the major aim of this research is to identify additional attributes which are reliably associated with the original cluster of symptoms and signs and which are usually thought to be antecedents of this original cluster. When researchers first identify a pattern, they might claim to have discovered a new disease; if they identify antecedents of this pattern, they might claim to have found the cause of the disease.

The relationship of medical research to diagnosis

If medical research can be conceptualised as a process of pattern identification, or discovery and refinement, then diagnosis can be thought of as a later process of recognising new exemplars of the originally 'discovered' pattern. Following the initial stage of pattern discovery, the activities of research and diagnosis become inseparable, for the following reasons. First, the 'disease' concept which is originally inferred by researchers has as its referents the cluster of symptoms and signs whose hypothesised relationship led to the inference of the new concept. In other words, this set of symptoms and sign(s) is a statement of what needs to be observed for the concept to be inferred. If we use medical language, this statement of what needs to be observed, becomes the diagnostic criterion for the concept. We are, of course, unused to talking about 'concepts' in this context and instead, and very misleadingly, talk about 'diseases', 'illnesses', 'conditions' or 'disorders'. Diagnosticians are therefore engaged in the task of recognising new exemplars of patterns originally identified by researchers and then inferring the same concepts as were originally inferred by researchers. So, when your doctor says, 'You have diabetes' what they are actually saying is, 'Researchers have identified a meaningful relationship between certain bodily phenomena and inferred the concept of diabetes from that pattern. You show the same pattern as the one identified by researchers, so I am inferring the same concept'. Perhaps it's not surprising that doctors rarely make speeches like this, but it would give a much more accurate account of the diagnostic process than the highly misleading 'You have diabetes'.

Diagnosis and research are related, secondly, because researchers are dependent on diagnosis to provide participants for their studies. It is through diagnosis that people showing particular clusters of bodily phenomena are separated out from those who may at first glance seem similar; for example, people diagnosed as suffering from lung cancer show features similar to those diagnosed as suffering from tuberculosis. Finally, research and diagnosis are related in that successful research, i.e. that which identifies further attributes shared by a particular group, leads to changes in diagnostic criteria or, to put it more generally, to changes in the statement of what must be observed for a particular concept to be inferred. For example, the diagnostic criteria now used to infer Down's Syndrome are different from those used fifty years ago, as a result of research which linked the original cluster from which the concept was inferred to particular characteristics of chromosomes. These changes are usually seen as a process of refining diagnosis, and of increasing the probability that we are identifying a distinct and separate group. This process, of course, is always incomplete, so that we cannot know whether future discoveries will show that our present confidence in any particular diagnostic category was misplaced.

Some problems and misunderstandings about diagnosis

I have emphasised that diagnosis is a process of recognising new exemplars of patterns which have previously been 'discovered' by researchers and of inferring the same concepts from these patterns as were originally inferred by researchers. Most of what we think of as diagnostic labels are therefore more accurately thought of as concepts, as abstract ideas. The distinction is crucial, for two related reasons. First, concepts are provisional, that is, they are always subject to abandonment or change if challenged by new observations. Second, concepts are just that: concepts, or abstractions, rather than things with a spatiotemporal location. Yet the way we talk about medical diagnosis obscures this, as when we say 'she *has* multiple sclerosis' or 'he *is* diabetic', or when the World Health Organisation claims that diagnostic terms are 'the names of diseases' (1978). The problem with this language is that it confers on these concepts a permanence and solidity which is quite unjustified, and suggests that they are entities that people possess. This language can also give the impression that diagnosis is a process of searching for and identifying a material entity and obscure the fact that it is a highly abstract and assumption laden process. As we shall see, these misunderstandings are likely to have contributed to the acceptability of what is actually a highly problematic system for thinking about behaviour and experience.

Diagnosis in psychiatry

I suggested earlier that psychiatric diagnosis gains its legitimacy by adopting the language and assumptions of medical diagnosis. This implies that psychiatric diagnostic systems have been developed by following the same procedures that underlie medical systems. A good starting point for the critical examination of psychiatric diagnosis is therefore to ask whether this is in fact the case.

Making a diagnosis, whether medical or psychiatric, involves two assumptions: first, it's assumed that researchers have already 'discovered' a relationship amongst certain phenomena and have therefore justifiably inferred the concept which is now being used as the diagnostic label. Clearly, if this has not been done, then the diagnostic process is conceptually meaningless as you cannot recognise new instances of a pattern which has never been observed. Second, it is assumed that underlying processes, whether biological or psychological, are 'holding together' the cluster identified by researchers. It is these underlying processes which researchers are seeking to discover and understand when they carry out research using the diagnostic label or when they talk about looking for the causes of a particular disease. A large part of the problems which surround psychiatric diagnosis arise from the fact that the validity of both of these assumptions — about the previous 'discovery' of patterns by researchers and about the existence of underlying processes — has been seriously questioned in relation to psychiatric diagnosis. For example, there is no evidence whatsoever that the original introduction of the concept of schizophrenia was accompanied by the observation of a meaningful relationship amongst the many behaviours and experiences from which the concept was inferred. Nor is there any evidence that the diagnostic criteria listed in the American Psychiatric Association's Diagnostic and Statistical Manual of Mental Disorders refer to any meaningful pattern — indeed, it would be quite remarkable if they did, given the lack of evidence to support the original introduction of the concept (Boyle, 1990). In addition, statistical studies of groups given a diagnosis of schizophrenia, have found no evidence that their 'symptoms' cluster together in a meaningful way (Bentall, 1990; Slade and Cooper, 1979). Given this, the question of an underlying process, whether biological or psychological, which holds together a pattern of signs and symptoms becomes irrelevant, as no such pattern has been demonstrated in the first place. Similar criticisms have been made of other diagnostic concepts, for example, depression (Hallett, 1990; Wiener, 1989); panic disorder (Hallam, 1989); agoraphobia (Hallam, 1983); borderline personality disorder (Kutchins and Kirk, 1997); self-defeating or masochistic personality disorder (Caplan and Gans, 1991).

What are the results of this state of affairs? First, the groups who receive any particular diagnostic label are highly heterogeneous. People may, of course, share some behaviour and experiences, for example, many of those diagnosed as schizophrenic are likely to hear voices, but since no-one has demonstrated that this similarity is *important*, in the sense that it signifies other, antecedent, shared features, then the group is likely to show a whole range of other shared and unshared characteristics with no indication of which might be significant. The same result would be expected in any group who shared characteristics which had never been shown to be meaningfully related, for example, headache, obesity, flat feet and nausea. A second result is that the use of the diagnostic label in research which seeks antecedent shared features in the group, the 'underlying processes', will produce highly unreliable results. As we would expect, then, the psychiatric and psychological literature is characterised by a failure *reliably* to identify the processes — whether biological, genetic or psychological — said to underlie the 'symptoms' of any diagnostic group. Indeed, the most consistent feature of this literature is its inconsistency. Sarbin and Mancuso (1980), for example, called the research on cognitive functioning in schizophrenia 'chaotic', and the situation has changed little since then, for schizophrenia and other diagnostic categories and across different research areas (Chua and McKenna, 1995; Ross and Pam, 1995) Kendall (1976) titled a paper on depression, 'A review of contemporary confusion', while another paper on the topic (Robins, 1988) asks 'Why are the results so inconsistent'? . Of course, if a shared underlying process were to be found for any diagnostic category, then the diagnostic criteria would change to accommodate it, in the same way that the criteria for Down's Syndrome changed to include particular features of chromosomes. That this has not happened for any psychiatric category is eloquent testimony to the entirely predictable failure of research based on categories with such poor conceptual and empirical foundations. A final result of the conceptual muddle which lies behind psychiatric diagnosis and of its pretence to science, is that the reliability of diagnoses are often unacceptably low (Kirk and Kutchins, 1992). It is important to emphasise that low reliability is not an inevitable result of the use of a problematic diagnostic concept or diagnostic system. It is quite possible to have a set of diagnostic criteria which are not based on the prior identification of a meaningful pattern but which can nevertheless be used in a highly reliable way. Such criteria, however, would have to be rigidly and rather forcefully imposed because, in the absence of a clear empirical justification for one set of criteria over another, clinicians tend to diagnose in accordance with their own varied experiences and biases.

Attempts to improve psychiatric diagnosis

Many of those who use psychiatric diagnosis are aware of the problems of heterogeneity, low reliability and the disarray in the literature. Unfortunately, they have made little attempt to address the fundamental problems which surround psychiatric diagnosis; instead, superficial measures have been taken which obscure these problems while giving a false impression of progress.

Attempts to address the problems of psychiatric diagnosis have centred around efforts to develop reliable diagnostic criteria through the deliberations of committees, and to disseminate these via the American Psychiatric Association's Diagnostic and Statistical Manual of Mental Disorders. These criteria were first published in the third edition of the Manual in 1980. Before that, in the first and second editions of the manual, diagnostic categories had been accompanied only by a brief description purporting to give the major features of each 'disorder', rather than by a list of the specific criteria which were to be used in making a diagnosis. Although the publication of these committee-devised lists in 1980 was presented as a significant advance, it in fact represents, scientifically speaking, an extraordinary state of affairs. This is because the original justification for using a concept is that it has been inferred from the observation of a pattern of relationships; for medical concepts, it is this pattern which becomes the diagnostic criteria. In other words, concepts come ready equipped with the criteria for inferring them. That is not to say that these criteria will not be refined and elaborated by later research; but to have to set up committees to search for basic diagnostic criteria is to engage in a parody of scientific activity and tacitly to admit that the crucial first stage of concept formation, without which the idea of diagnosis is meaningless, has not been carried out. It cannot be argued that the devisors of the DSM were carrying out this first stage, because their search depended on research which already used the diagnostic categories for which committee members were now seeking criteria. Nor is there any indication that serious consideration was given to the possibility that the search might be unsuccessful; yet there was no *a priori* reason to assume success, unless, of course, one assumed the validity of the diagnostic concept, in which case it is difficult to see why the search was necessary in the first place: as I pointed out earlier, valid concepts come ready equipped with the criteria for inferring them. Given this back-to-front version of science, it was inevitable that the diagnostic criteria which did emerge from the search should still be subject to disagreement and still have failed to advance the search for underlying processes.

Why has this state of affairs come about?

No single factor can account for the persistence of psychiatric diagnosis in spite of its lack of empirical support. Discussions of this issue have emphasised professional, social, political, commercial, inter-personal and cognitive factors (e.g. Szasz, 1987; Pilgrim, 1990; Boyle, 1990; 1994; Breggin, 1993). Although all of these are important, I am going to focus here on a relatively narrow range of factors which may help to explain why psychiatric diagnoses seems plausible or even necessary.

The plausibility of diagnosis

I suggested earlier that psychiatric diagnosis obtains its professional and social legitimacy from its links to medicine, which in turn obtains its legitimacy from its public allegiance to science. Psychiatric diagnosis is thus linked to a scientific ideal in a way which does not necessarily involve public scrutiny of its scientific status. One result of this link to science is that 'non-experts' either see no need, or do not feel able to challenge a process which claims to be based on scientific 'truths' to which they do not have access. This problem is confounded by the fact that the language of medicine and diagnosis gives little or no clue about what researchers and clinicians are actually supposed to be doing, so that it is very difficult for most people to know whether the shared language of medicine and psychiatry does in fact reflect shared activities, or whether the activities of the two professions are actually quite different.

The plausibility of psychiatric diagnosis is reinforced by at least three further factors. The first is that we tend to underestimate just how difficult is the process of identifying patterns amongst various phenomena and how poor our judgement often is (Kahneman *et al*, 1982). The fact that medical textbooks tend only to describe the successes, and the fact that patterns often look obvious with hindsight, do not help. Thus, when a diagnostic concept is introduced, our response may not be as sceptical as it should. Second, there appears to be a strong tendency to reify diagnostic concepts, to treat them as entities and to confuse observation and inference. Thus, the *diagnosis* of , say, depression, becomes confused with the description of the behaviours from which the concept is inferred, so that to criticise a diagnostic category can be (and frequently is) made to seem like claiming that the behaviours and experiences on which it is based do not exist. Finally, the idea that psychiatric diagnosis identifies some internal attribute which explains behaviour and experience is echoed by dispositional and individualistic accounts of behaviour within psychology and more generally within western culture. Moreover, the more unusual the behaviour, the more likely we are to reach for dispositional explanations (Ross, 1977). This means that although psychiatric diagnosis is couched in medical language, the ideas behind it — that people possess attributes which hang together as a result of underlying biological and psychological processes — are very much in line with cultural beliefs about behaviour. Psychiatric diagnosis therefore gains much of its plausibility not only from its claimed links to science but also from the fact that it seems to confirm something we already 'knew' about behaviour. This, of course, is one of the reasons the system was able to become established in the first place, in spite of its lack of empirical support.

The necessity of diagnosis

Psychiatric diagnosis, however, is not simply an extremely plausible activity; it also often seems to be a *necessary* procedure. One important reason for this is that the establishment of a diagnostic category inevitably creates or draws attention to a group who conform in some ways to the category description, e.g. children who are inattentive and difficult to control. This in itself may be sufficient to create the impression that the diagnostic concept is valid. But the establishment of a category is also often accompanied by the development of services specifically to cater for people assigned to the category (e.g. a post-traumatic stress disorder clinic) and by the development of interventions which are presented, however misleadingly, as specific to the category. This combination of the existence of a named group and of specific service structures and 'treatments' helps create the impression that other people who fit the category must exist and are 'out there' waiting to be identified. Worse, the impression may be created that it is a professional failure *not* to identify them and to bring them into contact with services said to be most suited to their needs. The necessity of diagnosis is further implied by DSM –IVs claim to be 'atheoretical', thus creating the impression that diagnosis is merely a way of describing behaviour. The fact that psychiatric diagnosis is laden with assumptions about people and their behaviour and is therefore highly theoretical is then obscured and diagnosis is made to seem part of the natural order. If we combine the perceived necessity of diagnosis with its perceived plausibility — and both are partly rooted in the reification of diagnostic categories — then to criticise the categories or the diagnostic enterprise can seem little short of nonsensical. These factors, together with the professional, social and cultural factors mentioned earlier, present a formidable set of obstacles to the development of alternatives to psychiatric diagnosis.

What are the alternatives?

Because psychiatric diagnosis is so plausible, and seems so necessary, it is easy to lose sight of the fact that it is a way of thinking about people's behaviour and their distress, not a way of describing it. Diagnosis involves many assumptions about behaviour and experience, not least that they can be thought about as the same sort of phenomena as bodily processes, and these assumptions have never been shown to be valid. To ask about alternatives to diagnosis is therefore to ask how else we might think about or understand disturbing behaviour and experience. Put like that, it seems likely that no single account from a particular theoretical viewpoint will be adequate to the problem. And using the term 'disturbing', rather than 'disturbed' emphasises that there is no 'natural' or culture-free subject matter for our study. It is important to remind ourselves that diagnosis is a particular, and particularly problematic, way of thinking about behaviour and experience, otherwise diagnostic concepts all too easily become the taken-for-granted entities which form the basis of what are thought to be alternative conceptualisations, for example, psychological approaches to schizophrenia. Thus, the fact that the diagnostic concept itself represents a conceptualisation of, and a set of assumptions about, behaviour and experience can be obscured. What we are seeking, then, is not an alternative account of depression or schizophrenia or post-traumatic stress disorder, but an alternative account of the behaviours and experiences from which concepts like these are inferred.

While it is certainly premature to say what this alternative account might be, especially in an area which has suffered from theorising well beyond the data, it is possible to suggest some characteristics which it should have. One of the most striking features of approaches based on psychiatric diagnosis is that they ignore, overlook or cannot account for, many of the observations which are made about behaviour and experience without providing a satisfactory explanation of why this neglect is justified. For example, the content of 'psychotic' experiences has been largely ignored (Boyle, 1996), while the fact that complaints of anxiety and complaints of depression so often co-exist has been downplayed in the face of the need to allocate people to separate diagnostic categories.

The suggestions which follow for alternatives to diagnosis are based on the assumption that at this stage, we are not justified in ignoring any observations about behaviour, experience and distress. First, the starting point of alternative accounts (i.e. what the account claims to be an account of) should involve as few inferences as possible. In practice, this would mean trying to account for what people do and what they say they experience, rather than trying to account for a hypothesised disorder or illness. Slade and Bentall (1988) for example, have provided a psychological analysis of hearing voices (as distinct from 'schizophrenia', although there is still a tendency to talk of 'symptoms'). A crucial aspect of a descriptive approach is that it must deal with the ways in which people's behaviour and experiences vary in different situations; in other words, it must take account of the social and interpersonal context in which the behaviour or experience happens. Psychiatric diagnosis has seriously neglected this issue and a reliance on diagnosis can lead to strange questions, such as, where is someone's schizophrenia when they are behaving 'normally' or where is their alcohol addiction when they are drinking in a controlled way? (see Heather and Robertson, 1997, for an alternative account of 'problem drinking' which addresses this issue). The answer 'in remission' or 'under control' hardly accounts for the extent of situational variability and tells us nothing about the processes which lie behind it.

A second feature of an alternative account is that it would deal with the content, meaning and function of experience and behaviour. These, of course, are closely related to the issue of context and, like context, have been largely neglected by theories dependent on diagnosis. I have suggested that diagnostic approaches to psychotic experiences find the issue of content not only theoretically difficult but also professionally threatening (Boyle, 1996). But it is difficult to see how we can understand people's distress if we do not take meaning and function into account. For example, the American Psychiatric Association suggested a diagnostic category of 'Self-Defeating Personality Disorder' (DSM-111R, 1987) whose 'symptoms' included 'choosing people and situations that lead to disappointment, failure and mistreatment, even when better options are available' and 'engaging in excessive self-sacrifice that is unsolicited by the intended recipients of the sacrifice'. Depicting these as symptoms of a mental disorder suggested that they stemmed from a pathological attribute of the individual and could not be seen as rational responses to particular situations. But Caplan (1986) argued strongly that not only were some of the 'symptoms' of SDPD socially encouraged for women (e.g. sacrificing your own desires for others; rejecting opportunities for pleasure), but other 'symptoms' could be understood as reasonable outcomes of abusive relationships (e.g. being unable to deal with kindness and caring) or as attempts to make the best of a very negative situation. Similarly, it is very difficult to understand the 'disorder' 'agoraphobia', most of whose 'sufferers' are women, without taking account of the different meanings which home and going out have for males and females in our society. Women are far less encouraged to go out alone than are men; they are told that 'outside' is a dangerous place where they are vulnerable to attack. This, and the phrase 'a woman's place is in the home' are arguably more important in understanding a reluctance to go out than is a diagnosis of agoraphobia (Gelfond, 1991).

Third, an alternative account needs to acknowledge that people actively construct their behaviour and experiences, even when they are distressing to them, rather than being passive victims of them. This is not at all the same as blaming people for their problems but it emphasises that what are labelled as mental disorders might actually be attempts to cope with very difficult situations and moreover, that these 'symptoms' can be successful in making a situation less aversive. For example, Gotlib and Colby (1987) have suggested that some of the behaviours we think of as indicating depression (withdrawal, low rate of speech) can be successful in reducing domestic violence. This is emphatically not to say that the person who shows these behaviours is not very distressed or that the behaviours are not genuine, but it does emphasise that treating the behaviours as symptoms of a disorder which needs to be removed can obviously be a very short-sighted approach. Similarly, believing that you have special powers or are chosen for a special mission, can be very protective of fragile self-esteem (Winters and Neale, 1983).

Finally, adopting an alternative approach to diagnosis highlights the need to study people who do not come to psychiatric attention. For example, far more people experience auditory hallucinations than are diagnosed as schizophrenic (e.g. Posey and Losch, 1983; Romme and Escher, 1993). Similarly, the idea of 'delusion' becomes very problematic if we try to apply it only to psychiatric patients and not to ourselves (Heise, 1988). Studying the non-psychiatric population presents us with a new and often neglected set of questions about those who do come to psychiatric or psychological attention, for example, what is it about the experience of hearing voices that is upsetting or disruptive for this person, when others may welcome the experience? Or, why has this person sought or been sent for psychiatric treatment when others with the same experiences have not?

An account of disturbing and distressing behaviour and experiences which acknowledged these factors is likely to be much more complex than one which takes psychiatric diagnosis as its starting point. It is also much more time-consuming to try to understand the function and meaning of someone's distress and the ways it is linked to their social situation, than to make a diagnosis based on the claimed presence or absence of certain symptoms. More than that, however, adopting a non-diagnostic approach often shifts attention from the individual to the social contexts which foster distress and this is perhaps one of the reasons it is less popular.

I suggested at the beginning of this chapter that diagnosis was central to psychiatry because it helped create an impression of similarity to medicine and because classification was claimed to be central to science. I have argued, however, that the similarity between medical and psychiatric approaches to diagnosis is more apparent than real, while a classification system is only as good as the assumptions on which it is based. The assumptions behind psychiatric classification are extremely problematic, which is hardly surprising as they were developed by medicine to suit bodily processes not people's behaviour and experience. Non-diagnostic approaches demand a very different set of assumptions which in turn demand a different set of social and therapeutic responses.

References

American Psychiatric Association (1980) *Diagnostic and Statistical Manual of Mental Disorders (3rd edition) Third edition (revised)*, 1987; *Fourth edition,* 1994.

Bentall, R.P. (1990) The Syndromes and Symptoms of Psychosis. In R.P. Bentall (ed.) *Reconstructing Schizophrenia.* London: Routledge.

Boyle, M. (1996) Schizophrenia Re-evaluated. In T. Heller, J. Reynolds, R. Gomm, R. Muston, and S. Pattison (eds) *Mental Health Matters.* London: MacMillan

Boyle, M. (1994) Schizophrenia and the art of the soluble. *The Psychologist* 7 399–404

Boyle, M. (1990) *Schizophrenia: A Scientific Delusion?* London: Routledge.

Breggin, P. (1993) *Toxic Psychiatry.* London: Fontana

Caplan, P. (1986) *Women's Masochism: The myth destroyed.* London: Methuen

Caplan, P. and Gans, M. (1991) Is there empirical justification for the category of Self-Defeating Personality Disorder? *Feminism and Psychology* 1 263–78

Chau, S.E. and McKenna, P.J. (1995) Schizophrenia: A Brain Disease? *British Journal of Psychiatry,* 166, 563–82

Gelfond, M. (1991) Reconceptualising agoraphobia: A case study of epistemological bias in clinical research. *Feminism and Psychology* 1 247–62

Gotlib, I. And Colby, C.A. (1987) *The Treatment of Depression: An Interpersonal Systems Approach.* New York: Pergamon

Hallam, R.S. (1983) Agoraphobia: Deconstructing a clinical syndrome. *Bulletin of the British Psychological Society* 36 337–40

Hallam, R.S. (1989) Classification and research into panic. In R. Baker and M. McFadyen (eds) *Panic Disorder.* Chichester: Wiley

Hallett, R. (1990) *Melancholia and Depression: A Brief History and Analysis of Contemporary Confusions.* Unpublished Masters Thesis, University of East London

Heather, N. and Robertson, I. (1997) *Problem Drinking.* Oxford: Oxford Medical Publications

Heise, D.R. (1988) Delusions and the Construction of Reality. In J.F. Oltmanns and B.A. Maher (eds) *Delusional Beliefs.* New York: Wiley

Kahneman, D., Slovic, P. and Tversky, A. (eds) (1982) *Judgement Under Uncertainty: Heuristics and biases.* New York: Cambridge University Press

Kendall, R.E. (1976) The classification of depressions: A review of contemporary confusions. *British Journal of Psychiatry*, 129, 15–28

Kirk, S.A. and Kutchins, H. (1992) *The Selling of DSM: The rhetoric of science in psychiatry.* New York: Aldine de Gruyter

Kutchins, H. and Kirk, S. (1997) *Making us Crazy: DSM: The psychiatric bible and the creation of mental disorders.* New York: The Free Press/ Simon Schuster

Pilgrim, D. (1990) Competing histories of madness: Some implications for modern psychiatry. In R.P. Bentall (ed.) *Reconstructing Schizophrenia.* London: Routledge

Posey, T.B. and Losch, M. (1983) Auditory hallucinations of hearing voices in 375 normal subjects. Imagery, *Cognition and Personality,* 3, 99– 113

Robins, C.J. (1988) Attributions and depression: why is the literature so inconsistent? *Journal of Personality and Social Psychology* 54 880– 89

Romme, M. and Escher, S. (1993) *Accepting Voices.* London: Mind Publications

Ross, C.A. and Pam, A. (1996) *Pseudoscience in Biological Psychiatry: Blaming the body.* New York: Wiley

Ross, L. (1977) The intuitive psychologist and his shortcomings: distortions in the attribution process. In L. Berkowitz (ed.) *Advances in Experimental Social Psychology Vol 10* New York: Academic Press

Sarbin, T.R. and Mancuso, J.C. (1980) *Schizophrenia: Medical diagnosis or moral verdict?* New York: Pergamon

Slade, P.D. and Bentall, R.P. (1988) *Sensory Deception: A scientific analysis of hallucinations.* London: Croom Helm

Slade, P.D. and Cooper, R. (1979) Some difficulties with the term 'schizophrenia': An alternative model. *British Journal of Social and Clinical Psychology,* 18, 309–17

Shepherd, M. (1976) Definition, classification and nomenclature: A Clinical Overview. In D. Kemali, G. Bartholini and D. Richer (eds) *Schizophrenia Today.* Oxford: Pergamon

Szasz, T. (1987) *Insanity: The idea and its consequences.* New York: Wiley

Wiener, M. (1989) Psychopathology reconsidered: Depression interpreted as psychosocial interactions. *Clinical Psychology Review*, 9, 295–321

Winters, K.C. and Neale, J.M. (1983) Delusions and delusional thinking in psychotics: A review of the literature. *Clinical Psychology Review*, 3, 227–53

World Health Organisation (1978) *Mental Disorders: Glossary and guide to their classification in accordance with the 9th revision of the international classification of diseases.* Geneva: WHO

CHAPTER 5

Drugs

DAVID CREPAZ-KEAY

I N PSYCHIATRY, JUST like real life, everything has its costs and benefits. Psychiatric medication (hereinafter referred to as drugs) is no different. The main benefit of psychiatric drugs is that they relieve symptoms. None of what follows should be seen as undermining the value of this, it is merely designed to offer a view of these drugs that is not often aired.

What you are told . . .
People are told at length about the risks of not taking medication, but this discussion is rarely extended to cover risks of complying with the treatment prescribed by your doctors. Some people are lucky enough to have doctors who will admit that the drugs that they are giving you may have what they refer to as 'side effects'. The phrase 'side effects' is carefully chosen to give the impression that the drugs are almost entirely *a good thing* but that they may have some marginal consequences that are less desirable.

. . . and what you are not told
What few doctors are prepared to acknowledge is that the negative effects are as likely to occur as the so called therapeutic effects. The key issues for individuals in distress who are offered drug treatments should therefore be choice and informed consent.

The negative effects of the drugs can be wide-ranging. Almost any organ of the body is at increased risk of damage; co-ordination and balance can be badly affected; peoples' energy levels and ability to function on a day to day basis can be markedly reduced.

Many of the images of madness that the public have are the

consequences of drug treatment rather than symptoms of any 'mental illness'. These include: staring, dribbling, shuffling, shaking, nervous tics, and pacing up and down. Also some of the adverse effects of psychiatric drugs described in the British National Formulary are psychiatric symptoms or diagnosable illnesses (e.g. anxiety, depression, insomnia and hallucinations).

The negative effects of drugs can reinforce the process of reduced self-esteem that follows a psychiatric diagnosis. In addition to those outlined above, weight gain, impotence, and memory loss are common. Many of the everyday things that build confidence and protect people from mental health problems can be harder to get as a result of taking the drugs: it is hard to get a job when you cannot muster the energy to get out of bed; it is hard to get a girlfriend when you cannot get an erection. Even the reparative effects of sitting in the sun may be denied to a person due to high photosensitivity and increased risk of sunburn.

Informed consent

The concept of informed consent underlies all areas of treatment for physical conditions. The 1983 Mental Health Act gives professionals the legal powers to override an individual's right to decline treatment on the basis that they, the professionals, know best and that someone with a psychiatric diagnosis forfeits that right. For people who are not detained under the 1983 Mental Health Act, the law affords them the same rights as any other human being. In practice, however, people with a psychiatric diagnosis are denied the chance to give informed consent (regardless of their legal status) in two important ways.

Information

People are rarely given adequate information in an appropriate form to enable them to assess the balance of pros and cons of what is offered to them. This is made worse when those who are responsible for dispensing the drugs are not able to answer the questions posed by those who are prescribed them. In order for someone to give informed consent:

- The information should be clear and comprehensible
- The information should be accurate
- The dispensing staff should assume that people receiving treatment are competent to make treatment decisions, rather than assume they must be treated at any cost.

Consent
Although, in theory, consent should be a fairly simple concept, in practice it is widely abused.

- *Consent is not simply the absence of dissent.*
  Just because people are not making very loud noises in objections to proposed treatments, does not mean that they understand the implications of agreeing or declining the treatment and have chosen the former.
- *Agreeing to take a single treatment is not an undated blank cheque.*
  A decision to agree to take a dose, or even a course of psychiatric medication, does not imply that someone is happy to undergo a second treatment or course. Nor does agreeing to undergo a regular treatment, for example a monthly depot injection, mean that the person is committed to it for all time.

Consent should be always be actively sought. It should be given on the basis of an understanding of the costs and benefits of both agreeing and declining the treatment in question. This is not extreme libertarianism, nor is it a utopian dream; it is simply a statement of how other branches of medicine behave.

Objective goals of treatment with psychiatric drugs
One of the most significant problems with current prescribing practice is the lack of a focus and stated objectives. When people are given drugs they are often not given an idea of what the treatment is expected to achieve, or the timescale.

At present, if a treatment fails to achieve anything after three months, many people face an increased dosage for the next three months, followed by a similar increase if there is still no positive result. This often leaves people locked into long-term high dosage use with little or no therapeutic benefit, but with an increased risk of long term damage.

If psychiatrists, when they start a course of treatment, were explicit about its desired effect and gave criteria by which it could be judged as having succeeded or failed, then people could assess for themselves both the efficacy of the treatment and the accuracy of the psychiatrist.

Withdrawal

Much is made of the dangers of people coming off medication. All of this centres around the idea of relapse and the return of symptoms. Even though the problems associated with addiction to and withdrawal from minor tranquillisers are well known and widely discussed, they are still often ignored (or, worse still, denied) in relation to neuroleptics and the new antidepressants.

As this chapter makes clear, there are many good reasons why people choose to stop taking their drugs. People coming off prescribed drugs, however, face three challenges, all of which make the process one of the most difficult activities a person may undertake.

- *Physiological effects*
  Like any other mind-altering drug (remember that these are being prescribed precisely because they are mind-altering drugs), psychiatric medication can have strong withdrawal effects. These can take a number of different forms. Many of these effects (for example: mood swings, irritability, hallucinations), can be mistaken for 'relapse'. The nature, degree and duration of these physiological effects are as individual as they are unpredictable.

- *Removal of professional support*
  Many, if not most people decide to come off psychiatric drugs against medical advice. A large number of services and mental health professionals simply refuse to support people who decline treatments prescribed by psychiatrists, who are still regarded as unchallengeable in the field of diagnosis and treatment. Even when a service or support is not withdrawn or refused, people who actively decline drugs are treated as troublemakers and can become marginalised within services.

- *Domestic conflict*
  Many younger people with a psychiatric diagnosis are living with parents. Many more people of all ages are living in housing with some degree of support, often provided by statutory or voluntary sector organisations. The people offering support, whether they are paid professional carers, or informal carers like family members or friends, often find that people are more manageable when drugged. When this manageability goes, and is replaced by the mood swings or irritability that accompany the physiological withdrawal, it is not surprising that domestic tensions become a serious block to successful withdrawal.

Successful withdrawal requires people to address all of these issues in an appropriate manner. Peer support from someone who has come off the drugs themselves is of enormous value. A sensible timetable for withdrawal is also important, and six to eighteen months is not unusual for someone who has been on medication for a long period of time.

Withdrawal from depot injections is made more difficult by the way they work in the body. The drug is stored in body fat and released slowly over time. People often put on weight as a result of the medication, so when it is stopped, the body has a store of it that is released as the fat breaks down and normal weight is restored.

Masking problems

Many people find that the effects of the drugs alter their perceptions and feelings to the extent that they find it difficult to remember the original feelings and perceptions that brought them into contact with psychiatric services in the first place. Often the treatments and environments that people have to deal with, such as the institutional settings of psychiatric hospitals, create their own problems and manifestations of distress that require even more treatment. And so the spiral of decline continues.

There is also the anaesthetic effect of psychiatric drugs. If you stick your hand in a pot of boiling water, it is possible to reduce or remove the pain by taking a local or general anaesthetic. It is possible to continue holding your hand in the boiling water for a considerable period of time by simply numbing the pain. Psychiatric drugs often take on the role of anaesthetic. Perhaps more doctors should encourage people to take their hands out of the boiling water.

Exclusion

Drug issues are also caught up with people being excluded from services that might help them. Paradoxically this can occur both ways:

Exclusion of people using drugs

A significant number of practitioners of alternative, complementary and, particularly, talking treatments will not work with people who are taking some types of psychotropic medication.

Exclusion of people refusing drugs

There are also services that refuse to take people who decline their prescribed medication. Some professionals simply refuse to offer any support at all if an individual refuses to comply with their drugs.

Conclusion: treating the whole patient

In theory, every mental health professional likes to believe that they treat the whole person, not just 'the illness'. In practice, however, psychiatric drugs remain the first and last port of call for those delivering services. People must be allowed to give proper, informed consent to all treatments, and assisted to come off medication if that is their choice. We hear so much about those who kill after refusing treatment, but nothing of the rather greater number who die whilst taking it.

Governments talk of choice and quality care, and of meeting the needs of individuals, but their actions speak of the single goal of compliance. This chapter only exists at all because I was able to come off medication *against medical advice.*

The current government has stated that under their policy non-compliance is not an option. If they are allowed to make this law, many thousands of people will be denied the opportunities that I and many colleagues in the survivor movement have fought (and in some cases died) for.

CHAPTER 6

ECT: The facts psychiatry declines to mention

KATY J. ARSCOTT

ELECTROCONVULSIVE THERAPY [ECT] was introduced in the 1930s by an Italian psychiatrist, Ugo Cerletti (see earlier chapter by Newnes) and involves an electric current being passed through the brain in order to produce a grand mal seizure. In many hospitals in the 1950s and 1960s, ECT was the treatment of choice for people diagnosed as having schizophrenia (Oxlad and Baldwin, 1996). ECT is now more commonly used to 'treat' depression. Technological advances have led to the modification of ECT techniques, the modern procedure involving administration of a muscle relaxant and an anaesthetic, to prevent the types of problems that were previously associated with the treatment such as broken bones and teeth. Modified ECT machines deliver a string of high voltage electric pulses (about 150 volts) either unilaterally, (electric current delivered to one side of the brain) or bilaterally (electric current delivered to both sides of the brain simultaneously). Breggin (1991) states that most people receive 6–10 sessions of ECT and MIND (1995) report that most people have a course of 4–8 treatments. The ECT Handbook (Freeman, 1995) states that a set number of treatments should not be prescribed and that a patient should be re-assessed after each treatment to see if further ECT is necessary. The Handbook suggests that 2 to 3 treatments should be given a week and that ECT should not be given daily.

ECT facts and figures
Two (Freeman, 1995) to 4.5 (MIND, 1995; Rogers, Pilgrim and Lacey, 1993) ECT treatments in every 100,000 are reported to prove fatal. ECT has been banned by psychiatrists in Germany, Holland and

Italy (Baker, 1995; MIND, 1995) and there are restrictions on compulsory treatment in Canada (MIND, 1995). In the UK the National Association for Mental Health has called for a ban on the use of ECT with children under the age of eighteen years and on all compulsory use of ECT (Baker, 1995). Many people today believe that ECT is used rarely, if at all. In fact, approximately 20,000 to 22,000 people receive ECT treatment in England every year (Baker, 1995; ECT Anonymous, 1996; Johnstone, 1989; MIND, 1995). In the year ending March 1991 (the year in which the method of collecting data changed and the last year for which accurate statistics are available) approximately 105,000 treatments were administered. This is likely to be an underestimate as not all ECT treatments are reported and the statistics do not include ECT administered in private or special hospitals. ECT Anonymous (a self-help group for ECT survivors and their carers) estimate that 140,000 treatments are given every year in British hospitals. Figures for children are also high, with an estimate of between 500 and 3500 minors being given ECT in the U.S.A. every year (Thompson and Blaine, 1987) and at least 60 young people aged 12 to 17 being given ECT in the UK in the ten years up to 1992 (Jones and Baldwin, 1996). The youngest child reported to have received ECT was 34.5 months old (Bender, 1955).

Approximately two-thirds of people given ECT are women; Pippard and Ellam (1981) suggest a ratio of 2.27 women to every man. There has also been a dramatic increase in the number of elderly people receiving ECT (Jones and Baldwin, 1992; Oxlad and Baldwin, 1996). Karagulla (1950) documented that in the 1940s only 4% of people given ECT for depression were over 66 years of age. Current figures in the USA indicate that over half of the people receiving ECT are over 65 years of age (Oxlad and Baldwin, 1996). A recent study of death certificates by U.S.A. Today in Texas found that one in 200 elderly patients died shortly after ECT, many from heart attacks or brain haemorrhaging brought on by the treatment (see Johnston, 1996). In the same article the author also cites a study by a British psychiatrist which found that deaths from ECT in an elderly population could be as high as one in ninety.

ECT and informed consent

To give informed consent to any medical treatment individuals must fulfil three criteria. They must possess the capacity to make the decision in question; they must possess the relevant information required to make the decision; and they must give their consent voluntarily, free from pressure (Appelbaum, Lidz and Meisel, 1987). ECT can only be given *without* an individual's consent under Part IV of the Mental Health Act, 1983 and if authorisation is given by a second opinion doctor appointed by the Mental Health Act (MHA) Commission (see MHA Code of Practice, Department of Health, 1993). A recent report published by ECT Anonymous (1996) analysing the official reports for the Royal College of Psychiatrists (RCP; Pippard and Ellam, 1981; Pippard, 1992) states that 10% of people who are given ECT are treated without their consent. This appears to suggest that 90% of people who receive ECT fulfil the criteria for having given an informed consent i.e. they are competent, volunteer their consent and possess adequate information about the treatment to be given.

Possession of information and voluntary consent
The Mental Health Act Code of Practice (Department of Health, 1993) recommends that people should receive full information about the purpose and nature of any treatment; the likely effects and risks of that treatment; the likelihood of its success; and any alternatives, including the alternative of no treatment at all. Similar regulations have been outlined in the American Psychiatric Association Task Force Report (1990; see Leong and Eth, 1991). Despite such recommendations, a survey of service users conducted by MIND (1995) found that only 14% of people had been given any information about ECT and only 9% remembered being told of any adverse effects. A further study by Jenaway (1993) found that although over 85% of the people in their study were satisfied with the consent procedure for treatment with ECT, fewer than 50% could recall being told of certain side effects including memory difficulties, headaches and confusion. Similar figures were found by Riordan, Barron and Bowden (1993) when interviewing 49 people about to undergo treatment with ECT. Fifty-seven percent of their sample recalled details of the procedure, 50% recalled that an anaesthetic would be involved, 38% recalled the use of electricity and only 10% recalled that a fit would be induced. In the same study 40% of people had no recollection of being told of any side effects and over a third felt that they had not been given adequate opportunities to discuss their treatment.

In order to give a valid consent an individual must do so voluntarily and free from coercion. However, a study of patients' perceptions of ECT at one hospital (Malcolm, 1989) found that nearly half of the patients who had experienced ECT thought that they could not refuse it and some did not know whether they could or not. Forty-five percent knew that it was possible to refuse, but many commented that it was futile to do so because they would be given the treatment anyway. Older people and women were found to be the least aware of their rights. Johnstone (1999) interviewed twenty people who reported having found ECT upsetting. She concludes that many people may consent to ECT despite inadequate explanations about the treatment due to their feelings of extreme desperation and powerlessness. She quotes one person as saying 'they asked me if I would agree to it, but they did say if I refused they'd go ahead with it anyway…being forced to stay there is bad enough but being forced to have something that you don't want is ten times worse, so I did agree, yes.'

The Royal College of Psychiatrists' fact sheet on ECT

The ideal opportunity to remedy this situation arose when, in 1995, the Royal College of Psychiatrists published their ECT Handbook. This provides practical guidelines on the clinical use of ECT, its administration and the position with regard to the law and consent. The guide includes in its appendices a fact sheet to inform patients and their families about the nature, purpose, and likely effects of ECT, as well as alternatives to treatment with ECT. On first sight this document appears to provide a comprehensive guide to ECT. On further examination a very different picture emerges.

What the Royal College of Psychiatrists' fact sheet says – and what it leaves out

- 'Most people who have ECT are suffering from depression'

Historically ECT has been used to treat many kinds of mental distress. Although the fact sheet is correct in suggesting that it is now most commonly used to treat depression, the Handbook endorses the use of ECT for a large number of diagnoses including mania (2–3% of people receiving ECT according to MIND, 1995), some cases of schizophrenia, catatonia, postpartum psychosis and even neuroleptic malignant syndrome. MIND (1995) also report the use of ECT in neuropsychiatric conditions such as epilepsy and Parkinson's disease. The fact sheet makes no allusion to this, leading the reader to believe that treatment with ECT for any condition other than depression is rare.

- '[The] current produces a seizure which affects the entire brain, including the centres which control thinking, mood, appetite and sleep. Repeated treatments alter chemical messages in the brain and bring them back to normal'

This is stated as a fact which most people consulting the information sheet are unlikely to question. However, the truth about how ECT works is far from clear. Shock treatments were initially developed to be used with patients diagnosed as schizophrenic on the basis that epilepsy and schizophrenia could not coexist. Although many theories exist (Johnstone, 1989; Fink, 1990; Gordon, 1948), the actual mechanism by which ECT works is not known (Frank, 1990). Dr Green (cited in MIND, 1995, p.13) agrees with the RCP that ECT has its effect through changes in brain chemistry, but goes on to say:

> ... comparing this favourably with the current generation of pharmacologically specific drugs would be similar to the assumption that a broken television could be mended as readily with a sledgehammer as with a screwdriver: you might jog the right bit.

Breggin (1991) argues that ECT works by causing organic brain damage, with memory loss, confusion and disorientation disabling the brain – an argument that was widely accepted in the early years of its use, even by some proponents of ECT. As recently as 1973 Dr Max Fink, a leading proponent of ECT in the USA, has stated that 'where there is no evidence of impaired mental function and no electroencephalo-graphic alteration [changes in brain waves indicating damage] clinical improvement does not occur' (MIND 1995, p.13).

- 'Once you are fast asleep a small electric current is passed across your head and this causes a mild fit in the brain. There is little movement of your body because of the relaxant injection that the anaesthetist gives'.

What people are not told is that the 100–150 volts passed through their brain, if applied to the chest, would have serious consequences (Frank, 1990). The ECT Handbook (Freeman, 1995, p.73) states that the minimum instrument setting required to induce a seizure ranges from 25 millicoulombs (mC) to 800 mC depending on the individual, implying a 40-fold inter-individual variation in seizure threshold. This suggests that great care is needed when assessing the requirements of each person undergoing treatment. However, recent audits of ECT (Duffett and Lelliott, 1998; Pippard, 1992) indicate that much confusion exists concerning instrument settings and the timing of seizures, practice varying greatly between clinics.

0Anaesthetics and muscle relaxants are central nervous system depressants, sedating the brain and necessitating the administration of higher voltages of electricity in order to produce a convulsion. It has been argued that this can increase the risk of amnesia and damage to the brain (Breggin, 1991; Jones and Baldwin, 1992). Further worrying evidence comes from a report compiled by Pippard and Ellam (1981). The authors found that 50% of clinics regularly used trainee anaesthetists, that in 68% of cases the anaesthetist met the client for the first time in the clinic and that in 19% of cases they had not been advised of the client's current medication regime. The authors witnessed several incidents where muscle relaxants were administered while the client was still conscious and some cases where no muscle relaxant was administered at all because 'they couldn't find a vein'. Although the recent audit of ECT (Duffett and Lelliott, 1998) indicates that there has been some improvement in this area, 15% of clinics still report difficulties in obtaining anaesthetic cover resulting in cancelled clinics or people being transported between hospitals for treatment.

- 'Some people wake up with no side-effects at all and simply feel very relaxed. Others may feel somewhat confused or have a headache' (and later in the fact sheet) 'Some patients may be confused just after they awaken from treatment and this generally clears up within an hour or so'.

The fact sheet provides an abbreviated version of the information provided in the Handbook which states 'immediately after treatment patients may experience headaches, muscular aches, nausea, drowsiness, weakness, anorexia and amenorrhoea. . .in the first week after ECT, memory problems and headache have been found to be the most prominent side-effects' (p.67). The Handbook also informs us that 'some patients may switch into a manic illness during treatment with ECT' (p.68), but patients are not informed of this. Abrams (1988) states that 'a patient recovering consciousness from ECT understandably exhibits multiform abnormalities of all aspects of thinking, feeling and behaving, including disturbed memory, impaired comprehension, automatic movements, a dazed facial expression and motor restlessness' (pp.130–1). However, the most reliable information regarding side-effects is likely to come from people who have actually experienced ECT. Rogers, Pilgrim and Lacey (1993) found that many people report memory loss. One client reported 'terrible loss of memory of considerable duration. I had to retrain my brain to remember things. Mainly the worrying aspect was long-term memory loss where I could not remember things which I knew that I knew'. Other quotes include: '[the] only side effect was that final treatments pushed me into a hypermanic state. Memory loss and headaches at the time'; 'headache, temporary amnesia, concussion'; and 'loss of memory which *didn't* right itself, bad headaches and sickness directly afterwards'.

The fact sheet also fails to address the psychological side effects of ECT. Johnstone (1999) found her participants to describe a wide range of emotional responses including 'feelings of humiliation, increased compliance, failure, worthlessness, betrayal, lack of confidence and degradation, and a sense of having been abused and assaulted.' One person said: 'afterwards I felt as if I'd been battered...I was just incapacitated, body and mind, like a heap of scrunched-up bones.' A survey of 306 people who had received treatment with ECT (United Kingdom Advocacy Network, UKAN, 1996) also reported many psychological effects including loss of confidence, dignity and self-esteem; fear of hospitals and psychiatry; anger and aggression; loss of self; and nightmares.

- 'Your memory of recent events may be upset and dates, names of friends, public events, addresses and telephone numbers may be temporarily forgotten. In most cases this memory loss goes away within a few days or weeks, although sometimes patients continue to experience memory problems for several months. *ECT does not have any long-term effects on your memory or your intelligence*' (my italics).

The Handbook itself states: 'the evidence suggests that neither new learning nor memory for information from the past are permanently impaired. Objective memory impairment (on specific memory tests) is reversible. Some patients may, however, be left with discreet memory gaps for specific autobiographical events, the explanation for which is unclear' (p.68). Although possible memory problems following ECT are acknowledged in the fact sheet, we are not told of the large body of evidence (including both subjective reports from people who have experienced ECT and the findings of empirical studies) that confirms the frequency of long-term negative effects of ECT on a wide range of cognitive abilities, predominantly memory function (Breggin, 1991; Frank, 1990; Freeman and Kendall, 1980;

Squire, 1977; Squire and Slater, 1983). Freeman and Kendall (1980) interviewed 166 patients who had had ECT during either 1971 or 1976. They concluded: 'we were surprised by the large number who complained of memory impairment [74%]. Many of them did so spontaneously without being prompted and a striking 30% felt that their memory had been permanently affected' (p.16). Squire and Slater (1983) found that some people who had received ECT were still complaining of memory loss three years after the last shock, forgotten events spanning an average of seven months surrounding treatment. A survey conducted by the UK Advocacy Network (UKAN, cited in Johnston, 1996) found that one third of 300 respondents believed that ECT had damaged them. Eighty percent of these claimed that it had irreparably destroyed their memory. Many said that the treatment had made them more depressed. In a recent case a woman from Scotland sued her Health Board for negligence due to memory loss following treatment with ECT (McKay, 1998). She said 'I found it almost impossible to remember anything that happened prior to the ECT treatment...I'm also unable to retain and remember new information. If someone tells me something it vanishes from my mind. My memory for years after the treatment is blanked too'.

ECT Anonymous (1996) summarise the conclusions of the 1981 and 1992 official reports by the Royal College of Psychiatrists. They conclude that 1) excessive currents of electricity can cause brain damage; 2) routine settings are bound to be excessive for many patients and as clinics cannot determine safe doses, dangerous routine settings are frequently used; and 3) brain damage is routinely caused to many patients. The RCP fact sheet does not adequately reflect the above research.

- 'Over eight out of ten depressed patients who receive ECT respond well, making ECT the most effective treatment for severe depression' (and later in the fact sheet) '. . . severely depressed patients will become more optimistic and less suicidal'.

A number of research studies have shown that ECT does produce short term improvements on depression rating scales for some patients, but that this is not sustained beyond four weeks (Buchan, Johnstone, McPhearson, Palmer, Crow and Brandon, 1992; Weiner, 1984) or at three and six-month follow-up (Johnstone, Deakin, Lawler, Frith, Stevens, McPhearson and Crow, 1980). This is not mentioned in the fact sheet. One of the studies most frequently cited to confirm the efficacy of ECT is that of Freeman, Basson and

Crighton (1978). However, on closer inspection the methodology of this study is shown to be unsound. The authors 'felt it ethically unjustified to withhold for a complete course a treatment generally regarded to be effective' (p.738). Despite the protocol of the study they gave the simulated ECT group real shocks for their third and subsequent treatments, thus rendering the study flawed and invalid. A reputedly 'double-blind controlled study' by West (1981) made a similar error, allowing ten of the eleven non-ECT patients to transfer to the ECT group during the research. Such studies are not good advertisements for scientific research or for ECT.

Wide regional variations in the rates of treatment (Rogers, Pilgrim and Lacey, 1993; Newnes, 1991) suggest there to be little consensus as to the efficacy of ECT. Jones and Baldwin (1992) cite discrepancies in prescribing rates as wide as 125 treatments per 100,000 population in Oxford to 400 per 100,000 in Wessex. It could be argued that these figures reflect regional differences in the number of people presenting with depression. However, a study by Gill and Lambourn (1981), which found very large differences in the prescribing rates of ECT between consultants working in the same geographical area, suggests that differences in consultants' attitudes towards ECT is a more likely explanation.

Fink (1990) provides further evidence to refute the above statements from the fact sheet, reporting that ECT patients who are not receiving medication relapse at rates as high as 70%. The Handbook acknowledges that nearly half of the depressed patients who recover from ECT will relapse within twelve weeks without drug treatment (Barton, Mehta and Snaith, 1973) and MIND's booklet on ECT (1995) raises doubts about whether ECT can prevent suicide. The fact sheet fails to provide patients with such information.

- 'If you choose not to accept your doctor's recommendation to have ECT, you may experience a longer and more severe period of illness and disability than might otherwise have been the case'.

There is a noticeable lack of conclusive evidence to support the truth of the latter part of this statement, there being few valid studies comparing people who have had ECT with those who have not or with those who have had simulated ECT. Of the studies that do exist, many do not report results in support of long-term benefits from ECT above no treatment or simulated ECT (Johnstone et al., 1980; Lambourn and Gill, 1978).

- 'People who have responded to ECT report it makes them feel 'like themselves again' and 'as if life is worth living again".

There is mixed opinion amongst people who have experienced ECT as to its benefits. Rogers, Pilgrim and Lacey (1993), in a survey of service users, found that 43% of people said ECT had been helpful or very helpful and that 37% reported it as unhelpful or very unhelpful. A further 20% reported no effects. The fact sheet does not provide quotes from people who said 'I permanently lost all memory of myself and my family. I couldn't even remember how to read and write. The person I used to be died the day I had ECT' or 'please inform others never to have this treatment. I had ECT many years ago and am still trying to recover' (ECT Anonymous, 1996) or 'I never want ECT again, I'm afraid of it' (Rogers, Pilgrim and Lacey, 1993). Many such statements exist.

- 'The alternative is drug therapy which also has risks and complications, and drug treatment is not necessarily safer than ECT'.

The only alternative treatment mentioned in the fact sheet is antidepressant medication. Other ways of helping depressed people, such as psychotherapy, are ignored. It is likely to be difficult for a patient to refuse treatment with ECT if they believe that this is their only chance of a cure. Unless, that is, they opt for the alternative of medication which also has 'risks and complications'. The RCP Handbook on ECT acknowledges that little is known about the combined effects of many drug groups and ECT on seizure thresholds and on cardiac function. Few clinical studies have been undertaken in this area, most research being conducted on animals, particularly rats (Freeman, 1995, p.55). The RCP accept that the effects of psychotropic and anaesthetic drugs on the efficacy and safety of ECT are neglected areas of research. However, the fact sheet does not mention possible concomitant use of other medication for diagnoses such as schizophrenia, a subject that merits seven pages of discussion in the Handbook.

- 'You can refuse to have ECT and you may withdraw your consent at any time, even before the first treatment has been given. The consent form is not a legal document and does not commit you to have the treatment . . . withdrawal of your consent will not in any way alter your right to continued treatment with the best alternative methods available.'

The fact sheet is clear about patients' rights to withdraw consent. However, patients are likely to find it difficult to refuse ECT in the light of the information that is provided in the fact sheet and with the only alternative treatment offered being medication. Riordan, Barron and Bowden (1993) questioned 49 people undergoing ECT. They conclude that '...although patients had a low understanding of treatment, they were still compliant, with most rating highly the doctor's role in decision-making. This may reflect a high level of trust, or a resigned lethargy, in part reflecting mental state, but also a feeling of lack of involvement in their own management' (p.533).

The need for adequate information

The issue of informed consent is complex. It is not easy to define *adequate information*. How much should people be told? Too much information may be overwhelming, but too little may be inaccurate and misleading. A compromise is obviously needed. What is not in debate is that people should have access to the facts about the treatment they receive. Although individual quotes have been selected from the fact sheet to illustrate my arguments, much of its content has been included in the above discussion. It is clear that the information presented to patients about ECT is inadequate and, at times, inaccurate. It could be questioned whether patients who have only read the fact sheet would be able to give truly informed consent to treatment with ECT. Many people who agree to have ECT will be completely unaware of issues which should have played a part in the decision and are unlikely to have access to literature exposing the risks. It is important to note that the RCP fact sheet is intended to be used as an adjunct to information about the purpose, nature and implications of treatment presented by the psychiatrist prescribing ECT. There is thus an opportunity for discussion to take place in order to address any questions and concerns that an individual may have. However, research exploring the nature of additional information given in such a consultation appears to be lacking and it is not clear whether people are ever presented with adequate information on which to base a decision about treatment with ECT.

Why conceal the truth about ECT?

Jones and Baldwin (1992) argue that ECT has been repackaged in a way that is designed to censor public and user opinion. ECT is routinely sold as a harmless intervention with no serious long-term side effects, the only alternative to which is medication. Reasons for this are unclear. Some possibilities are explored below.

Time pressures and a belief in the efficacy of treatment
With the increasing pressure placed on all professions by escalating case loads, increased bureaucracy and the complexities of peoples' presenting problems, it is arguable as to whether people are offered adequate explanations about all sorts of medical and psychological treatments. Psychiatrists are likely to suffer the same pressures, with little time to spare and ever-increasing responsibilities. When professionals possess a belief in the absolute efficacy and the minimal risk of harm relating to their offered treatments they may not feel it possible, or even necessary, to spend valuable time ensuring that consent from their patients is fully informed.

The need for reassurance and illusion
Patients and their relatives place a great deal of faith in the medical profession; they have to. Desperate for a cure, it is understandable that they are willing to place their faith in a professional person who promises to provide an explanation for, and a solution to, their distress. The consultant (also desperate for a cure and acutely aware of the respect and responsibility the role brings) is under pressure to maintain the confidence placed in the profession. This is likely to involve protecting patients from the uncertainty surrounding the likelihood of a cure. Psychiatrists alone hold the power to prescribe a course of ECT and have been doing so since the 1940s. Not surprisingly there is a reluctance to acknowledge the potential damage that ECT can cause – it would be unthinkable to suggest that psychiatrists (for over 50 years) have been administering a treatment that is destructive to those whom they aim to cure. Psychiatrists are also in the unenviable position of carrying the responsibility for dealing with emergency psychiatric cases. It is often with a sigh of relief that other professions place at their door those people in extreme distress or who are the most difficult to help, with the expectation that they will be 'treated'. With such pressures and expectations placed upon them, and very few options available, it is possible that ECT is embraced by psychiatrists with a similar sigh of relief, providing them with at least 'something' that can be done for people in extreme distress. The hope of patients, relatives and professionals for a 'cure', especially a rapid, dramatic cure, is therefore not dashed.

The Medical Model of distress
Much of psychiatry is based on the medical model which holds that depression is a physical illness caused by a chemical imbalance

in the brain and is genetic in origin. Patients are encouraged to believe they have an illness which will remain with them for the rest of their lives. If their symptoms decrease or disappear they are in remission, the depression waiting to return with a vengeance and without warning. An organic illness begs an organic cure and it is not therefore surprising that the interventions offered by psychiatry are medication and ECT. To offer alternatives such as psychotherapy would not make sense. It is therefore imperative that patients accept the physical treatments on offer as there is nothing obvious to take their place. However, not all clients are able or willing to consent to treatment with ECT. As ECT is often claimed to be used as a last resort when drug treatment has failed, refusal of treatment exposes the lack of an alternative and may leave psychiatrists feeling helpless to intervene. It is possible that this results in an increased number of people being administered ECT *without* their consent. Statistics compiled by the Mental Health Act Commission (1993; 1997) do indicate an increase in ECT treatments given to patients detained under section 58 of the MHA 1983. In the two year period from 1985 to 1987, 3362 people were given ECT under the provisions of the Act. In the period from 1993 to 1995 (when overall ECT figures showed a gradual decline) this figure had risen to 4607.

Lack of knowledge

For any treatment there exists a wealth of conflicting information as to its relative benefit and harm. The possibility that professionals in any discipline are unaware of the extensive body of literature that undermines their practices cannot be ignored. In any profession it is difficult to keep up-to-date with current literature. The RCP Handbook does provide a fairly comprehensive literature review on ECT, but it seems unlikely that everyone prescribing ECT is fully conversant with the listed studies. A recent audit of ECT (Duffett and Lelliott, 1998) confirmed this. Fifty-five ECT clinics in Great Britain were visited and interviews were conducted with the consultant psychiatrists identified as responsible for each. Only 36% of consultants claimed to have read the ECT Handbook (Freeman, 1995). Even those reading the Handbook may look only at the conclusions at the end of each chapter and these are generally more positive about ECT than the literature referred to in the main body of the text.

The way forward

A movement against the use of ECT in Great Britain is slowly gaining force. People who feel they have been damaged by ECT are coming forward and are being given a voice. Organisations such as ECT Anonymous are organising demonstrations and lobbying the Royal College of Psychiatrists in London. Health Authorities are being sued for damages. Two major positions appear to exist within the anti-ECT lobby: some people feel strongly that ECT should be banned and others that ECT practices, including those around the provision of adequate information, should be reviewed and improved.

Should ECT be banned?

In my opinion the answer is 'yes'. ECT Anonymous (1996) eloquently dispel what they term the 'myth of the ECT controversy'; that is, the case for and against ECT. They argue that there is in fact no controversy – when examining ECT there is evidence that it both provides help and causes harm. The questions that we should be asking are 'what is the degree and frequency of help and of harm'? and 'is the ratio of one to the other acceptable'? They reveal that treatment with ECT provides a 50:50 risk of real harm: it appears to harm as many people as it helps. Is this an acceptable risk? Should such a treatment be so widely prescribed in the 1990s? Is it not time for ECT to be confined to the past and regarded with the same condemnation as treatments such as insulin coma and Metrazol shock (seizure's induced by the injection of Metrazol into the bloodstream)? It will perhaps be some years before this debate reaches the highest levels of policy-making, current emphasis appearing to remain on monitoring treatments and making the existing procedure as non-aversive as possible.

How could current practices be changed?

Increasing pressure is being placed on psychiatry to question and change its practices. Sadly, such initiatives have not yet had a major impact. The recent audit of ECT in England and Wales (Duffett and Lelliott, 1998) failed to show a marked improvement in standards of administration from the previous audit of Pippard (1992). Only one-third of clinics were rated as meeting the Royal College of Psychiatrists' standards, only 16% of responsible consultant psychiatrists attended their ECT clinic weekly and only one-third of clinics had clear policies to help guide junior doctors to administer ECT effectively. The report concluded that 'these problems have not been resolved by 20 years of audit and College activity. There should be a continuing debate as to what further interventions might be considered' (p. 405). Recommendations are made regarding improvements to practice, however the issue of informed consent is not addressed. This must also be an area for further consideration. The RCP fact sheet needs to be revised to provide patients with a more balanced and accurate picture of ECT. Below is an alternative fact sheet that addresses some of the above issues and that provides patients with at least some of the facts which psychiatry declines to mention.

An alternative fact sheet

This alternative fact sheet (see below, pages 114-118) follows the outline and format of the Royal College of Psychiatrists' fact sheet which can be found on pages 103–105 of the *ECT Handbook* (Freeman, 1995). The reader is also referred to the MIND Booklet *'Making Sense of Treatment and Drugs: ECT'* (1995) which provides a comprehensive and balanced guide to ECT. (Readers may photocopy the fact sheet on pages 114-118.)

References

Abrams, R. (1988) *Electroconvulsive Therapy*. New York: Oxford University Press

Appelbaum, P.S., Lidz, C.W. and Meisel, J.D. (1987) *Informed Consent. Legal Theory and Clinical practice*. New York: Oxford University Press

Baker, T (1995) The minor issue of electroconvulsive therapy. *Nature Medicine,* 1(3), 199–200

Barton, J.L., Mehta, S. and Snaith, R.P. (1973) Prophylactic value of ECT in depressive illness. *Acta Psychiatrica Scandinavia,* 29, 386–92

Bender, L. (1955) The development of a schizophrenic child treated with electric convulsions at three years of age. In G. Caplan (Ed.), *Emotional Problems of Early Childhood*, pp.407–25. New York: Basic Books

Breggin, P.R. (1991) *Toxic Psychiatry. Drugs and Electroconvulsive Therapy: The truth and the better alternatives.* New York: St Martin's Press

Buchan, H., Johnstone, F. McPhearson, K., Palmer, R.L., Crow, T.J. and Brandon, S. (1992).Who benefits from electroconvulsive therapy? Combined results of the Leicester and Northwick Park trials. *British Journal of Psychiatry,* 160, 355–9

Department of Health (1993) *Mental Health Act, 1983, Code of Practice.* London: HMSO

Duffett, R. and Lelliott, P. (1998) Auditing electroconvulsive therapy. The third cycle. *British Journal of Psychiatry,* 172, 401–5

ECT Anonymous (1996) *The Royal Colleges' Own Case Against Electric Shock Treatment in British Hospitals.* West Yorkshire: ECT Anonymous

Fink, M. (1990) Electroconvulsive therapy. *Current Opinion in Psychiatry,* 3, 58–61

Frank, L.R. (1990) Electroshock: Death, brain damage, memory loss, and brainwashing. *The Journal of Mind and Behavior,* 11(3–4), 489–512

Freeman, C.P. (1995) *The ECT Handbook. The Second Report of the Royal College of Psychiatrists' Special Committee on ECT. Council Report CR39.* London: Royal College of Psychiatrists

Freeman, C.P.L., Basson, J.V. and Crighton, A. (1978) Double-blind controlled trial of electroconvulsive therapy (E.C.T.) in depressive illness. *The Lancet,* April 8, 738–40

Freeman, C.P.L. and Kendall, R.E. (1980) ECT: I. Patients' experiences and attitudes. *British Journal of Psychiatry,* 137, 8–16

Gill, D. and Lambourn, J. (1981) The indications for ECT: A profile of its use. In: R.I. Palmer (Ed.). *Electro-Convulsive Therapy: An Appraisal.* Oxford: Oxford University Press

Gordon, H.L. (1948) Fifty shock therapy theories. *The Military Surgeon,* 103, 397–401

Jenaway, A. (1993) Educating patients and relatives about electroconvulsive therapy: The use of an information leaflet. *Psychiatric Bulletin,* 17, 10–12

Johnstone, L. (1989) *Users and Abusers of Psychiatry: A Critical Look at Traditional Psychiatric Practice.* London: Routledge

Johnstone, L. (1996) Inside psychiatry. The electric shock therapy scandal. *The Outreach Connection Newspaper (Toronto),* May, 29

Johnstone, L. (1999) Adverse psychological effects of ECT. *Journal of Mental Health,* 8 (1), 69–85

Johnstone, E.C., Deakin, J.F.W., Lawler, P., Frith, C.D., Stevens, M., McPhearson, K. and Crow, T.J. (1980) The Northwick Park electroconvulsive therapy trial. *The Lancet,* 20/27 December, 1317–1319

Jones, Y. and Baldwin. S. (1992) Shock, lies and psychiatry. *Changes,* 10(2), 126–35

Jones, Y. and Baldwin. S. (1996) ECT, infants, children, adolescents: Shocking abuse of power, or valuable treatment medium? *Behavioral and Cognitive Psychotherapy,* 24, 291–305

Karagulla, S. (1950) Evaluation of electric convulsive therapy as compared with conservative methods of treatment in depressive states. *Journal of Mental Science,* 96, 1060–91

Lambourn, J. and Gill, D. (1978) A controlled comparison of simulated and real ECT. *British Journal of Psychiatry,* 133, 514–19

Leong, G.B. and Eth, S. (1991) Legal and ethical issues in electroconvulsive therapy. *Psychiatric Clinics of North America,* 14(4), 1007–1019

Malcolm, K. (1989) Patients' perceptions and electro-convulsive therapy. *Psychiatric Bulletin,* 13, 161–5

McKay, N. (1998) Shock therapy case may lead to increase in patient claims. *Scotland on Sunday*, 16th August

Mental Health Act Commission (1993) *Fifth Biennial Report*, 1991–
1993. London: HMSO

Mental Health Act Commission (1997) *Sixth Biennial Report*, 1995–1997.
London: The Stationary Office

MIND (1995) *Making Sense of Treatment and Drugs: ECT*. London:
MIND Publications

Newnes, C. (1991) ECT, the DCP and ME. *Clinical Psychology Forum*,
36, 33–5

Oxlad, M. and Baldwin, S. (1996) The use of ECT in older people: Risks,
rights and responsibilities. *Health Care in Later Life*, 1(1), 39–49

Pippard, J. (1992) Audit of electroconvulsive treatment in two National
Health Service Regions. *British Journal of Psychiatry*, 160, 621–37

Pippard, J. and Ellam, L. (1981) Electro-convulsive treatment in Great
Britain. *British Journal of Psychiatry*, 139, 563–8

Riordan, D.M., Barron, P. and Bowden, M.F. (1993) ECT: A patient-friendly
procedure? *Psychiatric Bulletin*, 17, 531–3

Rogers, A., Pilgrim, D. and Lacey, R. (1993) *Experiencing Psychiatry.Users'
Views of Services*. Hampshire: McMillan

Squire, L.R. (1977) ECT and memory loss. *American Journal of Psychiatry*,
134, 997–1001

Squire, L.R. and Slater, P.C. (1983) Electroconvulsive therapy and
complaints of memory dysfunction: a prospective three-year follow-
up study. *British Journal of Psychiatry*, 142, 1–8

Thompson, J.W. and Blaine, J.D. (1987) Use of ECT in the United States
in 1975 and 1980. *American Journal of Psychiatry*, 144, 557–62

United Kingdom Advocacy Network (UKAN) (1996). ECT Survey. *The
Advocate*, Issue 1, Spring / Summer, 24–8

Weiner, R.D. (1984) Does electroconvulsive therapy cause brain damage?
Behavioral and Brain Sciences, 7, 1–22

West, E. (1981) Electric convulsive therapy in depression: A double-blind
controlled trial. *British Medical Journal*, 282, 355–7

Acknowledgement

The author wishes to acknowledge Craig Newnes for his supervision on
issues regarding this chapter and Guy Holmes, for commenting on a
previous draft.

ECT: A Fact Sheet for You and Your Family

Introduction

This leaflet tries to answer some of the questions you may have about electro-convulsive therapy (ECT). For example, what is ECT? Why is it used? What is it like to have ECT and what are the risks and benefits?

Don't worry if you find it difficult to read through the whole leaflet at once. You can come back to it later. You may need someone to help you to understand some parts of the leaflet and you may wish to use the information below to help you to ask questions of staff, relatives or other patients.

Some facts about ECT

- Over 20,000 people a year are given ECT.
- ECT has been banned by psychiatrists in Germany, Holland and Italy and there are restrictions on compulsory treatment in Canada.
- In the UK the National Association for Mental Health has called for a ban on the use of ECT with children under the age of eighteen years and on all compulsory use of ECT.
- Approximately two-thirds of people given ECT are women; there has been a dramatic increase in the number of elderly people being given ECT.

Why is ECT used?

Most people who are given ECT have been diagnosed with depression. However, ECT is also sometimes prescribed for people with a number of other diagnoses including mania, schizophrenia, catatonia, postnatal psychosis, epilepsy and Parkinson's disease.

ECT is often suggested for people who have not been helped by tablets, although this is not always the case. Some people believe that ECT is the best treatment in cases of severe depression and that it can be life-saving. MIND state that 'although ECT does sometimes prevent death when someone is profoundly depressed, no longer eating and drinking and is in a critical state, there is no evidence that ECT prevents suicide'.

How does ECT work?

Nobody really knows how ECT works, but there are many different theories. The Royal College of Psychiatrists believes that repeated treatments with ECT alter chemical messages in the brain and bring them back to normal. Other psychiatrists argue that ECT works by causing brain damage, with memory loss, confusion and disorientation disabling the brain.

How well does ECT work?

ECT has been shown to produce short term improvements on depression rating scales for some people, but this improvement has not been found to continue beyond four weeks and has not been found to be present three and six-months later. ECT patients who are not receiving medication have been found to relapse at rates as high as 70% and research has also shown that nearly half of the people who receive ECT for depression will relapse within twelve weeks without treatment with medication.

There is mixed opinion amongst people who have experienced ECT as to its benefits. In one study 43% of people said that ECT had been helpful or very helpful and 37% reported that it had been unhelpful or very unhelpful. A further 20% reported no effects. People who have found ECT helpful report that it makes them 'feel like themselves again' and 'as if life was worth living again'. Other people have said 'please inform others never to have this treatment. I had ECT many years ago and am still trying to recover' and 'I permanently lost all memory of myself and my family. I couldn't even remember how to read and write. The person I used to be died the day I had ECT'.

What ECT cannot do

The effects of ECT will not help all of your problems. The way you are feeling may be the result of a whole number of problems, for example at home or at work. These problems may still be present after your treatment and you may need further help with these. ECT will not prevent future 'episodes of depression'.

Why has ECT been recommended for me?

ECT is given for many reasons. If you are not sure why you are being given ECT, don't be afraid to ask your doctor. It might be possible to have an advocate with you if you need support in asking questions.

How many treatments will I be given?

ECT is usually given two or three times a week. It is not possible to say exactly how many treatments your psychiatrist will prescribe. Some people are given as few as two or three treatment sessions, others are given as many as twelve and sometimes more. ECT treatments should not be given daily.

What will happen immediately before treatment?

Before having ECT you will be given an anaesthetic and a muscle relaxant. You will therefore need to fast (have nothing to eat and drink) from about midnight the night before each treatment. This will involve having no breakfast on the morning that you have ECT. Anaesthetics and muscle relaxants sedate the brain. They prevent your bones being broken during treatment with ECT, but mean that higher voltages of electricity will have to be administered to produce a seizure than was previously the case. Some psychiatrists have argued that this can increase the risk of memory loss and damage to the brain.

What will actually happen when I have ECT?

Treatment with ECT will take place in a separate room and other patients will not be able to see you having it. The procedure itself takes a few minutes. The anaesthetist will ask you to hold out your hand so you can be given an anaesthetic injection. This will make you go to sleep and cause your muscles to relax completely. You will be given some oxygen to breathe as you go off to sleep. Once you are fast asleep a current of 100–150 volts will be passed across your head and this will cause you to have a grand mal seizure. This is equivalent to an epileptic fit. The seizure affects the entire brain, including the centres which affect thinking, mood, appetite and sleep. There will be little movement of your body because of the relaxant injection that the anaesthetist gives.

When you wake up you will be back in the waiting area. There will be a nurse with you to offer you reassurance and make you feel as comfortable as possible. Once you are wide awake you will be offered a cup of tea.

For the treatment you should wear loose clothes, or nightclothes. You will be asked to remove any loose jewellery, hairslides or false teeth if you have them.

How will I feel immediately after ECT?
Immediately after treatment you may experience headaches, muscular aches, nausea, drowsiness, weakness, a lack of appetite, and amenorrhoea (loss of periods in women). Other reported effects include disturbed memory, impaired comprehension and motor restlessness.

What are the longer term side-effects of ECT?
In the first week after ECT, memory problems and headache have been found to be the most prominent side-effects. One research study found that 74% of people who had had ECT complained of memory impairment and 30% felt that their memory had been permanently affected. Another study found that people were still complaining of memory loss three years after treatment.

ECT may also exacerbate existing psychological problems. Psychological after-effects can include loss of confidence, dignity and self-esteem; fear of hospitals; nightmares, anger and feelings of depression.

A survey by the UK Advocacy Network found that one third of their sample believed that ECT had damaged them and that many said the treatment had made them more depressed. Some people may become very manic during treatment with ECT.

Are there any serious risks from the treatment?
The Royal College of Psychiatrists state that the risk of death or serious injury with ECT is about one in 50 000 treatments. MIND cite a figure of 4.5 deaths per 100,000 treatments. Older people are at a much higher risk than younger ones and one study by a British psychiatrist found that deaths from ECT in an elderly population could be as high as one in ninety. Deaths are usually because of heart problems. If you do have heart disease it may still be possible for you to have ECT safely with special precautions such as heart monitoring. Your doctor should ask another specialist to advise if there are grounds for concern.

What other treatments could I have?

Alternatives include medication, talking therapies (e.g. counselling and psychotherapy) and complementary therapies (e.g. acupuncture, aromatherapy and homoeopathy). MIND have published a series of booklets which will inform you about all of these different approaches.

Will I have to give my consent? Can I refuse to have ECT?

Your doctor must have your consent to give you ECT. ECT can only be given *without* your consent if you are sectioned under Part IV of the Mental Health Act (1983) and authorisation is given by a second opinion doctor appointed by the Mental Health Act Commission.

At some stage before the treatment you should be asked by your doctor to sign a consent form for ECT. If you sign the form you are agreeing to have up to a certain number of treatments (usually six). Before you sign the form your doctor should explain what the treatment involves and why you are having it, and should be available to answer any questions you may have about the treatment. You can refuse to have ECT and you may withdraw your consent at any time, even before the first treatment has been given. The consent form is not a legal document and does not commit you to have the treatment. It is a record that an explanation has been given to you and that you understand to your satisfaction what is going to happen to you. Withdrawal of your consent to ECT should not in any way alter your right to continued treatment with the best alternative methods available.

What if I decide not to have ECT? Are there any risks in not having ECT as recommended?

If you decide not to have ECT this should in no way alter your right to continued treatment with the best alternative methods available. Some people would argue that refusal of treatment may lead you to experience a longer and more severe period of disability that might otherwise have been the case. Others would argue that by refusing ECT you are avoiding the possible negative side-effects outlined above and may find better ways of coping with your difficulties.

CHAPTER 7

Do families cause 'schizophrenia'? Revisiting a taboo subject.

LUCY JOHNSTONE

THE ISSUE OF whether family dynamics play a causal role in the development of conduct that is labelled 'schizophrenia'[1] has for many years been one of the most controversial in the whole of psychiatry. In the 1960s Laing and his colleagues, among others, made the challenging claim that so-called 'symptoms' were in fact understandable responses to impossible dilemmas in family relationships (Laing and Esterson, 1964). Although Laing also emphasised that parents are partly the product of their own family backgrounds, and that all families exist within a less than ideal society which exerts its own pressures on them, the message that was picked up by more traditional psychiatrists, by the media and by the relatives themselves was that 'families cause schizophrenia.' This misleading inference has been used to discredit such work ever since, with the current position being that such links are unproven and damaging, part of an outdated theory that caused much unnecessary distress to relatives. For example:

> You only have to live with someone who in fact is going mad to realise that it's not your narrow, pinched refusal to tolerate the discourse of the mad that's at fault, but actually that people are ill. I think that a great deal of harm was done to the families and to the ill themselves by the great sixties denial of mental illness. (Miller, 1991)

[1.] I have used the term 'schizophrenia' in inverted commas throughout, in order to indicate reservations about its validity as a concept (see earlier chapter by Mary Boyle).

*Theories of family pathogenesis have in the past been
widespread and are still held by some professionals. This
has resulted in relatives being blamed and stigmatised
for the patient's illness.* (Tarrier, 1991)

*Advances in the understanding of the biological basis of
schizophrenia have left most of the philosophical objections
to the medical view of it as an illness, the so-called 'anti-
psychiatry' argument, looking distinctly old hat. (*Appleby,
1992)

Professional literature, voluntary organisations such as SANE
(Schizophrenia: A National Emergency) and the National
Schizophrenia Fellowship in this country, and in the USA, the
National Alliance for the Mentally Ill, educational videos and media
articles all maintain the same line. To challenge it is to arouse a
storm of protest, to be accused of being ignorant of the research,
callous to the relatives and impervious to the distress of the patients.
It is consistent with this position that psychotherapy or family
therapy with 'schizophrenia' is seen as at best irrelevant and at
worst damaging (with the exception of the Family Management
approach to be discussed below). In the words of the distinguished
American psychiatrist and analyst Michael Robbins: 'Schizophrenia
is now generally believed to be an organic disease like diabetes or
cancer . . . (Psychotherapeutic models) . . . are looked on as relics of
antiquity, even of the age of magic and witchcraft' (Robbins, 1993,
p.3).
    In examining these opposing views about family aetiology, I
am starting from the basic assumption that theories about human
nature do not simply arise in a vacuum. The social constructionists
would argue that all scientific theories are structured by factors
such as personal and political interests that need to be explored
and acknowledged rather than hidden away under the guise of
scientific objectivity and neutrality; science is seen as a form of
knowledge that creates as well as describes the world. A powerful
demonstration of how this happens in psychiatry can be found in
Richard Warner's book, *Recovery from Schizophrenia*, in which he
demonstrates, with the help of a detailed analysis of recent and
past studies from all over the world, that there is a close link between
recovery rates from the condition and political economy. At times
of labour shortage, the emphasis turns to rehabilitation and social
causes of mental distress and the outlook for patients improves,

whereas in economic downturns there is a swing towards biological theories and treatments, with correspondingly negative prognoses. His striking conclusion is that 'psychiatric ideology is influenced by changes in the economy...rather than psychiatric treatment having a big impact on schizophrenia, both the course of the illness and the development of psychiatry itself are governed by political economy' (Warner, 1994, p.139).

Starting from the premise that psychiatric theories represent something rather more complex than an impartial, objective search for the truth, we can understand the rejection of ideas about family aetiology at various levels. Patients, relatives and professionals may all find it easier to work with an account that distances them from pain in relationships, and from blame, anger, guilt and responsibility. Non-medical hypotheses can be seen as a threat to medical dominance in psychiatry and to psychiatry's scientific status. There are powerful financial interests involved, such as those of the pharmaceutical industry, which has a major role in shaping research agendas by providing funding. And there has been a general shift away from social/psychological explanations and towards biomedical ones for reasons which are surely as much to do with politics as with science; for example, suggestions in the prestigious journal *Science* that there may be genes for unemployment, domestic and social violence, and homelessness (Lewontin, 1993). Thus, when the current orthodoxy is challenged, the responses consist not just of legitimate scientific arguments but also, I suggest, of anger and resistance as vested interests are challenged and personal dynamics touched upon.

Of course, the fact that there are vested interests in a particular theory does not necessarily mean that the theory is wrong. However, it may well mean that alternative views get a less than fair hearing, and that the currently accepted 'facts' give a less than complete picture of the evidence.

Before proceeding any further, I want to establish some points of logic which, although extremely obvious, can tend to get lost in a debate that is sometimes very heated.

If families do play a role in the emergence of 'schizophrenia' . . .

. . . does this imply that this is the *only* causal factor? The answer is obviously no. There is plenty of evidence for the relevance of factors such as socio-economic status, racism and external stresses. There also seems to be a role for individual vulnerability, although we are not yet clear exactly what it consists of. Almost certainly, like every other mental or physical state that human beings can experience, the causes will turn out to be complex and multi-factorial.

... would explanations that draw in part upon family dynamics necessarily apply to *all* cases where a diagnosis of 'schizophrenia' is made? This is highly unlikely. Because of the well-documented variations in diagnostic practice resulting from the lack of reliability and validity of the term, (see chapter by Boyle in this volume), it would be very surprising if any factors emerged which applied to every individual so labelled.

... do such theories imply that families are in some way 'to blame'? No, they do not, for the obvious reason that parents are themselves at least partly the products of their own families of origin, and so on in an infinite regression. Moreover, families are themselves shaped by powerful pressures that are beyond their control. For instance, it is known that extended family structures may be able to bear the burdens of breakdown and promote recovery far better than nuclear ones (Warner,1994). This is not to deny a role for individual responsibility. However, psychotherapists working in the field find that the most useful position is one that assumes that relatives are doing the best they can in their own very difficult circumstances (Karon and Vandenbos, 1981).

... does this mean that identified patients are merely passive victims? No; systemic formulations would see them as contributing actively to the family dynamics, and there is evidence to support this (Scott 1973b). Nevertheless, it is unarguable that the parents were there before the child, with the implication that with a different parenting style the condition might not have developed.

... would such theories mean that biological processes play no part at all? Of course, we are bodies as well as minds, and all human experience presumably has its biological correlates in brain chemistry changes. The question is whether we see such processes as having a primary causal role, as in the diseases of general medicine, or whether they will turn out to be simply the correlates, or even the results, of psychosocial factors. No such biological factors have yet been identified in 'schizophrenia', but even if they were, there would be several logical hurdles to leap before we could be confident that they were *causal* in any way. The undoubted involvement of biological processes in some ways and at some levels does not in itself justify the use of the term 'illness' to describe 'schizophrenia'.

Having spelt this out, we can briefly overview the evidence for theories of family aetiology. Here, we may note a curious paradox. Biological theories of 'schizophrenia' are frequently presented as established facts ('Schizophrenia ...is caused by a biochemical abnormality in the brain', Haydn Smith, 1998), although one can occasionally find admissions in official sources that there is actually no evidence to support these confident assertions ('Although the concept of schizophrenia has been in existence for nearly a century...there has been no identification of any underlying causal pathology', Chua and McKenna, 1995.) On the other hand, as we have seen, theories involving family dynamics are generally dismissed as completely unsubstantiated, although the evidence supporting them is arguably far stronger.

The literature on family aetiology is extensive; some key articles and overviews are listed at the end of the chapter. To summarise the work very briefly, we can note that certain themes in family relationships have consistently emerged over several decades in work from a variety of therapeutic orientations – psychoanalytic, psychotherapeutic, existential, systemic, humanistic and cognitive-behavioural. These are:

- extreme difficulty in separating and achieving independence
- blurred boundaries in relationships
- fundamental confusions about identity
- confused and contradictory family communications
- emotional and physical/sexual intrusiveness
- difficulty in dealing with anger and sexuality
- severe marital disharmony
- social isolation

The model that emerges from this large body of research and therapy can perhaps be summarised as one in which parents, due to psychological difficulties that may date back several generations, are unable to facilitate their infant's very early development of boundaries and a sense of self. The child's identity becomes inextricably linked with parental identity, projections and defences. The consequences become apparent when the child's attempts to separate in adolescence or early adulthood are met with terror and resistance due to the crucial role that he or she plays in the parents' precarious psychological adjustment. The expression of anger and sexuality are particularly threatening because of their potential to disrupt the status quo. However, because these psychological difficulties are largely out of the parents' conscious awareness, and conflict with their (genuine) love and concern, they cannot be expressed directly but emerge in the form of confusing and contradictory communications. The child, torn between overt and covert messages, lacking a secure sense of self and isolated from healthier outside influences, is left with no room to manoeuvre. He or she may resort to expressing in metaphor what cannot be said or acknowledged openly. This carries the danger of being labelled as 'mad', with the false solution of locating family difficulties within an 'illness' suffered by one individual.

A particularly interesting example is provided by the Genain quadruplets, better known in the USA than in the UK. These four genetically identical girls, born in America in the 1930's, became the focus of possibly the most detailed investigation ever undertaken into one family when they were all diagnosed as 'schizophrenic' in their early twenties. They were admitted to NIMH (the National Institute of Mental Health) for a three-year period of intensive treatment involving numerous physical and psychological tests, while family, friends, neighbours, colleagues and teachers were all interviewed at length. The picture emerged of a highly disturbed family environment with a violent, jealous, unfaithful and sexually abusive father, and a mother who was unable to gainsay him or allow her daughters any independence of thought or feeling.

The researchers were initially anticipating confirmation of genetic influences; 'When one first learns that the quadruplets are both monozygotic and schizophrenic, one can hardly help but wonder what further proof of a genetic aetiology anyone would want to have' (Rosenthal, 1963). However, no such proof was found, although Rosenthal, who summarised the mass of information, still favoured a model in which a non-specific hereditary factor such as an introverted and placid temperament made the quads more vulnerable to environmental influences. Instead, the results provided evidence for the causal influence of family dynamics in the emergence, timing, form, content and outcome of the quads' breakdowns. High levels of control, which included emotional over-involvement, excessive contact and intrusiveness, seemed to play a primary role in the *emergence* of the condition, while levels of parental hostility, which varied towards each quad, gave a perfect correlation with *outcome*. Thus the most favoured quad was eventually able to marry and have children, while the least favoured of her genetically identical sisters spent most of her life on a locked psychiatric ward. In addition, the characteristic pattern of 'symptoms' displayed by each quad seemed to reflect a different aspect of Mrs Genain's own intrapsychic life; for example one quad , who became aggressive and sexually active in her breakdowns, seemed to be acting out her mother's repressed sexuality and anger, while another, who was eventually able to marry and leave home, seemed to represent her mother's strivings for independence. 'The detailed history obtained from so many sources all tends to...indicate that the pattern of parental behaviour existed long before the girls became ill and in fact dated back to their infancy'(Rosenthal, 1963, p571).

Anticipating the response that this research has long since been contradicted by new findings, let us turn to some recent work from Finland. Tienari and his colleagues compared 155 adopted children whose biological mothers had been diagnosed as 'schizophrenic' with a control group of adopted children of mothers who had not been so diagnosed (Tienari et. al., 1994). The percentage of 'schizophrenia' and other severe diagnoses was significantly higher in the index group. However, a clear difference between the two groups emerged *only in adoptive families which were themselves rated as disturbed.* All children – even those who were presumed to be carrying some genetic tendency to a 'schizophrenic' breakdown – did well in healthy adoptive families. Two conclusions may be drawn. One is that the quality of relationships within the family appears to be a crucial factor both in leading to, and protecting from, serious psychiatric breakdown. The other (in line with Rosenthal) is that any inherited component may, as the Finnish researchers suggested, consist of a non-specific predisposition such as general sensitivity to the environment rather than a gene or genes for a biologically-based illness. 'If this turns out to be the case, the diagnosis of schizophrenia as a distinct disease entity may also need revision' (Lehtonen, 1994).

The few longitudinal prospective studies on families with high levels of communication deviance (a measure closely related to high expressed emotion) also find that their offspring have a much increased chance of later being diagnosed with a range of severe psychiatric disorders (Goldstein, 1985; Douane et. al., 1981). It is important to note that neither these nor the Tienari studies tell us anything about 'schizophrenia' as such. If the concept is neither reliable nor valid, one would not expect to find precise links between pre-existing family disturbance and particular psychiatric labels. However, they do lend support to the common-sense but controversial notion that disturbed families tend to produce disturbed children.

It follows from this model that psychotherapy may, at least in some cases, be the most effective form of treatment for 'schizophrenia.' Some of the large and almost entirely neglected literature supporting this position is listed at the end of the chapter. A particularly important recent project comes, once again, from Scandinavia, and is based on a model which draws on the literature of the 1950s and 1960s but avoids a rigid division between the biological and the psychological. Pre-existing disturbances in the parents are believed to lead to family relationships characterised by blurred boundaries, projections and symbiotic dependency, which play a crucial causal role in the child's subsequent breakdown. However, the condition is seen as multi-causal. Biological factors are also relevant, but not necessarily in the sense promoted by orthodox psychiatry. It is argued that interactionality with other people is part of human biology and inevitably has effects on cerebral development and functions (Alanen, 1994).

Based on this model, a nation-wide project was set up in Finland offering 'need-adapted treatment' to all patients with a diagnosis of 'schizophrenia.' In an initial meeting shortly after admission, all members of the family are helped to 'conceive of the situation rather as a consequence of the difficulties the patients and those close to them have encountered in their lives than a mysterious illness the patient has developed as an individual.' As they note, 'this is an important difference compared with the psycho-educational family therapy approaches, which usually regard schizophrenia as an organically determined illness' (Alanen et. al., 1991). A flexible and individually-designed treatment package, consisting of various combinations of individual, couple, family and group psychotherapy, is set up and re-assessed as it progresses. The package often starts with system-oriented family therapy to help the patient achieve a degree of separation, at which point he or she may be more able to make use of long-term individual therapy. Social needs, for example help in getting a job and developing social skills, are also addressed. Neuroleptic medication is used at the minimum levels and often discontinued entirely in the second year. Follow-up studies show a reduction in symptoms, inpatient days and disability pensions compared to a control group (Pylkkanen, 1997).

To summarise the argument so far
There is an accumulation of evidence over the years in support of the hypothesis that disturbed family relationships can have a causal

influence on the emergence of 'schizophrenia', and that psychodynamic and other therapies can be an effective form of treatment. At the same time, there are powerful pressures on the psychiatric profession not to acknowledge this. This has resulted, as I now hope to show, in various unhappy compromises in current theory and practice.

The first type of compromise is found in the internationally known school of Family Management, which has been heralded as 'the most significant breakthrough in schizophrenia since the discovery of neuroleptic medication' (Kavanagh, 1992). It is based on a model of 'schizophrenia' as a biological illness, which may be triggered or made worse by environmental factors such as stress: the so-called 'vulnerability-stress' model. Researchers have found that a proportion of relatives score highly on a scale of Expressed Emotion which includes hostility, critical comments and over-involvement (e.g. excessive self-sacrifice, inability to lead separate lives and over-protectiveness), and that a patient living in such a family has a much greater chance of relapse. Intervention is aimed at reducing levels of Expressed Emotion, and hence the rate of relapse, by problem-solving, improving family communication and encouraging patient and relatives to spend more time apart.

This list of family characteristics has a very familiar ring to anyone who has read the literature of the 1950s and 1960s, as do some of the clinical observations: 'Separation is always the key issue...for some families it was possible to work towards hostel placement, in others the intensity of closeness was so great that the focus had to be on small issues...Attempts to reduce contact were often met with fierce resistance and reflected the central problem of being unable to tolerate separation, so often seen in these families' (Berkowitz, 1984).

However, it is important to note that Family Management workers explicitly distance themselves from theories of family aetiology. Families are 'educated' that 'the symptoms of schizophrenia seem to be caused by a chemical imbalance, which is partially or fully corrected by the medication' (Falloon et. al., 1984), and that 'THERE IS NO EVIDENCE THAT FAMILIES CAUSE SCHIZOPHRENIA' (Smith and Birchwood 1985, their capitals). High Expressed Emotion is seen as relevant to relapse, but not to initial breakdown: 'We consider that families do not exert a *causal* influence, although they can modify the *course* of the illness' (Kuipers et. al., 1992b). This preserves the orthodox biomedical view of 'schizophrenia' in line with all the vested interests that were discussed at the start of the chapter, but at some cost, as I have argued elsewhere, to logic and conceptual clarity (Johnstone, 1993).

For example, Leff has admitted that over-protective parental attitudes seem to develop very early in life (Leff et. al., 1982). This makes the claim that High EE has a causal influence on relapse but not on the development of the condition in the first place, highly implausible. Nevertheless, the preferred explanation is that High EE is *caused by* the stress of having to live with the patient's disturbance. Even the strangest behaviour described by the researchers, such as a mother sharing her bed and all her leisure time with her adult daughter while father was banished to another room, have to be understood in this way. This leads us into further improbabilities; patients are apparently able to cause disturbance in relatives, but not vice versa (or at least, not until the first breakdown has occurred.)

It is consistent with the vulnerability-stress model that clinicians, in the words of one of them, 'do *not* view the family as being in need of treatment. Hence we avoid calling our interventions 'family therapy.' Our aim is to help the family to cope better with the sick member who is suffering from a defined disease' (Kuipers et. al., 1992a). However, the same book gives several examples of interventions that are borrowed from standard family therapy practice; thus, it is suggested that separation can be facilitated by changing seating arrangements, positive reframing and paradoxical injunction. The message to families can come across as 'There is nothing wrong with you' and, simultaneously, 'You need to change'. In other contexts this could be described as a double-bind. These confusions in practice spring directly from confusions in the theory, in which 'Blame is avoided only at the expense of conceptual clarity–by declining to address the issues of aetiology altogether' (Terkelson, 1983).

Genuine growth and change may be another casualty of the apparent need to preserve an illness model of 'schizophrenia' at all costs. Most reviews report that overall gains are modest: 'Globally, patients appear better but not well...relatively few patients appear to achieve independent living and continued employment' (Hogarty et. al., 1991). Over-involvement, as rated on the EE scale, is particularly resistant to change. This is exactly what one would predict from a psychotherapeutic model which sees separation difficulties as a central causal factor, rather than the by-product of dealing with a relative's biological illness.

Family Management researchers thus find themselves in a

very awkward position. While denigrating supporters of family aetiology for not having any evidence to support their theories, they themselves have inadvertently uncovered much of this evidence but cannot afford to acknowledge it.

The second type of compromise is found in the work of those who, while acknowledging the importance of exploring the meaning of so-called psychotic experiences and beliefs, still retain the medical term 'schizophrenia.' This is true of most of the recent work on cognitive therapy with psychosis (Haddock and Slade, 1995; Fowler et. al., 1995). It is also true of the Scandinavian groups and Robbins in the USA, who, although seeing family dynamics as having clear implications for aetiology, appear to find the concept of 'schizophrenia' unproblematic. In this way they are, I believe, avoiding the full implications of conceptualising the condition as a psychological or psychosocial phenomenon. Medical and psychotherapeutic models are based on incompatible assumptions. It is contradictory to imply that someone is suffering from a biological illness and, at the same time, having an understandable emotional response to their situation; that the cause is internal, individual and biological on the one hand but rooted in relationships on the other; to categorise experiences as symptoms while at the same time looking for meanings; to relate to someone simultaneously as a patient (whose role is to take expert advice) and as a client (who needs to take an equal role in exploring the meaning of their distress).

This mixed and contradictory model also creates problems in practice which are bound to have adverse effects on psychotherapeutic interventions. Scott, in some classic papers from the 1970s, coined the term 'treatment barrier' to describe what happens when one member of a disturbed group is officially labelled as 'the sick one' by the process of applying a medical diagnosis. The drawing of a line that, in his words, 'rigidly divides the sick from the well' means that 'human relationships are then maintained in a severed and disconnected state.' This false solution to unbearably painful conflicts is, according to Scott, often reached at a crisis point in family life, when professionals are called in to verify what is essentially lay people's selection of one person in the group as 'mad' or 'ill.' Although this initially brings relief, the long-term effect is disastrous. 'The parents deny that forms of relationship threatening to themselves are relationships; they are seen as forms of disturbance in the patient. Thus, symptomatology is maintained by the conventional approach while relationship issues are depersonalised and evaded' (Scott, 1973a). All clinicians will be familiar with the scenario in which relatives complain, 'He's been answering his mother back/ playing his music too loud/ not telling us where he's going – he must be getting ill again.' The use of a medical diagnostic label may well put families beyond our therapeutic reach even before our first meeting with them.

We also need to be aware of the devastating impact of the label on the identified patient, to which many service users have testified: 'I walked into (the psychiatrist's office) as Don O'Donoghue and walked out a schizophrenic...I remember feeling afraid, demoralised, evil' (O'Donoghue, 1997). 'The diagnosis becomes a burden...you are an outcast in society. It took me years to feel OK about myself again' (Lindow, 1997). Barham and Hayward (1995) have vividly documented how a psychiatric diagnosis introduces people into a life of stigma, isolation and discrimination in which 'an impoverished conception of what they can reasonably do and hope for – of their significance and value – have been brought to merge in a painful experience of exclusion and worthlessness.'

The way forward
The central message of this overview, it seems to me, is that we need to return to the key tenet of Laing and others from the 1950s and 1960s: 'schizophrenia' is, in many cases, best understood as a meaningful response to psychological conflicts arising within damaged and damaging family relationships.

We also need to acknowledge the full implications of such a hypothesis. One is that rather than a *diagnosis,* we need a *formulation*; an understanding of the meaning of the individual's experience that links past and present, external and internal, conscious and unconscious. Here we can recall, in conjunction with more recent critiques, the contention by another key figure from the 1960s that since the mind cannot be 'sick' in any but a metaphorical sense, the term 'mental illness' should be abandoned (Szasz, 1961).

Another implication is that the primary form of intervention should be psychotherapeutic rather than medical, with a range of individual, couple, group and family therapies on offer.

As well as forgetting many of the lessons from 40 years ago, we have also learned a great deal. As we have seen, large-scale studies such as those from Scandinavia lend some empirical support to theories of family aetiology, while giving valuable indications of how such ideas might be put into practice nationally. At a broader level, we also know much more about the complex effects of poverty, inequality and racism on mental health (Thomas, 1997; Gomm, 1996; Fernando, 1991.) With sophisticated analyses like that of Warner putting individuals and families into a socio-economic context, and demonstrating how the pressures inherent in industrialised societies can impact upon recovery, we no longer have to fall back on a vague conviction that society drives people mad. Instead, we can develop (as Warner has) a detailed blueprint of social and political strategies to back up our psychotherapeutic interventions. We have the theoretical and practical knowledge to justify abandoning the medical model of 'schizophrenia', along with the term itself, and adopting a psychosocial one instead.

However, we cannot afford to be naïve about the forces arrayed against such a shift in our understanding of what has been called 'the prototypical psychiatric disease' (Boyle, 1990). Warner, as we have seen, has argued that promoting good outcomes for patients is actually secondary to psychiatry's main function of social control, and 'Ideological views which emerge counter to the mainstream of psychiatric thought make no headway in the face of a contrary political and social consensus' (Warner, 1994, p.139). Commenting on the same phenomenon from a psychoanalytic perspective, Robbins (1993, p.190) has said, 'Because the recognition and validation of certain elements of genuine thought and feeling within the schizophrenic and his disturbed family have the potential to disrupt family structure... and hence pose threats to the stability of society, society appears to enact and support the totalitarian forces within the family designed to suppress and deny them.'

If 'schizophrenia' is a dramatic manifestation of some of the central contradictions of our Western industrialised way of life, filtered through family dynamics, it is not surprising that the debate surrounding it has been so controversial, so heated and so inconclusive. Robbins has argued that current psychiatric theories are little more than pathological processes writ large, designed to suppress the individual in order to support 'the myth of the happy family and the myth of treatment' (Robbins, 1993, p.470). The question of how to intervene thus becomes not just a scientific but a moral one. Are we ready to admit our own collusion with the denial and repression that leads to breakdown? Do we have the courage to meet the person behind the label? Whose side are we on?

References

Alanen, Y., Lehtinen, K. and Aaltonen, J. (1991) Need-adapted treatment
of new schizophrenic patients: experiences and results of the Turku
Project. *Acta Psychiatrica Scandinavica*, 83, 363–72

Alanen, Y.(1994) An attempt to integrate the individual– Psychological
and interactional concepts of the origins of schizophrenia. *British
Journal of Psychiatry*, 164 (suppl 23), 56–61

Appleby, L. (1992) Pain and paranoia. *Observer magazine*, 2.2.92

Barham, P. and Hayward, R. (1995) *Relocating Madness: from the mental
patient to the person*. London: Free Association Books

Berkowitz, R,(1984) Therapeutic intervention with schizophrenic patients
and their families: a description of a clinical research project. *Journal
of Family Therapy*, 6, 211–33

Boyle, M. (1990) *Schizophrenia: a Scientific Delusion?* London, New York:
Routledge

Chua, S.E. and McKenna, P.J. (1995) Schizophrenia– a brain disease?
British Journal of Psychiatry, 166, 563–82

Douane, J.A., West, K.L., Goldstein, M.J., Rodnick, E.H. and Jones, J.E.
(1981) Parental communication deviance and affective style. *Archives
of General Psychiatry*, 38, 679–715

Fallon, I., McGill, C. and Boyd, J. (1984) *Family Care of Schizophrenia*.
New York: Guilford Press

Fernando, S. (1991) *Mental Health, Race and Culture*. Basingstoke:
Macmillan/Mind publications

Fowler, D., Garety, P. and Kuipers, L.(1995) *Cognitive Behaviour Therapy
for Psychosis: Theory and Practice*. Chichester: Wiley

Goldstein, M.J. (1985) Family factors that antedate the onset of
schizophrenia and related disorders. *Acta Psychiatrica Scandinavica*,
71, suppl 319, 7–18

Gomm, R.(1996) Mental health and inequality. In: *Mental Health Matters:
A reader* T. Heller, J. Reynolds, R. Gomm, R. Muston, and S.
Pattison, (eds) Basingstoke:Macmillan/OUP

Haddock, G. and Slade, P.D. (1995) (eds.) *Cognitive Behavioural
Interventions with Psychotic Disorders*. London: Routledge

Haydn Smith, (1998) Letter to *The Guardian*. 26.10.98

Hogarty, G.E., Anderson, C.M., Reiss, D.J., Kornblith, D.P., Ulrich, R.F.
and Carter, M. (1991) Family psychoeducation, social skills training
and maintenance chemotherapy in the aftercare treatment of
schizophrenia. *Archives of General Psychiatry*, 48, 340–7

Johnstone, L.(1993) Family management in 'schizophrenia': its
assumptions and contradictions. *Journal of Mental Health*, 2, 255–
69

Karon, B.P. and Vandenbos, G.R. (1981) *Psychotherapy of Schizophrenia:
the treatment of choice*. New York: Aronson

Kavanagh, D. (1992) Recent developments in expressed emotion and
schizophrenia. *British Journal of Psychiatry*, 160, 601–20

Kuipers, L., Leff, J. and Lam, D. (1992a) *Family Work for Schizophrenia: a practical guide.* London: Gaskell

Kuipers, L., Birchwood, M. and McCreadie, R.D. (1992b) Psychosocial family intervention in schizophrenia: a review of empirical studies. *British Journal of Psychiatry,* 160, 272–5

Laing, R. and Esterson, A. (1964) *Sanity, Madness and the Family.* London: Tavistock

Leff, J., Kuipers, L., Berkowitz, R., Eberlein-Fries, R. and Sturgeon, D. (1982) A controlled trial of social intervention in the families of schizophrenic patients. *British Journal of Psychiatry,* 141, 121–34

Lehtonen, J. (1994) From dualism to psychobiological interaction: a comment on the study by Tienari and his co-workers. *British Journal of Psychiatry,* 164 (suppl 23), 27–8

Lewontin, R.C. (1993) The dream of the human genome. *The New York Review,* 28th May, 31–40

Lindow, V. (1997) Personal communication.

Miller, J. (1991) The doctor's dilemma: Miller on madness. *Openmind,* Feb/March

O'Donoghue, D. (1997) Misdiagnosis. *Openmind,* 87, p.8

Pylkkanen, K. (1997) The Finnish National Schizophrenia Project, in C. Mace and F. Margison, (eds.) *Psychotherapy of Psychosis.* London: Gaskell

Robbins, M. (1993) *Experiences of Schizophrenia: an integration of the personal, scientific and therapeutic.* The Guilford Press, New York, London

Rosenthal. D.(1963) (ed.) *The Genain Quadruplets.* New York: Basic Books.

Scott, R.D. (1973 a) The treatment barrier: Part 1. *British Journal of Medical Sociology,* 46, 45–55

Scott, R.D. (1973b) The treatment barrier: Part 2. The patient as an unrecognised agent. *British Journal of Medical Sociology,* 46, 56–67

Smith, J. and Birchwood, M. (1985) *Understanding schizophrenia.* Health Promotion Unit, West Birmingham Health Authority

Szasz, T. (1961) *The Myth of Mental Illness.* New York, Harper

Tarrier, N. (1991) Some aspects of family interventions in schizophrenia: 1. Adherence to treatment programmes. *British Journal of Psychiatry,* 159, 475–80

Terkelson, K.G. (1983) Schizophrenia and the family: Adverse effects of family therapy. *Family Process,* 22, 191–200

Thomas, P. (1997) *The Dialectics of Schizophrenia.* London, New York: Free Association Books,

Tienari, P., Wynne, L., Moring, J., Lahti, I., Naarala, M., Sorri, A., Wahlberg, K., Saarento, O., Seitmaa, M., Kaleva, M., and Laksy, K. (1994) The Finnish adoptive study of schizophrenia: implications for family research. *British Journal of Psychiatry,* 164 (suppl 23), 20–6

Warner, R. (1994) 2nd edn. *Recovery from Schizophrenia: psychiatry and political economy*. London: Routledge

Additional references on family aetiology and psychotherapeutic interventions:

Bateson, G., Jackson, D., Haley, J., Weakland, J. (1956) Towards a theory of schizophrenia. *Behavioural Science*, 1, 251–64

Berke, J.H. (1979) *I Haven't Had to go Mad Here*. Harmonsworth: Pelican

Breggin, P.R. and Stern, E.M. (eds.) (1996) *Psychosocial Approaches to Deeply Disturbed Persons*. New York: The Haworth Press

Esterson, A., Cooper, D.G., and Laing, R.D. (1965) Results of family-oriented therapy with hospitalised schizophrenics. *British Medical Journal, 18 Dec, 1462–1465*

Fromm-Reichmann, F. (1950) *Principles of Intensive Psychotherapy*. Chicago: University of Chicago Press

Foudraine, J.(1974) *Not Made of Wood: A psychiatrist discovers his own profession*. London: Quartet Books

Jackson, D.D. (ed.) (1960) *The Etiology of Schizophrenia*. New York: Basic Books

Jung, C.G. (1939) On the psychogenesis of schizophrenia. In A. Storr (1983) *Jung: Selected Writings*. London: Fontana

Laing, R. D. (1960) *The Divided Self*. London: Tavistock

Lidz, T., Fleck, S. and Cornelison, A.R. (1965) *Schizophrenia and the Family*. New York, International Universities Press

McGlashan, T.H. (1984) The Chestnut Lodge follow-up study. *Archives of General Psychiatry*, 41, 573–601

Reilly, S,P.(1997) Psychoanalytic and psychodynamic approaches to psychosis: an overview. In C. Mace and F. Margison, (eds.) *Psychotherapy of Psychosis*. London: Gaskell

Schiff, J.L. (1975) *Cathexis Reader: Transactional analysis treatment of psychosis*. New York: Harper and Row

Sechehaye, M. (1951) *Autobiography of a Schizophrenic Girl*. New York: Grune and Stratton

Selvini Palazzoli, M. (1989) *Family Games*. London: Karnac Books

Steiner, C. (1974) *Scripts People Live*. New York: Bantam

Sullivan, H.S. (1953) *Schizophrenia as a Human Process*. New York: Norton

Werbart, A. and Cullberg, J. (1992) (eds.) *Psychotherapy of Schizophrenia*. Stockholm: Scandinavian University Press

Wynne, L.C., Cromwell, R.L., and Matthysse, S., (eds.) (1978) *The Nature of Schizophrenia*. New York: John Wiley and Sons

CHAPTER 8

Psychiatric hospitals and patients' councils

MARESE HUDSON

I married a psychiatric nurse. It was April or May 1965, when we moved into the hospital houses. There was this damn big wall, I never even went in the grounds – for all intents and purposes we were living outside, we didn't have any contact with the hospital. To get money I worked a couple of days a week on Ward One for the women. There were a lot more patients than there were on the books. It was just a few weeks later they decided that they would unlock the wards – the staff weren't pleased at all. It meant they had to chase after people outside. They would call patients 'old chronics', not because of age but because of the length of time they'd been there. I was a nursing assistant. It was mostly staffed by nursing assistants. We had no training. We had a few lectures after we'd been there a while. The job was just to supervise and organise patients and definitely not to talk to them. You'd have about nine or ten in the bathroom, women stripped stark naked. We had to make sure that every patient got one bath a week. I thought it was pretty deadly. I was quite shocked, but felt sort of covered . . . 'this will never happen to me'. You don't consciously think of it; I was just thinking, 'You poor sods'.

TWO WORLD WARS in the 20th century resulted in a great weakening of the class system. 'The rich man in his castle, the poor man at his gate. God made them high and lowly and ordered their estate' was vigorously questioned by an increasingly cynical public. The powerful upper classes had proved to be incompetent in a time of crisis and the nation would not forget because the common man had paid the price and would no longer accept that a government was always right. Women gained the right to vote and all its entitlements that they had fought so long, bitterly and passionately for. Trade unions emerged with the power to change working conditions and society came to realise the value of solidarity and campaigning. After the second world war the educational system embarked on a comprehensive method of teaching with a much broader curriculum, eventually abolishing the selective 11 plus system and the school leaving age was raised gradually to 16 years of age. The old 'ordered estate' had had its day.

The late 1950s and the '60s saw a strong civil and human rights movement emerging and growing in many countries and the movement was appalled at the often inhumane and corrupt psychiatric services. In the '60s and '70s inmates of the psychiatric hospitals emerged from their former incarceration with horrific individual testimonies of the conditions, the barbaric treatments, the brutality and the debasement endured by the afflicted humanity imprisoned in these so called 'asylums'. No-one could remain unmoved by their plight – a plight that society had collaborated in and condoned. The time was right and ripe for change.

The user movement

The first country to act for reform was the Netherlands. As more and more patient experiences of the psychiatric hospitals were made public and taken up as an issue of concern the Government was forced to investigate and act.

Patient Action Groups were formed, and many hospitals took the initiative in trying to redress the balance of power between patients and therapists. In 1980 the Dutch parliament endorsed and insisted on an experiment in patient advocacy. In 1987 this project was positively evaluated and became common practice. The National Foundation of Patient Advocates in Mental Health now takes care of the administration of patient advocacy. Patients' councils are now active in *every* Dutch psychiatric establishment.

In Britain there was also pressure for change. Mental health groups leaned on all the powers that be for better conditions, treatments and safety for all the patients in their care. Many questioned the care and therapies that were being provided for the 'good' of the patient. Notably, the national charity MIND (the National Association for Mental Health) in the middle 1960s began to campaign for 'Care in the Community'. Some mental health professionals whose humanity and integrity had not been eroded by the frustrations and politics encountered in their professional lives also joined the call for better services. This made the time right for the emergence of a user movement throughout the country and thus some modern-day user groups were formed.

In 1985 there were only around half a dozen user groups. This led to the first national user network – Survivors Speak Out (SSO) – being set up in 1986. The first large gathering of users from all over Britain was at Edale in 1987. This was a very important moment for self-advocacy and gave users a vision. In 1991 the United Kingdom Advocacy Network was set up by a conference and its first meeting was held in September 1992. UKAN is still a good support and information provider for psychiatric sevice user groups. Meanwhile . . .

It was like something out of a horror story. Lying on that operating table and coming to during my first Caesarean section. The excruciating pain and the panic; the total helplessness. Why couldn't the anaesthetist tell I was awake? 'Oh God, let me faint'. I came to again while clips were being pushed into my flesh. Later, my heart stopped. That night I couldn't sleep for fear I would dream about the operation. I began to wonder if they could burn you or bury you alive when you were supposed to be dead. I'm sure this all affected my reaction to my father's death. He dropped dead in 1979, I was thirty nine. This was a big shock. He was a strong man, took care of his diet and physical fitness and all that. One minute he was going up the stairs, saying no he was NOT going to watch the golf on television because 'there were women in it', and then he came and he died in front of me. It was quite horrific really. And that opened up, 'God, we're all going to die, how will they know when I'm dead?'. I was getting near that age when people confront their own mortality. God had fallen from the sky and I didn't know what had hit me. So within the next 24 hours I had a few panic attacks, but I didn't know they were panic attacks. I passed out with one. I was up in Liverpool. This little GP arrives and just patted my hand and said 'Oh yes, you English don't know how to cope with death, these are just panic attacks, take these tablets.' They didn't touch me. I was still so frightened of death. I wouldn't sleep in case I didn't wake up. I went to my own doctor and I think we went through all the tablets he could think of. I was on Valium three times a day, I was on four Nitrazepam at night. I didn't sleep in a bed properly for eighteen months, I was so frightened I had to stay up. I knew that if I went to sleep I was going to die. I'd also been bringing up my children single handed for quite a while, on benefits, so I'd taken a part-time job as a dinner lady to get some money and be with the children. I struggled on for a year. A lot of it was the psychiatric drugs I was on . . . I was getting the children up and seeing them out, going back to bed, setting the alarm for dinner time, on the way home from school getting the assembly kit for dinner and going back to bed before they came home – I was hardly awake. Nobody ever questioned the drugs; they just decided I was in a deep depression. I do remember one visit to the GP, she was so sweet and I felt so much better and all she did was let me talk. But that was rationed, that was obviously going to be my only chat, that was meant to clear it up. When she suggested I should see a psychiatrist, I told her exactly what I thought of psychiatrists and no bloody way and they needed one more than me. After fifteen minutes she talked me round to it.

Patients' councils

Patients' councils are groups focused on the well-being of users of mental health establishments. Members are, if possible, made up of users or ex-users of that particular service. The first patients council in Britain started in Nottingham at Mapperley Hospital – an initiative which later became the National Patients' Council Support Group and then the Nottingham Advocacy Group. There are now two main types of patients' council in Britain (MacLachlan, 1996). The first consists of elected members who are currently attending the hospital (e.g., St Clement's in East London, and the two special hospitals of Ashworth and Broadmoor). MacLachlan suggests that in the case of the special hospitals this structure reflects 'the lengthier and more custodial nature of the patients' stay. Ashworth Patients' Council has a written constitution and a written agreement outlining its relationship with the hospital management group. In this agreement the management group agrees to consult with the council on matters of policy that relate to the care, treatment and quality of life of patients and that this consultation takes place before final decisions are made, except in exceptional circumstances. They also agree to respond to issues raised by the council within a reasonable time limit, to meet formally with the council at least four times a year and to provide continuing financial and administrative support. Ashworth Patients' Council, for its part, agrees to respond to requests for comments on matters referred for consultation and not to pursue the cases of individual patients' (p.19).

The second type of council is one in which visits are made to mainly acute wards in psychiatric hospitals by patients' council visitors: patients are either consulted individually or a meeting is arranged and held without staff present. MacLachlan found a wide variation in the relationship of the patients' councils to advocacy networks. She notes that 'in some cases there is a fully formed advocacy system set up and managed by the patients' council, for example, at Springfield Hospital in South London. At Springfield there is a referral service from the patients' council to a patient advocate if an issue is raised by a patient that is of a personal nature' (p. 20). Other councils are establishing links with existing advocacy groups in their area, for example, at Broadgreen Hospital, Liverpool.

Several patients' councils have a support group or management committee that will meet monthly or bi-monthly to cover any issues raised by patients' council members. As in our local council in Shropshire, support group members tend to be NHS Trust employees who are sympathetic to the council, such as members of a Trust's Quality Assurance Department, management and psychologists. Support groups vary in their degree of formality, some having an elected chair and secretary and a set agenda, while others operate more like ongoing consultation or steering groups (MacLachlan, 1996).

The Patients' Council at Shelton Hospital, Shrewsbury was formed following a study day, 'Advocacy in Action', in 1992 attended by Colin Gell from the Nottingham movement and Viv Lindow of SSO. This was supported by local professionals and members of the Shropshire Advocacy Forum, and resulted in the formation of a steering group interested in establishing a patients' council at the hospital.

Later we visited some of the other patients' councils we knew about to tap into their expertise and experiences and to gain some practical ideas. We were warmly welcomed by all of them and information, advice, support and their time was very generously given.

First of all we visited the Nottingham movement who are recognised to be the most advanced in the country and they inspired us with a goal to aim for, i.e., a patients' council for all psychiatric services networking within the geographical area of the responsible local Health Authority. Later we visited Broadoak and Talgarth Patients' Councils and gained more knowledge. I was also given the privilege of visiting Ashworth Patient Council; I found this extremely sobering and thought provoking. This visit highlighted the complete disempowerment and almost criminalisation of the user. It was brought home to me, first hand, that outside those high walls existed a public that neither knew nor cared what went on inside. Any sort of abuse could happen to those confined. The State and the existing Mental Health System hold the patients completely within their power – some may never see the outside again – a potent recipe for human injustices and disaster.

We have now been operating at Shelton hospital in Shrewsbury since 1994 and have gone through various growing pains and struggles as does any voluntary organisation. At first it was a bit like being part of a travelling circus because we couldn't get a permanent base, and we kept getting moved around the hospital while a building programme took place on the hospital site. At one point we were nearly put in the Chapel. We now have a permanent office base in the main part of the hospital.

Until this year (1999) our funding was felt by Patient Council members to be most unsatisfactory with bits and pieces of funding being accessed from other budgets for us by the Quality Assurance Director. We have had a breakthrough and have just been granted our own designated budget. MacLachlan (1996) found that some patients' councils are run on an almost entirely voluntary basis with visitors receiving only travel expenses (as is the case with Shelton Hospital Patients' Council). The Whittington Patients' Council visitors receive travel expenses up to the limit of pay that can be received for work when on income support. Others have received more funding and have appointed development workers. For example, the Susan Britton Wills Centre in Bristol appointed two development workers to replace the volunteers. In other cases development workers are employed to support the work of the volunteers.

Some councils manage to operate with little funding. Others, such as Ashworth's Council, have over £2000 per annum for administrative resources. MacLachlan's work revealed that despite apparent sanctioning of councils the support was poor, administration being carried out on an informal basis by a secretary or a manager of a Trust, which clearly compromises the independence of a council. Councils such as Springfield Patients' Council have been more successful in securing funding in that they have a substantial administration budget and a part-time administrator.

We have seven full visitor members and five trainee visitors. Recruitment presents a continuing challenge and retention of volunteers can be difficult as ex-users find visiting wards nerve-racking (Newnes and Shalan, 1998). The members are made up of current users and ex-users of the psychiatric system and three others who have an interest in mental health. This is not ideal as there can be a very real risk of disempowerment to the users and ex-users in the patients' council. We now, after many appeals, have an administrative support worker, paid for by the Trust, but directed by us. We visit all four adult acute admission wards twice a month and the elderly admission ward once a month.

We give support to patients who want their voice to be heard and will act as their voice if that is their wish. We maintain complete confidentiality. This makes it possible to bring the concerns and complaints of vulnerable patients to the attention of managers. Feedback on the council has been positive: 'The Patients' Council is a good idea. It makes you feel, as a patient, that there really are people who care how you are being treated, how you are getting on, other than just the nurses who are paid for doing so!' (Holmes, 1996).

Before the interview with the psychiatrist I'd asked a friend who worked at the hospital who was the best one to be referred to. She'd said that they were all pretty much the same, but, 'for God's sake don't go to Z'. It happened to be Y. You had to take somebody with you in those days, and I had no carers, I didn't want my family around, so I took my friend. I sat just inside the door and told him that was as far as we were going. He suggested the usual thing, 'a rest'. That was very seductive, because I was worn out. If they'd have put me in a hotel with some good food, taken the drugs away, and given me time to think and talk, fine.

I got onto the ward ... he said, 'just for a week'. I was petrified they'd take my children away from me. I did have medication and I know antidepressants came into it, but I never ever thought, 'Oh God, I'm leaving here'. I somehow felt I didn't have that right. I never questioned it from week to week to week. Y's under-doctor was Dr. S., who was a trainee at the time, and we had long in-depth interviews about this, that and the other, especially delving into childhood. I had no access to talk to anyone about bereavement. Now this puzzled me and I thought well perhaps this person gets upset by it and can't handle it. He got really excited when we found out that when I was nearly six my brother, who was nearly four, was killed in an accident. You could see them pricking their ears up. But I said, 'No, that's fine. It's not a problem. I've been through that. I've got a very supportive family, it's been talked over for years and I'd say by about my middle teens that had all been resolved.' Dr. Y wanted me to have ECT and there was a lot of pressure and I wouldn't at that time. So I was sent to the day hospital. And I was really scared. Well this was a whole new world. 'Psychotherapy' they called it. Dr. Z was in charge. It started off with this morning assembly, big group, and Mondays they used the one way mirror and the microphones. The staff, some in-house and others from outside, were behind the mirror. Then they would walk in and everybody would go quiet, and we'd think, 'Who are you going to target today?' They would come in and they would position themselves, everybody would stay quiet, and then one of the staff would say, 'I feel there's a lot of anger in this room'.

It is very difficult for a patient within the system to speak out in opposition to that system; consider the following patient comments made to visitors over the last five years: 'I feel scared about complaining and saying what I think'; 'I'm frightened that the staff will spit in my food as retaliation for food complaints'; 'If I complain they will probably give me an injection'; 'Nobody believes me – staff just say I'm ill and don't know what I'm saying'; 'It's no use saying anything – they don't listen to us patients' and, 'I can't complain if things aren't right because it would be ungrateful to criticise. I think patients should just put up with the conditions'.

Sometimes visitors can only listen because patients are very frightened of the very real power the service has. They want to share their difficulties with us but do not want us to raise them with staff. The following patients' comments illustrate this: 'In hospital I feel intimidated. If I don't conform, I feel that physical action will be taken against me'; 'I won't speak to my key nurse because of bullying and being shouted at'; 'The ward staff are using sectioning as a threat – a stick to make me do what they want. It isn't to do with the way I feel'; 'My consultant has said that he will give me ECT if my discharge doesn't work out – it's making me anxious and scared.'; 'I was a voluntary patient so I thought I could leave when I wanted, but when I tried to they wouldn't let me go and now I'm under a six-month section'.

All these patients' comments are evidence of a flawed and inappropriate mental health system that is often found to be less than therapeutic to its users. Although we get favourable comments which we do pass on also we have to take notice of the fact that of the 392 individual comments recorded in our Patient Council report 1996/97, 97 comments were positive and 295 were negative.

The main aim of our patients' council is to get better mental health services – a fairer deal for patients – services that are more therapeutic and holistic, and above all to get choices of services for users and to make the services accessible. It is also vital that full information about the services and the different therapies available is willingly and freely given so that a service user may evaluate them as to their appropriateness to relieve their individual distress, and thus be in the position of making a real informed choice. It never seems to occur to the services that if they made this possible then the user, by making a choice, will have already made a commitment to that therapy and will have a much better chance of success. Distress is an individual condition and users must be treated individually.

As patients' council visitors we are accountable always to the patient. I don't know who professionals are accountable to. We inform managers and campaign on patient issues and make them aware of the patient as a person. We point out that patients often tell the services what they want to hear rather than risk being marked out as an ungrateful troublemaker or challenge their oppressive power. It is much easier to make one's path through the services a smooth one – especially if it is an enforced route.

We are often cheated by the lack of commitment of managers to listen – you don't just listen with your ears, you act. We don't want excuses like, 'It's against policy'; 'There's no money'; or, 'Clinical decisions and issues cannot be challenged'. 'We haven't the staff' is popular. Policies can be changed and some money can always be found for we never really want the earth; our ideas and preferred requirements are usually very cost effective.

We continually guard against allowing ourselves to put most of our energies into 'playing offices' and reflecting bureaucratic practice or accepting the managers' timescale, which is always too long.

Local achievements
Many issues come up on a regular basis: the quality and quantity of food and issues about patients receiving the special diets requested; boredom and lack of activities on and off the wards, especially during the winter months; concerns about leave and discharge arrangements, especially concerning suitable accommodation to which patients can be discharged; complaints from voluntary patients who are subsequently sectioned and who resent this very much.

During the last year the council had many successes, listed in the annual report: visiting more wards (including new visits to an admission ward for elderly people); agreement from the Mental Health Services Trust to fund a support administration worker for the (permanent, at last) office; a meeting with the Chief Pharmacist, which led to furthering and improving drug information to patients; putting great pressure on the Trust to quickly resolve a bed crisis; introducing 'Welcome Packs' of toiletries to avoid embarrassment for patients arriving in hospital without any; negotiating an Emergency Loan system on a trial basis for patients admitted with no money.

We attend Trust meetings and these vary from the very formal to more friendly affairs. We always try to get permission for two of us to attend together. It can get lonely out there. All meetings have an obvious preponderance of men in attendance so if you are female one immediately feels doubly disadvantaged. As a member of the patients' council you are very aware that you are entering their world – it is often very difficult to know exactly when they will think it appropriate for you to speak – it's a bit like doing a dance and heaven help you if you get the steps wrong. If you do choose an inappropriate slot they can stare at you with an ill-concealed disapproval, and you can just curl up inside. (Why is it so hard for professionals to accept criticism? There is bound to be a Therapy for it and after all they are in the business). Trainers have assured us that nobody can invalidate your feelings – want to bet? Professionals often have a damn good try. They often trivialise your views that you base on first hand experience if they don't fit in with the existing policies and their 'expert' opinions and practices. Users have only felt the effects and often suffered from their policies, opinions and practices – so who are the 'experts'? We don't purport to be experts but suggest that our views and opinions are formulated on the most solid base of all – experience.

The balance of power
Patients' councils challenge the psychiatric empire. It is one of blatant inequality, minimum choices and dubious treatments – of diagnostic labels, *not* people. Mental health professionals are often ignorant of patients' real concerns yet they believe they 'know best' and will invalidate and dismiss patient views. However we have been there – *we have witnessed* – and because of our experiences we have a special bond, each to the other, and will celebrate a person's good experience but mourn the bad.

It often seems impossible to redress any balance of power because the whole system is operated under the Mental Health

Act. This Act allows for compulsory imprisonment, medication and even ECT. It can also dictate where you can live and can lead to a lifetime of supervision from psychiatric staff. At its worst it tries to criminalise mental distress. The monies allocated by Government must first of all be used for *their* vision of mental health provision and adhere to *their* policies.

I was put on Section for a month in the locked ward after an interview with a GP from outside the hospital. That was the lowest ebb, that time, because I hadn't known about the procedure, I wasn't playing by their rules in a way they could understand, I didn't know the way they functioned, and that was a time when I felt there was nothing left, and it got so bad that I didn't see anything in colour. There was no hope left. I wouldn't let the children visit, not to a locked ward. My eldest boy was home then – he was 22. I wanted him to sign me out. And he wouldn't because he was more inclined to believe them, like carers do. In later years he said, 'I was only 22. I had the staff telling me one thing, my mother telling me another, and I was too young to cope with it.'

In every branch of medicine doctors have established a unique immunity to serious challenge – the 'I am God' syndrome, and many doctors really believe it (see 'All Mighty' by Richter, 1984). The Mental Health Act gives doctors legal powers over the user, and by doing so it gives them the right to consider themselves the ultimate experts. The other factor in this omnipotent delusional state is often the collusion of users themselves, because of the strong urge to believe in their therapists and so give themselves hope in their distress. Some need to feel that doctors hold the key to a cure for themselves – they will even blame themselves for 'failing' in therapy – it is unsustainable that their therapist could be wrong because by acknowledging this their hope would be lost.

It's so total: they order your getting up, your going to bed, your meal times, what you eat. You hear about the penal system, they're locked in the cell 22, 23 hours a day. You could be in the same big room 24 hours a day. You could do nothing. If you cried, you were depressed, if you didn't co-operate, that was interpreted as a sympton of illness. Everything was ordered. So all you could do was sit there and seethe.

Psychiatry is so hard to challenge. Patients' council members are told quite explicitly that they cannot challenge clinical decisions. This is ironic. After all, in psychiatry it really is no joke that 'if you have six psychiatrists you will have six diagnoses'. Psychiatry is, at the moment, built on theory, each theory cancelling out another, but these theories are a rich source of academic acclaim and kudos for the expounder (see Newnes, this volume), and are often totally inflexible: like all organised religions each thinks they are right and the only one. Despite its obvious flaws psychiatry has been given the power to label distress as illness, treat, contain and forcibly restrain people. With so much power it doesn't have to bother much with 'user satisfaction' with its therapies. The power of the user is negligible. Perhaps mental health professionals in training should be forced to spend two weeks on a psychiatric admissions ward to feel some of that powerlessness themselves. The imbalance of power is only partly redressed by groups like patients' councils. Changes we help bring about often seem cosmetic and without real shifts in attitude or power. Psychiatry needs to recognise the unique expertise of the user perspective. We have made some progress here; recently local patients' council members participated on interview panels for the appointment of clinical psychologists.

It is an indictment of the present mental health system that many emerge feeling weak, flawed or that our opinions are no longer to be trusted. We feel stigmatised and judged by the system. We are seen as different from normal people and will always be treated this way. Before entering the system many users felt that to enter psychiatry was to be deemed mad. After our first brush with the system we felt tainted; failures who would no longer be considered whole again. This invalidation contrasts sharply with those who suffer mental distress but don't enter the system. They have not been officially diagnosed, labelled and documented.

Generally, users want to turn their back on the system. It takes particular courage to re-enter it as a patients' council member. Those still in the system are wary of being seen as trouble makers. Patients' council members must be prepared to be unpopular with the service staff. Going back evokes powerful feelings: 'Going back to the hospital brings back memories that are hard to cope with, memories of what they did to me. I was damaged by the treatments, by the ECT and the drugs'; 'It feels like we are under observation from the staff when we do our visits'; 'There is a sense we can change very little. There's just a slow drip, drip of complaints into the system'; 'Ex-patients visiting gives hope to patients that they can get out and have a better life' (Holmes, 1995).

All over the British Isles patients' councils are feeling their way, discovering the enormity of their task. Pooling experiences is one means of self-empowerment. We need to develop effective strategies to ensure that ex-users continue to enable current psychiatric patients to be heard.

References

Holmes, G. (1996) Bringing about change in a psychiatric hospital: the Patients' Council at Shelton two years on. *Clinical Psychology Forum, 95,* 25–8

Holmes, G. (1995) Report on the patients' council at Shelton. Shelton: Unpublished

MacLachlan, A. (1996) A survey of patients' councils in Britain. *Clinical Psychology Forum, 98,* 19–22

Newnes, C. and Shalan, D. (1998) Fear and loathing in patients' council visitors. *Clinical Psychology Forum, 111,* 27–30

Richter, H.E. (1984) *All Mighty: A study of the God complex in western man.* Claremont, Ca: Hunter House

CHAPTER 9

Hearing voices and the politics of oppression

RON COLEMAN

FOR MANY PSYCHIATRISTS, schizophrenia is considered to be a disease of the central nervous system characterised by abnormalities of the brain that have been observed through brain imaging technology. Furthermore, it has a strong genetic component that has been identified by recent DNA studies which show schizophrenia to be part of a group of genetically caused brain disorders. Finally, there are studies that point to additional biochemical factors which are providing a more sophisticated understanding of the role of dopamine in causing schizophrenia. Case closed. Or is it? In this chapter I shall explain why I think psychiatrists are mistaken.

Every time someone writes about mental health they start with a case study which they always claim proves their particular theory. So as not to disappoint I will do likewise.

Case study

The subject is male, about 30 years of age. He wanders off and stops looking after himself, then he starts to hear voices. There are two voices, one is the voice of God and the other is the voice of the devil. He is told that he can jump from high places and not harm himself, he is also told that he can own half the world if he surrenders to the voice. The man comes through this experience unscathed, then goes into a big civic building, trashes the place and throws people out.

What would our society do with this man?
The answer is obvious. Acting in the way that he is clearly represents a danger to himself and to other people. His delusional thoughts

and hallucinations are controlling his actions. As a result he would probably be arrested, be seen by a police surgeon and taken to the local psychiatric hospital where, if he did not accept being admitted voluntarily he would be sectioned and treated, again against his will if need be. The psychiatrist would then try all sorts of combinations of drugs to eliminate the voices. The view of all the service providers will be a simple one – here is a sick person, we must make him better. What actually happened in this case, for it is a real case, was that the voice hearer was crucified and we now call him the Son of God, or Jesus. Remember, we are told in the bible how Jesus wanders off into the desert, starts hearing not only his father's voice, but also the voice of Lucifer. He is told that if he jumps from the top of the cliff he will not be dashed on the rocks and if he follows Lucifer he will be given half his kingdom to rule. Later, Christ goes to the temple where he finds the moneylenders plying their trade, upon which Christ threw tables all over the place and threw the money lenders out of the temple.

So right at the very beginning of this chapter we can see that just describing behaviour patterns can lead us to make conclusions that are false. Most would by now have sectioned the Son of God and probably called him psychotic or schizophrenic. Moreover, if I were to go to see my doctor and tell him that whilst walking down the road one day I stopped by a bush that was on fire, only for the bush to start talking to me, then I'm afraid I would be in deep trouble. It would be straight to hospital, no messing, my number would be up; yet this very thing happened to Moses or so it is recorded in the bible. The Western world's moral, ethical and codes of law are based on the thoughts and writings of a whole series of voice hearers. Today, John's book of revelation could be described as a true journey through the madness of psychosis, yet within its own particular framework, that of religion, there is no problem associated with these experiences. All of the world's religions have been started by people who heard the voice of someone they allude to as God. Even today it is okay to talk to this God, whom you cannot see, hear or touch, but watch out if He talks back because the chances are you would then be considered schizophrenic by psychiatry.

What, if anything, does this case study prove?
I believe it shows one important thing and that is simply that you cannot make any assumptions until you are in possession of all the facts. In some cultures, far from being a sign of mental illness,

the hearing of voices is seen as positive or as a gift for the whole of society. It is mainly in the science-dominated West that the hearing of voices is stigmatised to such an extent that until now talking about it openly has been a definite one way ticket into the psychiatric system.

Voices – a primary symptom or a doctor's delusion?

DSM IV lists hearing voices as a first rank symptom of schizophrenia. The only thing that should be noted about the voices is the form they take i.e., whether the voices speak in the first, second, or third person or give a running commentary of what the person is doing or thinking. The content of the voices is regarded as being of no consequence; voices are seen as meaningless and without value. Yet study after study has shown that there is a link between life events and the onset of voices. Romme and Escher (1993) found that 70% of people they interviewed started hearing voices after a traumatic life event. Ensink (1993) found that 33% of women that she interviewed who had been subjected to sexual abuse heard voices that were consistent with a diagnosis of schizophrenia. Further studies in Europe and the USA have confirmed this relationship. Even with the weight of all this evidence most doctors reject the notion that there is a link between trauma and ongoing distressing voices.

The dominant theory used by psychiatrists is often called the medical biological model. The most common explanation given by this form of psychiatry for hearing voices and conduct labelled schizophrenia goes something like this: the brain over-produces a chemical called dopamine and it is this chemical which causes the person to hear voices and have the other so-called symptoms, and again this leads to the distress and behaviour problems that the person starts exhibiting. The doctor's response to someone presenting with these symptoms is the usual one of writing the person a prescription for neuroleptic medication (major tranquillisers) which they claim will alleviate the symptoms, that is get rid of the voices, thereby returning the person to more normal life.

But do the results fit the theory? I would suggest that they do not. The facts are that using the theoretical model above and the treatments it recommends, 33% of those treated recover fully and get on with their lives, 33% relapse on a regular basis and become what are called revolving door patients and 33% are eventually classed as chronic schizophrenic. The World Health Organisation international outcome study in 1979 found that the best recovery rates for schizophrenia varied greatly throughout the world. For example, London has a 24% recovery rate and Washington 23%, whilst Ibadan and Agra have rates of 57% and 48% respectively which shows that there is an unexplained variation in outcome in the developed and developing countries. The figures for the two best outcome studies in each country combined show this pattern continuing with London at 36%, Washington 39% whilst Ibadan is as high as 86% and Agra 66%. Does this show that the developing world is more advanced in their response to schizophrenia? On the face of it, it would seem so. In these terms it is clear the West continues to fail to increase its recovery rate in spite of the so-called advances in treatment and care. So the reality is somewhat different from the theory; only one in three recover fully, using the dominant belief about schizophrenia. This is surely not a record that we can brag about. Instead of talking about the recovery rate we should concentrate on the 67% failure rate. For this 67% are treated exactly the same way as the 33% who do recover or so it would seem on first glance; the reality is yet again something completely different.

Let us look behind the theory and consider what happens to everyone who is given the label of schizophrenic. As we have seen, all of them will be treated with major tranquilisers, but some in a different way. For instance the 33% who recover will normally be on a low dose of medication, sometimes called a maintenance dose, while the other 67% will normally be on a much higher dose of drugs yet still experience voices and other distressing 'symptoms'. The 67% are also more likely to be on drug cocktails, sometimes called polypharmacy, even though it is against the Royal College of Psychiatrists' own guidelines. Even when using this highly dubious and harsh drug regime, the studies show that over 50% still have ongoing problems with experiences such as voices. This fact has led to no discernible changes to the treatment offered by the doctors; indeed it is not uncommon to find people on three or four different drugs, plus another one to counter the side effects of the first four. Included within this cocktail it is not unusual to find two major tranquilisers. Dosages in these cases are often at or exceed the maximum recommended by the pharmaceutical companies. The doctors also rarely, if ever understand the implications of these sometimes lethal cocktails. Even with the relaunched so-called wonder drugs such as Clozaril (clozapine), known for their dangerous and potentially deadly side effects, the evidence that they are more effective is not conclusive.

Many psychiatrists have fallen into the trap of reducing all voice hearers' experiences down to a biological root leaving no room for the view that psychosis could be caused by an environmental or social factor. Even those who do accept this possibility still claim that environmental or social factors primarily cause the chemical response which causes the schizophrenic condition. Even when they have tried every physical treatment possible they still won't budge; instead they move the goalposts. Hearing voices, which was regarded as the primary symptom, is either reduced to a residual symptom or the person is called drug resistant. What arrogance these people have. A so called first rank symptom, indeed the very symptom on which the diagnosis is based is suddenly no longer important, it is only now a residual thing. This reasoning allows them to continue to use exactly the same treatments, even though the person is still being distressed by the voices (a primary symptom). Perhaps even worse, the person concerned is told that he or she is drug resistant, even when they are on massive doses, have no quality of life and are like zombies, unable to do much except sleep. For many people in the community this is their reality; living in a twilight world, seeing the world through a haze of prescribed drugs with nothing to look forward to apart from the next visit to the clinic to be overdosed once again. We have given this lifestyle a fine sounding name; we call it 'care in the community'; perhaps 'lost in space' would be a better title.

In the mid 1950s Largactil, the first major tranquiliser, was introduced and it was claimed it would revolutionise the prognoses of those with schizophrenia (see chapter by Newnes, this volume). What was the result of this revolution? William Sargent, an eminent Psychiatrist, presented a paper in 1966 entitled, *The recovery rate in schizophrenia prior to the introduction of neuroleptics*. This paper was presented to the Royal College of Psychiatrists and its conclusion was simple. The recovery rate prior to neuroleptics was 33%. The current recovery rate was now 33%. This effectively means that the increase in recovery since the introduction of these drugs was zero. These research findings are further supported by Richard Warner (1985) shows that recovery rates have remained constant since 1901. In the 1950s, the baby was thrown out with the bathwater. Perhaps it is not the same 33% that recover. Now if 33% recover using drugs and 33% recovered before the use of drugs using talking therapies then it follows that the recovery rate could be at least 66%.

One could argue that on this basis psychiatry is guilty of neglect, but another explanation could be that psychiatry is no longer psychiatry but is just another branch of physical medicine. That psychiatrists no longer look after minds but look instead to biology and chemistry to find answers means they are then no longer psychiatrists, they are physicians.

The trouble with drugs

Psychiatrists' arrogance goes further still. John O'Donoghue, a pharmacist in Liverpool, found that the norm amongst doctors was not to tell their clients about the side-effects of the drugs they were prescribing, because if patients knew the side-effects they would not comply with their treatment regime (O'Donoghue, 1997). Yet guidelines clearly state that people should give informed consent to treatment. Effects of medication can in some cases be even more distressing than the symptoms that they are meant to be dealing with. These effects include concentration and speed of thought and movement being adversely affected, dry mouth, blocked nose, difficulty in urinating, constipation, and blurred vision. Other side-effects include tardive dyskinesia, menstrual disturbances in women and impotence in men. With some of the new wave neuroleptics there is the possibility of serious blood disorders. Other more visible effects include drooling and violent movements or shaking.

The effects of neuroleptics are not welcomed by many people who are prescribed them. Those effects listed above are not the worst, the worst two effects of major tranquilisers are death and suicide. National MIND have stated that there are fifty deaths a year in hospital due solely to the use of neuroleptic medication. Indeed, in a twelve-month period there were five deaths directly caused by the re-launched drug clozaril. If this was to occur in any other branch of medicine then the drug would be immediately withdrawn. It would appear therefore that the continued use of these drugs is justified purely on the basis that they are agents of social control. Would you take a drug which has death as a possible side effect? What about suicide as a side effect? Research has shown that one of the effects of neuroleptic medication is the sudden onset of depression, which comes without warning, and it is at this stage that many people kill themselves. It is the 67% who do not respond to treatment who suffer these two side effects. Doctors are taking a blanket approach to something that is very individual and therefore requires individual attention.This generalised approach can have fatal consequences.

Pathologising the mind

The question that must be addressed is why this seemingly paradoxical situation occur. The answer to this may be found in the training that doctors undergo before coming into psychiatry, for in order to become a psychiatrist you must first spend five years studying medicine. It is important that we realise what happens during this initial training.

A psychiatrist usually starts as a young first-year medical student who may not know what they want to specialise in. They commence their training and soon meet their first patient. And who is their first patient? It is of course a dead body. It is with this patient that many of their attitudes are shaped and formed. It is here that many of them learn their bedside manner. For many this is the first time they have seen a dead person and they find it frightening.It is here that the idea of the human being as merely organic matter is set in concrete and it is here too that the notion of patholigising everything that is occurring to a person has its foundations. For the next five years the medical student learns medicine, medicine, medicine and more medicine; at the end of five years the student becomes a doctor and decides to go into psychiatry and what do they do there? Yes, they practice medicine. They get their patients and they pathologise their patients' feelings; hence sadness becomes depression, happiness equals mania, anger is classed as aggression and woe betide if you cannot be bothered cleaning your house one week, for this shows a lack of daily living skills, sometimes called a social dysfunction, which is of course a secondary symptom of schizophrenia. They try to do the impossible, they try to pathologise the mind. You can pathologise the brain, which is organic, but you cannot pathologise the mind which is not. How can you pathologise feelings? How can something which has no real physical presence be turned into a biological symptom?

DSM IV lays out the diagnostic criteria for schizophrenia. It gives a list of primary symptoms, one of which is voices, and then a massive list of secondary symptoms. An experiment which has been carried out by the Hearing Voices Network on many occasions has been to simulate the voice hearing experience with groups of professionals working in mental health. We do this by splitting the group into threes, then two members of the group have a conversation and the other one is a 'voice' in the ear of one of those conversing. Then they change places till everyone has had a turn. We then bring everyone together, and ask them what they think the consequences for them would be if this was an experience that lasted not only for a few minutes but all the time, and to imagine that there may be more than one voice. When we asked people to list the consequences for them, on every occasion the list was consistently the same as the list of secondary symptoms of schizophrenia.

This immediately begs the question are the things that happen to you after you hear voices consequences of the voices or are they, as the DSM IV states, secondary symptoms of schizophrenia? They cannot be both. Professionals we have worked with have at first been happy to list them as consequences when related to their own experience in the simulation. They have then become circumspect when shown how this list fits in with the DSM and schizophrenia. The one thing that is clear is that the very diagnostic tool used for schizophrenia is seriously flawed. This cannot be new evidence we are presenting, why therefore has it not been published before? Many people have stated that they have done similar exercises in the past, why then have they not followed it through and come to the same conclusions that we have reached? Could it be that it is not in the interests of medicine for a challenge such as this to be made? Indeed, if the challenge was successful, where would it leave psychiatrists in relation to so called secondary symptoms? For remember you only need two secondary symptoms, in conjunction with one primary symptom, and you're there; 'schizo' without a doubt, with all the stigma that entails, portrayed by the media either as a mad axe-wielder, or as an object of pity unable to function at any level of society.

Because you have admitted to hearing voices, the system that is meant to care for you becomes a system of rigid social control; a system where the voice hearer finds not sanctuary but fear; a system that does not enable independence but rather dependency; a system obsessed with curing the incurable (voices) rather than helping people to cope; a system of despair rather than hope. The reason for this is simple. The majority of psychiatrists have become biological reductionists, reducing every experience we have to chemical reactions in the brain.

It does not stop with doctors, nurses too are taught to work in a particular way with patients who hear voices. Hence if you are on the ward and say to a nurse that your voices are bothering you and you want to talk about it, you will receive the time honoured reply of 'let's play Scrabble', Scrabble may improve your vocabulary but it will do absolutely nothing for your voices. The other option the nurse might take is to see if you are written up for medication PRN i.e., as required. If you are, you are encouraged to take it. Why do they not talk to you about your voices? The answer is understandable, they are taught that to enter into dialogue with a person about their voices is dangerous and should never be done. Rather they should reinforce the idea that it is not really happening and find a way to distract the person from what is going on.

Who says it's dangerous, and why? Most doctors will say that it is dangerous to talk about the content of voices and the reason given is that if you collude with a person's delusion or voices then you are going to reinforce their belief in the experience, and they are less likely to come through it. Therefore if a person's voices are telling them to commit suicide and you talk to them about the voices then they are more likely to commit suicide, or if voices are telling someone to kill someone else you don't talk to them about the voice content on the basis that to do so would increase the chances of a murder being carried out. What nonsense. Common sense alone should tell us that these situations must be worked through if it is not going to end up in disaster and how can you work it through if you cannot talk to the person about the content of the voices, for it is within the person's experience of voices that the answer will be found.

The idea that it is dangerous to talk to people diagnosed psychotic seems to go back to Freud and his concept of dividing diagnosis into three categories – neurotic, psychotic and personality disorder – and apparently telling his followers not to talk to psychotics. Even here history has been distorted. Freud did say not to talk but believed that working with psychotics took longer and so analysts should work with neurotic people so as to prove that his theories worked in a shorter period of time. He never intended that work with psychotic people should never happen only that it should be put on hold in the short term.

Finally, where is the proof that it is dangerous? Where are the research findings that provide the evidence to back this prevailing idea? The answer is that there are none. No studies have shown this to be the case. In fact the opposite is true; studies consistently show that talking to people who hear voices is not only not dangerous but is very helpful in assisting clients to live and work in the community.

It can clearly be seen that the biological model, though working very well for 33% is not effective for everyone (67%) and though another 33% are helped on a temporary basis, the quality of life for these and for the other 33% is poor. As a 'caring' society we must assist voice hearers to speak and to make choices for themselves about their treatment. The days of doctor being God must end. Neuroleptic medication has been tried now for almost fifty years; with professionals ignoring the content and meanings of peoples' voices for even longer.

The genetic model

Let us now look at the genetic model. This model states that there are genes for mental illnesses such as schizophrenia and that finding the genes will then lead to a treatment that will eradicate the illnesses.

Most people know the story of Oliver Twist, either from the book or film or musical. Oliver is an eleven year old boy who was born in a workhouse in the East end of London, who spends his childhood there scrubbing floors and living in a workhouse, who because he drew the short straw is elected to ask for more food; but what is strange about Oliver is his ability to ask for more in a perfect middle class English accent, whilst all around him everyone speaks with a cockney accent. How can this be? He has never heard middle class English yet he speaks it perfectly. It is only as the story progresses that we find the answer – Oliver's parents are both middle class and so his breeding was bound to come through for it was in his blood. Here lies the basis of the genetic argument. Prior to science we called it God's will or divine right; with the dawn of the age of science it started as in the blood and ended with eugenics.

There have been two attempts to use this science to eradicate serious mental illness. The first was in the USA where one woman who was diagnosed as schizophrenic was ordered by a local court to be sterilised. She went through all the appeals procedures until finally the supreme court upheld the original decision. Sterilisation then became a widespread treatment, becoming law in twenty six states and yet *made no difference* to the rates of schizophrenia. Even today it remains on the statute books of twenty two states.

The second attempt was much more radical and was carried out by the Nazis from the late 1930s onwards when they took everyone with a diagnosed mental illness, learning disability or who was homosexual and killed them all. When the war was over, what difference did this radical intervention make to the rates of schizophrenia? Again the answer is *none*. But what about the recessive gene, some people argue. The answer to that must be what about it? You cannot kill off a whole generation and have no variation – but there was none. Still this is not enough. It runs in families they say, this proves it is genetic. Yes, if one member of a family is given a psychiatric label then it is more likely that other members of the family will be given the same label, but that does not prove the genetic theory. Family members are likely to be brought up in the same environment, share the same traumas or abuse or whatever is going on in the family, so it is no wonder then that they will share the same psychiatric fate.

The greatest weakness of the genetic argument is exactly this; it does not take into account any environmental or social factors. But in any case, how can you find a gene for the mind, and the workings of the mind? Where is the real scientific evidence for schizophrenia having an organic root? Even DSM IV concludes that there is no laboratory test for schizophrenia.

Genetics are useful when dealing with physical ailments such as cystic fibrosis but there is no evidence to suggest that they will help in mental health. Indeed the evidence shows that to date genetic theory has done nothing to advance our knowledge of mental health. If they were to claim to find the gene for schizophrenia what treatment could they offer? The only scenario I can foresee will be: 'Your foetus is carrying the schizophrenia gene and may become a schizophrenic when it grows into adulthood. Of course you can have an abortion and try again'.

The genetic road is therefore one fraught with dangers for the schizophrenic. It is a road we must challenge at all times. It is probably a road to nowhere.

The psychological model

Of the three clinical models the psychological model is the one least open to criticism, for within this model the client has the opportunity to understand the cause and nature of their experience. This model works on the premise that the voices are caused by external factors i.e. a traumatic life event. This in turn means that the voice hearer can do something to help themselves, it means that the voice hearer can be proactive in turning their lives around. It accepts that the person has the right to make decisions about their own treatment and that this treatment is not something which is done to them but done together in a partnership with the therapist.

In this model the voice hearer is able to explore their lives to look at their voices, to find out who the voices are, why they are there, where they come from and what they can do to deal in a more positive way with the voices. This allows for working with the person within their frame of reference. If a person believes their voices to be telepathic, the normal intervention is to call this maladaptive or delusionary and not enter into talk with the person about their frame of reference but rather to reject it outright, and try to change it. This way of working causes an immediate conflict to arise, with the professional refusing to budge and calmly claiming that the user lacks insight, i.e., they do not agree with the professional. However, working with the person's frame of reference means that you can develop ways of dealing with the voices together. Again, using telepathy as an example, you could work together to put in place psychic blocks that will not allow negative voices through. Too radical? Not at all if it works, for that must be the bottom line – either it works or it does not, and if it does then it must be accepted as of value to that individual.

Here then is the crux of the matter; is science king in mental health or is it, as many suspect, abused by psychiatrists, and is it not science at all but ideology dressed up to look scientific? If it is to be scientific then it should act as such which would mean that we would stop using the label schizophrenic until it could be proven to exist scientifically, i.e., in the lab.

The creation of a victim
These then are the three models that make up the clinical framework. The biological model which works well for 33%, the genetic model which works well for no-one and probably will never help anyone with a diagnosis of schizophrenia, and the psychological model which is not allowed to help many people because of the prejudices of those who hold power in the system. The first two models do have one main thing in common for the 67% who do not recover, and that is that it makes them victims. In fact it makes them passive victims who can do almost nothing to facilitate recovery except turn up to their depot clinic or take their medication. They are indeed helpless with nothing they can do but wait for the magic cure which may never appear. Indeed, if Romme (1993) is correct and there is no biological root to many people' voices, it will never appear.

Stop being a victim
In the early 1980s I was diagnosed as schizophrenic. By 1990 that was changed to chronic schizophrenic and in 1993 I gave up being a schizophrenic and decided to be Ron Coleman. Giving up being a schizophrenic is not an easy thing to do, for it means taking back

responsibility for your self, it means that you can no longer blame your illness for your actions. It means there is no disease to hide behind, it means no more running back to hospital every time things get a bit rough, but more important than all these things it means that you stop being a victim of your experience and start being the owner of your experience. For the voice hearing experience belongs to the voice hearer, not to the psychiatrist, not to the psychologist, not to the nurse, not to the social worker, not even to the carer or family but to the voice hearer alone. It is only if the voice hearer accepts ownership that growth is possible.

It is easy to remain the victim, for in the initial stages we are real victims of the system. The system creates us in its own image, we are seen as the modern day Frankenstein monster; our symptoms the body parts sewn together by some crazed doctors. We are given drugs that act like the electricity which flowing through us is meant to bring us to life, but which in reality turns many of us into the living dead; Parkinsonian parodies of people living as tardive retards held in a chemical prison with the very voices we seek either to lose or understand.

It is at this point that many of us think that our only power is this so called illness, this degenerative disease, this rumour of madness, that gives us the freedom to do what we want. If I throw a chair through a window, and I am asked why I did it and I answer, 'Did what?' I bring upon myself the ultimate in disempowerment. I maintain my own victim status for minutes after denying any knowledge of the now broken window. I go into the smoking room and boast to the rest of the patients about my actions.

Not only did I maintain my victim status. I also reinforced my illness in the eyes of the system. I remember early in my psychiatric career, I was being what we call 'specialed'. That is I had two nurses with me at all times, one either side of me always in touching distance, never allowed to be on my own. I was angry and frustrated by this intrusion on my privacy, so I decided to get my revenge. I would be sitting down, one nurse sitting each side of me, then I would stand up and walk across the room. The nurses would walk across with me then I would sit and as soon as the nurses sat down I would get up again and walk back across the room with the nurses following dutifully beside. Back and forth I would go, thinking to myself I am really pissing these nurses off, when in actual fact all that was happening was that they were writing in my notes 'Ron very agitated and unsettled today', and that would normally mean an increase in my medication. All I was achieving was the reinforcement of my diagnosis making it easy for the doctors to say, 'You're very ill and need to stay in hospital'. The doctors may have made me a victim but it was me that maintained the status by choosing a way of fighting back in which I was the only casualty. I believe many of us feel we have stayed victims long enough: we have to decide on a new way forward. We have a choice to make, and we can choose to stop being victims – not just victims of the system but victims of ourselves.

Professionals also must give up being victims. It is often the professional status itself that makes them victims also. Trapped as they are by their inability to look beyond the medical model; trying their hardest to convince themselves that there is a biological cure to problems with no proven biological cause. Victims of their inability to admit that, for many, drug treatments do not work. In effect the one thing that voice hearers and workers have in common is our mutual victim-hood. Is this then how it must be, where the common bond between worker and user is some kind of orgy of enmity and distrust? Where we remain forever locked in a mutual battle of victimhood, and can never meet together as equals seeking common cause against the real enemy, that being the distress that many voice hearers suffer? Must we the voice hearers be like Frankenstein's monster, condemned to forever decay in a pit of misery created by a lack of understanding of our real needs? I say that the answer to this is no, there is a way forward, there is a solution, there is hope for the future and that hope is ownership. We must be allowed to own our experience. Professionals must stop denying our experience. We must learn to work together in partnership, but it must be a partnership of equals based on mutual respect and trust.

As users we must give up our baggage and start being honest about our experience. We must give up using our supposed illness as our power. We must accept ownership of our experience. We must stand up and be proud of our experience, we must talk openly about our voices, we must make society listen and we can only do that by admitting and accepting our experience and by doing this publicly.

Professionals must give up their baggage as well. They must start listening to what their clients say. But not only must they listen, they must also learn to hear, for as I have found over many years workers' capacity to listen without hearing is amazing. They must give up this idea that they always know what is best for us. And finally they must learn to let us go, to let us make our own choices about our lives.

Partnership then is the key that opens the door to ownership and in turn ownership is the key to real power in our lives – ownership of our experience, ownership of our feelings, indeed ownership of our own lives. I wait for the day when like the scene in *Spartacus* after the final battle, where the slaves have been enslaved once again, the Roman soldier asks Spartacus to identify himself and the rest will be allowed to live. First one stands up and cries 'I'm Spartacus'; then another until they all claim to be Spartacus. They may have been enslaved physically but in their minds they owned their lives; they were no longer victims.

Perhaps one day the same will be true for us; when someone asks who is the voice hearer, we can all reply 'I am'. So let us own our experience, let us go forward to the future; a future where voice hearers and workers can work together as partners and in partnership find real personal growth. Finally, through growth perhaps the day will come when the rumour will no longer be that voice hearers are mad, but that madness itself is only a rumour.

References

Ensink, B. (1993) Trauma: A study of child abuse and hallucinations. In M. A. J. Romme and A. D. M. C. Escher (Eds.) *Accepting Voices*. London: MIND

O'Donoghue, D. (1997) Misdiagnosis. *Open Mind, 87*, p. 8

Romme, M. A. J. and Escher, A. D. M. A. C. (1993) The New Approach: A Dutch experiment. In M. A. J. Romme and A. D. M. A. C. Escher (Eds.) *Accepting Voices*. London: MIND

Warner, R. (1985) *Recovery from Schizophrenia: Psychiatry and political economy.* London: Routledge

CHAPTER 10

Collaborative conversation

PETER HULME

One hour's reflection is preferable to seventy years'
pious worship.
(Bahá'u'lláh 1982)

P EOPLE ARE SUCCESSFULLY questioning whether it is helpful to use
the term 'schizophrenia' as a label for certain kinds of
experience (Boyle, 1990). Visions, voices and 'delusions', or
the tendency to experience the world in those ways, are no longer
always lumped together as signs of an illness (Bentall: 1990). It is
accepted by more and more people that we are dealing with
dimensions not categories here. It's not a case of black or white but
shades of grey. Some of us find ourselves at one extreme or the
other: most of us are spread across the middle, bridging the distance
inbetween.

We no longer have to do violence to the rich subtlety of human
experience by distorting it to fit into narrow boxes. We are
increasingly able to capture each person's unique subjectivity. More
and more we are encouraged to listen carefully, to make the effort
to receive, in its own terms as far as possible, the story people tell
us of their lives.

This is a welcome shift in our thinking. However, it may not
be taking the matter quite far enough.

We still tend to place too much of the problem on the shoulders
of the individual rather than in his or her environment (Warner,
1985; Doubt, 1996; Sloan, 1996; and Smail, 1996). This is an
important consideration but is beyond the scope of this chapter.

Also, from the therapeutic point of view, the most troublesome characteristic or dimension of the experience currently labelled 'psychotic' or 'schizophrenic' has been pushed to one side at best or at worst completely missed. This characteristic is the main focus of this chapter. I shall call it 'fixity', a sort of stuckness that makes any kind of change difficult. I will explain it in more detail in a moment. Some of the implications for therapy will then be unpacked.

Potential replacements for the sacred cows

Different terms might capture better the experiences we are concerned with here.

Voices and visions are better terms[1] than 'hallucinations' for three interrelated reasons. First, these terms are usually more acceptable to clients. Second, they are more clearly dimensions we all might share to some extent. The third point is, for present purposes, the most important. These words do not have a built-in and implicit fixed and sticky quality which in my view should remain separate and explicit.

Psychiatry has seen an extreme resistance to change as the defining quality of what it calls delusions. It is at the core of the concept. In so far as hallucinations are intertwined with delusions, fixity all too often becomes their hallmark too: in practice they are seen as entailing almost by definition a more or less complete loss of perspective. I feel that psychiatry's position is fundamentally mistaken in this respect. One of the main purposes of this chapter is to analyse the nature of this fixity and explain why it is important to realise that psychiatry has got it wrong.

Beliefs almost certainly should be substituted for 'delusions'. None of us knows what the truth is. We develop a simulation of reality, a more or less useful approximation to the truth (Senge, 1992; Spinelli, 1994; Shweder, 1991; Reason, 1992; Kolstoe, 1985; 1995; and the Baha'i International Community, 1995). Most of us come to share a major part of how we see the world with other people from the same culture. We all have aspects of our worldview which are different from other people's to some degree or other. This is a question of degree not kind. Also these personal and shared views of the world (Berger and Luckmann, 1979; Tart, 1988) all fail, to some extent or other, to capture the essence of absolute truth which remains forever out of reach.

It is therefore not a question of whether you or I are 'deluded' and 'hallucinating': the real question in all our cases is, 'To what extent?'

Beliefs is also a better word to use because it does not imply we are stuck and cannot by definition change what we believe. As we shall see, the extent to which we are trapped by our worldview varies from person to person, just as the extent to which we are uncritically immersed in our experiences and powerless to step back from them also differs between individuals. This tendency to lose perspective and flexibility I am calling fixity and it is a separate dimension of experience all on its own.

To treat what people see, hear and believe and its degree of flexibility as a seamless whole is to pretend that a salad is a soup.

So, while the content of our voices, visions or beliefs may be making a contribution to our difficulties, it is by no means the only important component. The so-called bizarreness of these experiences and ideas may often not even be the key issue. There is also this quality of fixity and more often than not this is the main stumbling block to constructive change. This, in my view, has been unwarrantably neglected as an independent force. It is worth reminding ourselves that many people with mainstream beliefs hold them with unhelpful rigidity.

Fixity as a force to be reckoned with

The experience of unusual and nasty phenomena in the absence of critical distance generally earns the label of 'psychosis' or 'schizophrenia'. Why should this be so?

Fixity in the face of often extremely unpleasant phenomena causes an unacceptable and virtually inescapable amount of distress. The distress is what brings the sufferer to the attention of the psychiatric services. Psychiatry then applies the label schizophrenia. This label mixes up the content of the experiences with the person's relationship to those experiences in a most unhelpful way. Just as it is important to separate our perceptions (voices, visions and other internally generated experiences in other sensory modalities) from our understanding (beliefs, models, assumptions, meaning systems etc), it is crucial also to separate out, from the nature of these experiences in themselves, this loss of perspective and flexibility which I am calling fixity.

To give it a separate name locates it where it belongs. Fixity is an altogether different aspect of experience. It has its own characteristics (drowning, disowning and dogmatism) which will be examined later. When we see it this way and give it its own name, it reveals its true nature. It is a dimension along which we are all placed. We none of us can help but demonstrate some degree of fixity and too little may be as bad as too much. Without any, we are a leaf in the autumn wind: with too much we can become a fossil locked in rock. It is also a characteristic of group as well as of individual behaviour. It is a distinguishable aspect of other problems of the mind such as 'anorexia' and 'obessional/compulsive disorder'.

Perceptions and beliefs (from mainstream to idiosyncratic) and fixity are separate and independent dimensions along which people can vary. Some people may display one, two or all of these dimensions to an extreme and untypical extent. Others may display some or many such extreme phenomena in the context of different dimensions of human experience such as the intense and bleak darkness of the mind we call depression.

Only when you experience more than one of them with a sufficiently high degree of negative intensity would you seek or be forced towards professional help. When mental health professionals see only people who are experiencing several of these dimensions at the same time, they think they are all part of the same thing and call it an illness. This is an illusion, or may be even a delusion. This illusion confusingly denies the independence and meaning of these experiences in the life of the individual and can turn help into oppression.

It is tempting, but too complex for the purposes of this chapter, to explore the ways in which this framework maps onto such concepts as the 'self'. It clearly would also be intriguing and valuable to tease out whether the fixity described in this context is really the same as the fixation evinced by the fanatic, the authoritarian and the fundamentalist, but this too lies beyond this chapter's scope.

The roles of reflection, relatedness and relativism
Central to the present focus is the almost self-evident truth that many other states described as 'pathological' display this feature *fixity*. The success of many psychotherapies depends upon cultivating antithetical qualities such as reflection (Koestenbaum, 1978), relatedness (Spinelli, 1994)[2] and relativism (Shweder, 1991; Momen, 1988).

In the end true insight cannot simply lie in getting a better fix on reality for the reasons explored above. Even less does it lie in bringing the patient's view of the world into line with the therapist's. Insight must lie instead largely in improving our capacity to *reflect, to relate and to be relativist*.

What good conversations, when we are able to experience them, enable us to do is replace the inter-related forces of fixation with the inter-related forces of flexibility. Drowning, disowning and dogmatism are replaced by reflection, relatedness and relativism.

Drowning and reflection

When we are drowning in our experiences we are unable to separate ourselves from them. We are identified with or completely absorbed by them. They govern us absolutely.

A nightmare moment from Hazel's struggle with her inner life provides an example of drowning. She had been abused as a child and was tormented as an adult by voices. When her son was about four years old, the voices began to suggest that she should do something to stop him becoming an abuser when he grew up. One night she found herself walking up the stairs to her son's bedroom with a carving knife in her hand intending to castrate him at the instigation of her voices.

Fortunately, something broke their influence upon her. Until that point the experience had engulfed her. She had lost all perspective. For that period of time she could not see beyond the conclusions these experiences forced on her and, if something had not disrupted the process, it could have ended tragically for her as well as for her son.

Reflection is the capacity to separate consciousness from its contents (Koestenbaum, 1978). We can step back, inspect and think about our experiences. We become capable of changing our relationship with them and altering their meanings for us. We do not then replace one fixation with another: we are provisional and somewhat tentative in our new commitments which remain fluid in their turn.

For present purposes, the principal focus of reflection will be upon our models of reality and upon the experiences which give rise to them and to which they give rise in return. The capacity to reflect increases the flexibility of our models in the face of conflict and opens us up to new experiences: the adaptation and change that this makes possible enhances the potential usefulness of our models and their connected experiences.

Incidentally, this does not necessarily mean that they are 'true', whatever that is. It is only within certain cultures, and sadly ours is one of them, that truth and usefulness are seen as almost indistinguishable. For us also what is good is all too often reducible to what is useful and successful: the works of Machiavelli and the experience of the Third Reich give transparent illustrations of where that can lead. To be naive about the truth value of our suppositions is inherently dangerous. 'Psychotic' phenomena are only one illustration of that danger.

Dogmatism and relativism

Dogmatic certainty is just as dangerous. Dogmatism is to beliefs what drowning is to experiences. Transactional Analysis has a slogan: 'When in doubt, check it out'. When you're not in doubt, there's no need to check anything out.

Chris loves animals. She has a canary of which she is extremely fond. To her its claws became unpleasantly long. She came to believe she was a vastly experienced expert in exotic birds, much sought after by hundreds of people needing her help and advice. Though she had never in reality manicured a bird in her life, buoyed up by her absolute conviction that she had done it thousands of times, she took a pair of clippers to the small bird's claws. She was totally unaware of what might happen. At the first snip, blood came flooding out of the artery in its foot. Immediately, realistic doubts about her competence came flooding in. She knew instantly that she did not know what she was doing.

Until that moment, though, there had been no trace of doubt in her mind. In the absence of doubt there is little incentive to change one's mind about anything: we do not hesitate to put our beliefs into immediate action when the situation seems to us to demand it.

The antidote to dogmatism is relativism. Reflection and relativism not surprisingly are also interconnected. By placing our models and assumptions mentally in brackets or inverted commas, which is a necessary first step towards reflecting upon them, we inevitably acknowledge, at least implicitly, that we have no monopoly on the truth, that we understand and experience the world at best imperfectly from a particular viewpoint or perspective.

Disowning and relatedness

When we disown aspects of our experience, they do not necessarily cease to influence what we feel, think and do. The disowned aspect of experience generally retains a strong influence over us while evading our influence in return. We dance to a tune we have made ourselves powerless to alter.

We may sometimes disown experiences that would otherwise engulf us. We can disown conclusions experiences are forcing us to make when these conclusions conflict with deeply cherished beliefs we already hold. Disowned experiences, such as strong feelings, can be the breeding ground of other problems such as terrifying voices. Buried guilt for past actions, for instance, turned Ian's voices from friendly advisers to fierce persecutors who demanded that he kill himself.

By definition disowning is anything but obvious to the person who is doing the disowning.

Emma had rows with her husband and he beat her at times. She claimed to feel nothing as a result. She had provoked it, she felt. She was therefore responsible. There was nothing to feel. Shopping in town after one of these rows, she became convinced that a group of people in the shopping precinct were laughing at her and were part of a conspiracy against her. With her judgement already affected by tormenting voices, she was barely able to contain her feelings of anger and leave the vicinity before she physically attacked them. She was extremely distressed by the experience in town, in stark contrast to her indifference to the beating she had received at the hands of her husband. What she had disowned about her husband in her home appeared to be leaking destructively in a distorted shape onto the people in town.

Relatedness, in this context, is the capacity to consciously acknowledge and relate to what we are experiencing. It makes us sufficiently accessible to relationships with people and things to learn to accommodate to as well as assimilate experiences, to make appropriate adjustments to our selves or to our circumstances.

Disowning is in a way the opposite of drowning and dogmatism, but it is not an effective antidote. It can also be used to defend dogmatism and create the conditions for drowning. It is equally undesirable as a way of dealing with experiences and beliefs. What we have disowned is inaccessible to reflection: to that extent how much we can reflect depends upon the degree of our relatedness to our total experience. Without the capacity to own and reflect we frequently remain the helpless victim of our own inner life.

The uncertainty principle

We can become almost as sceptical of our own position as we tend to be of other people's. We can come to recognise that there are other points of view and types of experience that are equally if not more valid. We can become radical relativists. The Hulme Uncertainty Principle captures the essence of this position. This states that importance and certainty are inversely related. In the strong form it concludes that all certainty about matters of any importance is pathological: the only thing that is certain is that we can be certain of nothing important.

Koestenbaum (1978) optimistically contends that there is no identification with a particular worldview or experience that cannot be withdrawn: there are no contents from which consciousness cannot be separated. He acknowledges that all reflection is painful while at the same time implying it is always possible. Is this true for all of us all the time?

Can reflection, relatedness and relativism be acquired?

This brings us on to the crucial question. If part of the difficulty that some people experience in life is created and maintained by the difficulty they have in stepping back from painful experiences of an unusual nature and examining them, is it possible to help them acquire the closely related skills of reflection, relatedness and relativism? Given the fixity or rigidity attributed to what professionals have termed the 'psychotic' or 'schizophrenic' experience, how could this process of reflection ever be possible for anyone in the grip of such intransigent and autonomous phenomena?

This question only has meaning if we accept certain easily avoidable assumptions.

Obviously, if we approach such phenomena with the assumption they are inherently intractable, the not surprising consequence will be their dramatic intractability! Our a priori position will be confirmed by a process of self-fulfilling prophecy. If we approach the rigid dogmatism of the psychotic experience with the rigid dogmatism of the medical model, with all its disabling assumptions, such as that the professional knows what is true and right and the poor deluded patient is barking mad, and up, completely the wrong tree, it should be no surprise to find that professional rigidity meets psychotic rigidity in return.

We can observe this kind of phenomenon every day if we choose to attack someone else's core beliefs. Their immediate reaction is to defend them fiercely. If the attack continues they may withdraw from the interaction. Does that sound familiar?

If, on the other hand, we approach the psychotic experience with humility, respect, empathy and genuine curiosity, as well as an obvious and healthy scepticism about all world-views including our own, we are likely to find that our reflectiveness, our capacity to relate openly to our experience as a whole and our relativism, unfolded within a collaborative relationship, elicits similar responses in the client, who no longer stands in such grave need of his or her barricades.

Certain other conditions may need to be met. For instance, the client will need to trust the helper, which might take time to accomplish. The client will need to feel safe enough from harassment, or worse, to lower his or her defences. Perceived and real inequalities of power will have to be significantly reduced before dangerous vulnerabilities can reasonably be exposed. The overall environment within which the client has to operate will have to feel sufficiently benign[3]

Once you begin to look at things from this perspective, it becomes obvious that 'psychotherapy' is not a set of techniques but a relationship process with special characteristics.

We can build upon Smail's augmentation and modification of the Rogerian triad of congruence, empathy and unconditional positive regard: he added clarification, solidarity and encouragement. All six of these characteristics are of course crucial in building trust and creating safety. They have been described, perhaps exaggeratedly, as the psychotherapeutic equivalents of love. It is essential that a person feel deeply cared about if (s)he is to become able to break free of the gravitational field of his or her deep emotional investments in a particular worldview.

However, three more ingredients, reflection, relatedness and relativism, are essential if we are to capture the core of psychotherapy's efficacy most especially for those who find reflection in and of itself particularly difficult. If the therapist does not have and display these characteristics a client who is at the mercy of the forces of fixity is unlikely to move towards greater flexibility. The same can be said for the overall environment in which (s)he finds him/herself. Sedimented[4] environments are highly likely to create fossilised beliefs!

It is perhaps also the case that clarification, as Smail describes it, cannot be achieved without some degree of reflection, relatedness and relativism: it may also be true that those three forces of flexibility cannot be acquired through relationships devoid of congruence, empathy, warmth, encouragement and solidarity. Once present they may all be reciprocally potentiating.

One way of describing this is to see reflection, relatedness and relativism as fuels and caring relationships as rockets, by means of which we can heave ourselves above the surface of massive and hostile planets of meaning when they are holding us prisoner by the gravitational force of their attraction for us.

At worst we can at least fly above or orbit around them: at best, if we really desire it and have taken on board enough fuel, we can escape their gravitational field altogether. This does not mean these planets cease to exist or lose all their attraction for us. Just that we end up in a completely different and hopefully more fulfilling relationship towards them.

Of course there is always the possibility that, in the final analysis, we may have no real desire to blast off from the surface of a home planet which, however hostile, is all we have ever known of safety.

This is a complex inter-relationship, to which the rocket and fuel analogy does not entirely do justice. An example might help tease out this part of its complexity.

Reflection generally helps by modelling a creative and flexible way of looking at our inner experiences from a different perspective, of putting some distance between us and the heat of the inner moment. Sometimes, though, reflection (as well as the more obvious relationship qualities such as warmth) may help create a feeling of safety in the client.

Laura had been given a diagnosis of endogenous depression. She used to believe that her parents were more or less perfect. After a fruitful period discovering the limitations of this view with the help of a series of dreams, the work we were doing became very stuck and seemed to be going nowhere.

We had plateaued on bleak and distressing terrain, more tolerable than her previous habitat but too unwelcoming to live on comfortably for the rest of her life, and yet with no detectable path towards more hospitable ground.

Frustrated by the protracted lack of movement, I began to see discharge as a very attractive option. I discussed this with my peer supervision group. We decided that I should continue with the processes of exploration but make sure that I did not continue my habit of stepping in relatively early to rescue her in sessions from her frequent experiences of intense distress. I continued to see her, having agreed with Laura that I would allow her to sink right into the 'heart of darkness' in order to explore it more fully and understand it more clearly. The very next session, when we first put this plan into action, Laura came to a powerful realisation at the heart of a very intense darkness. She said, 'I think my mother threw me away even before I was born'.

It became immediately and rather frighteningly clear to me that, had I acted upon my professional sense that we were getting nowhere and moved to discharge[5] her, I would have been acting blindly in response to powerful messages from the depths of her being. I would have denied her the possibility of discovering the previously unacknowledgeable. It had obviously been imperative to bracket or place in suspension my own feelings and the action they implied. If I had not reflected in this way on my own processes and changed my plans accordingly, she would never have felt safe enough with me to acknowledge what she had previously disowned.

This led me to wonder also how often discharge is this same kind of blind response to subliminal processes and how often we should be stepping back from the impulse to discharge rather than unquestioningly acting it out.

Reflection, in this strong sense of the word, can be as much part of the relationship process as warmth and other such qualities. It is perhaps worth disentangling some aspects of its power.

This realisation of having been thrown away was the bedrock of much of Laura's self-hatred. It had, from her earliest days, always been part of the *I* through which she saw her personal world. It had become as invisible to her mind's eye as the eye with which she sees the physical world is invisible to itself. To see this *I* and its component parts we need a mirror, someone capable of a certain kind of reflection. When such a mirror is available we become aware of some of the characteristics of this *I* with which we see our personal world.

Obviously, we cannot work in this way if we are using mirrors with attitude, anymore than we could use a distorting mirror at a fairground to get a clear and accurate picture of ourselves. The more I as therapist intrude my unsuspected uninspected biases upon the client the less valuable I am as a mirror. The worse the mirror, the worse the therapist.

The medical model is powerful and has its uses. But in mental health, we need now to move beyond it. We should be careful not to replace it with any other single dominant model, including the psychological one in which I have been trained. The mirror of psychiatry, with its dismissive assumptions of disease, and the mirror of cognitive therapy, with its Socratic sense of superior wisdom, are seriously flawed. Any other single model would be similarly defective. Practitioners become biased and blinkered by their theories. The kind of collaborative conversation described here becomes impossible.

I believe the sceptical relativism I am advocating offers the best hope of protecting the client/therapist relationship from the abuses that inevitably ensue when any one model dominates. Clearly, although 'pluralism' is preferable to 'monism' (Robbins,

1993)[6] in this and most other social contexts, we can never completely overcome our human limitations and function with no biases at all. However, we can at least make the serious attempt to reduce our activated biases to as close to zero as possible, especially, but not only, when we sit down with a fellow human being experiencing the extremis of what our society has come to call 'psychosis'.

Collaborative conversation

'Collaborative conversation' (Andersen and Swim, 1993) is a good term with which to describe this cluster of transformative core processes. It avoids the undesirable connections of the word psychotherapy with disease and with steep differentials of status and power. Its invocation will not of course dispel those possibilities in some magical way; it simply explicitly commits the professional to reducing their influence as close to vanishing point as humanly possible.

Collaborative conversation places at the centre of its process[7] the triple essentials of reflection, relatedness and relativism. People who enter the psychiatric system and earn the label 'psychotic' or 'schizophrenic' experience a combination of phenomena, voices, visions, idiosyncratic beliefs and fixity, which has generally elicited dehumanising forms of help whose current embodiments are the tranquillizing drug and sectioning under the Mental Health Act. It is therefore particularly urgent that we exchange the tunnel vision of the psychotic model for the broader multidimensional view expressed here, without which collaborative conversation is virtually impossible. The words we choose matter, and will serve either to perpetuate the problem or resolve it.

References:
Andersen, H. and Swim, S. (1993) Learning as Collaborative Conversation: combining the student's and the teacher's expertise. *Human Systems: The journal of systemic consultation and management*, 4(3–4), 145–153.
Bahá'í International Community, (1995) *The Prosperity of Human Kind.* Sidney/London: Bahá'í Publishing Trusts (Australia/U.K.)
Bahá'u'lláh Kitáb-i-Iqán, (1982) *The Book of Certitude.* London: Bahá'í Publishing Trust
Bentall, R.P., (1990) *Reconstructing Schizophrenia.* London and New York: Routledge
Berger, P. and Luckmann, T., (1979) *The Social Construction of Reality.* Harmondsworth: Penguin

Boyle, M, (1990) *Schizophrenia. A scientific delusion.* London and New
    York: Routledge

Chadwick, P., Birchwood, M. and Trower, P, (1996) *Cognitive Therapy for
    Delusions, Voices and Paranoia.* Chichester: Wiley

Doubt, K., (1996) *Towards a Sociology of Schizophrenia: Humanistic
    reflections.* Toronto:University of Toronto Press

Kolstoe, J., (1985) *Consultation: A universal lamp of guidance.* Oxford:
    George Ronald

Kolstoe, J., (1995) *Developing Genius: Getting the most out of group decision-
    making.* Oxford: George Ronald

Koestenbaum, P., (1978) *The New Image of the Person: The theory and
    practice of clinical philosophy.* Greenwood

Momen, M., (1998) Relativism: a Basis for Bahá'í Metaphysics. In Momen,
    M. (ed) *Studies in the Bábi and Bahá'í Religions Volume 5.* Los
    Angeles: Kalimat Press

Reason, P. (Ed.), (1992) *Human Inquiry in Action: Developments in new
    paradigm research.* London: Sage

Robbins, M., (1993) *Experiences of Schizophrenia: An integration of the
    personal, scientific and therapeutic.* London: The Guilford Press

Senge, P. M., (1992) *The Fifth Discipline: The art and practice of the learning
    organisation.* City: Century Business, Random House

Shweder, R., (1991) *Thinking Through Cultures: expeditions in cultural
    psychology.* City: Harvard University Press

Sloan, T., (1996) *Damaged Life.* London and New York: Routledge

Smail, D., (1996) *How to Survive without Psychotherapy.* London: Constable

Spinelli, E., (1994) *Demystifying Therapy.* London: Constable

Tart, C.T., (1988) *Waking Up: Overcoming the obstacles to human potential.*
    Shafteshury: Element

Warner, D., (1985) *Recovery from Schizophrenia: Psychiatry and political
    economy.* London: Routledge

Notes

1. The terms 'vision' and 'voices' do have one main disadvantage. They
each relate to only one of our senses, hearing and sight respectively,
whereas the experiences we are concerned with are no respecters of such
boundaries. They can operate across all sensory modalities. It may be
necessary to retain the use of the term 'hallucination', but only for
experiences that extend beyond sight or hearing in the absence of external
stimulation.

2. For example on page 157 though he talks of 'ownership' where I talk of
'relatedness' I feel we are referring to the same thing in essence.

3. Medication is all too often used to make good these sorts of deficiency
in the situation. Hopefully we will eventually reach a stage when we no
longer feel it necessary to subject quite so many people to aversive 'side
effects' before we help them. At that stage we could more objectively
determine whether neuroleptics have a genuine residual role or whether

they can be safely discarded to join the straitjacket and insulin coma therapy in the dustbin of history.

4.   For a full and fascinating discussion of 'sedimentation' see Spinelli (1994) pages 345–351. I have taken the liberty of extending the concept of sedimentation from individual beliefs to the operating principles of wider social environments.

5. It also struck me, though not for the first time, how hostile a metaphor 'discharge' is. It has potent negative associations, such as the idea of a bullet from a gun or the notion of infected matter seeping from a wound.

6. Between pages 27–37 he discusses this issue in depth and develops his own interesting position in the process.

7. It is important to state certain caveats here. This process can be used to enhance coping or to explore inner states far more deeply. There may be reasons why using it for the latter purpose may not always be a wise thing to do. Sometimes the situations people find themselves in are genuinely too hostile. For instance, if a ward culture or a family of carers does not understand or does not have the resources to deal with the distress that sometimes follows this second kind of work, then they might resort to what would be experienced as punitive measures to eliminate the evidence of distress. The first goal, in this case, would be to decide whether it is possible to make the person safer. There are also dangers from within the person. The previously disowned pain that underlies the experiences of voices may be so intense that is cannot be contained within the existing mind-resources of the person experiencing it. Unless those resources can be strengthened and the person give clear consent to continuing the process, it would probably be best to find a different way of working. Sometimes it is impossible to discover this second danger without investing considerable effort. Occasionally the gain, such as a reduction in the intensity of malign voices, would not be experienced as sufficient to outweigh the pain of effective reflection, which can sometimes unlock unbearable emotions or realisations that are too distressing to assimilate. This makes the problem of securing informed consent an issue that has so be thought through and dealt with before both parties decide to go down the road of deep inner exploration. This is not to suggest that this approach is not worth using. It does indicate that it is not to be used lightly.

CHAPTER 11

User involvement in mental health service development[1]

DAVID PILGRIM AND LESLEY HITCHMAN

I N THE WAKE of the 1990 NHS and Community Care Act, most localities witnessed one or more consultation exercises which have informed mental health strategy documents produced by NHS and social service commissioners. This chapter reports a piece of action research about user involvement in one locality, which attempted to take users beyond the role of passive suppliers of opinion and encouraged their role as active negotiators of change. In order to understand both the achievements and limits of success of this exercise, the social context of user involvement in mental health service development is considered. Thus the chapter tacks to and fro between the study and its context in order to illuminate the question set in its title. The intention is to add to a slowly emerging literature about the pragmatics of user involvement in mental health services (Barnes and Wistow, 1994a and b; Williams and Lindley, 1996).

The study

The study was jointly financed by local health purchasers and providers in order to facilitate increased user involvement in mental health service development. The authors proposed a development project which would go beyond consultation to include direct negotiations for change between users and professionals. This open-ended notion was accepted by the funders and finance was supplied for one year (1996–1997) to facilitate a new users' group and supply

[1] A version of this chapter appeared in the *Journal of Mental Health* (1998) 7, 1, 95–104 and is reprinted with kind permission of Carfax Publishing.

a report of progress made with recommendations at the end for further service change and lessons learned about the facilitation of local user involvement.

The authors asked mediators in statutory and voluntary sector services to offer a list of mental health service users they knew who were likely to be willing and also able to work on service development. These identified patients were then invited to an initial exploratory meeting to establish their main interest. At the next meeting, the concerns of the attenders were recorded. The group met fortnightly and established priorities for change which came to be known as 'hobby horses'. Each participant agreed to take responsibility for an item on the list, either alone or in partnership with another group member. At its largest, at the outset, there were fourteen attenders. Over the year this dropped to a stable attendance of between eight and twelve members per meeting.

The authors acted as facilitators in the group but took no part in defining the hobby horses listed or the decisions about concrete negotiations (which are outlined below).

However, the facilitation role undoubtedly shaped outcomes in a number of positive and negative ways. For example, the facilitators opted not to provide a pedagogic role about chairing, recording or negotiating skills, but they occasionally confronted group members about motivation or disruptiveness. In the latter regard some of the interventions were close to those of group therapists although an explicit rule which was often repeated by the facilitators was that the group was *not* a therapy group. This was quickly internalised by the group.

The report produced for the research commissioners by the authors was lengthy (20,000 words), as it included a detailed description of lessons learned about the group's development. In this chapter we will only focus on the content of the group and the success it had in negotiating with service professionals about change.

Relevant content and negotiations
The 'hobby horse' list generated by the group is displayed in Table 1. The first on this list was the only item which referred to the group's internal structure. The rest of the items were a potential agenda for external negotiations. The vigour with which the items were pursued by group members varied for two reasons. First there were differences between the group members in terms of their skills and motivation. Second, the items implied variable degrees of external

constraint and opportunity. For example, the destigmatisation item came from a very broad lament by some in the group about the ways in which people with mental health problems are treated in contemporary society whereas the demand for greater out of hours access was a very specific demand for service development, where named managers could be approached for negotiations.

Table 1: List of priorities generated by the action group.

- Recruitment of ethnic minorities to the group
- Access to help from professionals of the same sex
- Employment opportunities for people with mental health problems
- Somewhere to scream and shout
- Help with bereavement
- Destigmatisation and discrimination
- Improved communication and information from professionals
- Out of hours access/24 hours services
- Advocacy for users of mental health services
- Quality of care in private residential settings

The three items which transpired to be the most satisfying for the group, in terms of achieved objectives within the year's study, were: out of hours opening; advocacy; and improved communication. Progress about these items can be summarised as follows:

- *Day centre out of hours opening* The group collected information via their own small survey of users of a social service day centre. From this they established a case for extending the opening hours of the centre beyond weekdays. The case was taken to social service managers who agreed to provide fortnightly Sunday opening after successfully bidding for new funds from the Mental Illness Specific Grant.
- *Advocacy* The group established that a generic voluntary advocate had recently been introduced to the local acute mental health inpatient unit by the local Council for Voluntary Services. The manager of the Council was invited to attend a meeting of the group and was offered support to publicise the new scheme. Whilst the group supported this innovation they felt strongly that a

dedicated paid mental health advocate should be appointed. The group contacted the person in the health authority responsible for mental health service development and established that some money was available from a re-settlement arrangement in the wake of the closure of a large local asylum. A letter was sent from the group formally requesting use of this money. The health authority responded by setting up a meeting with a variety of interested parties to discuss the principle and process of appointing a paid advocate. The health authority drew up a proposal and sent it to the group for their views about a person specification. An advocate was subsequently appointed.

- *Improved communication/information from professionals* The main objective of this hobby horse item was to make information about services more accessible. There was a view within the group that professionals were not good at providing information about their services. The group set about collating information about aspects of statutory services which they thought should be available to people with mental health problems. The information was published as a booklet and was financed by the local health authority.

The rest of the items produced less satisfying outcomes. Group members wrote to the Chair of the local psychiatrists' group asking if any new appointments locally could positively discriminate in favour of female candidates. (At the time of the study, there were four post holders, in the local psychiatric service, all of whom were male, and two unfilled posts.) The psychiatrist replied indicating that for reasons of equal opportunities it was not possible to endeavour to appoint female colleagues preferentially. The group were not happy with this response and sent another letter challenging the stance. This second letter was ignored. As a result, three members of the group made an appointment to see the psychiatrist who re-stated his position and argued that he had ignored the second letter because he assumed that the group would realise that nothing could be added.

A letter was also sent to a range of local companies regarding the employment of people with mental health problems. No replies were received. The concern about poor local private residential facilities kept recurring in the group meetings, but the enormity of the problem meant that no action was formally planned. Group members were fearful of losing their accommodation rights and thus were insecure about raising the issue as a complaint with either the NHS or Local Authority managers. However, this hobby horse did trigger a user-professional group which examinined the adequacy of local accommodation for people with mental health problems. Some items (somewhere to scream and shout, bereavement and destigmatisation) were simply not progressed by the group within the time span of the study.

This summary of the group's achievements and difficulties does not of course include a range of non-specific effects which were evident to various degrees at the level of individual group members. For example, all the negotiations, whether or not they were successful, entailed action and the development of skills. These included learning how to cooperate in a group setting; struggling with questions of democracy and autonomy within the group; negotiation with professional managers in writing, by telephone and face to face; reviewing progress and re-defining tactics and strategies. An overall personal impact was that group members were being given a valued social role which was being recognised explicitly by the facilitators and respected by the health and social service managers who were contacted by the group. Together these factors might constitute a notion which appears with high frequency in the discourse about service users – empowerment.

The socio-political context of user involvement
Having outlined the work of the group, we now turn to the context of the study in order to analyse the constraints and opportunities which might account for the priorities set and the partial but incomplete success achieved. The opportunities for user-involvement have been created by three main factors:

- *Deinstitutionalisation* The running down of the old large asylum system has placed more people with serious and long term mental health problems into community settings, such that the question of the *citizenship* of this client group is now a matter of concern for users themselves as well as for those providing and managing mental health services. Previously this question of citizenship was obscured by the mass segregation of psychiatric patients. With greater citizenship has come increased expectations of rights to good quality state-provided services.
- *The legitimacy of bio-medical theory and practice and the rise of the users' movement* The legitimacy of Western psychiatric knowledge with a strong biological bias has been brought into question recurrently over the past thirty years, first from internal

professional dissenters (so called 'anti-psychiatry'), then from clinical psychology and social psychiatry and, more recently, from disaffected service users. The latter have constituted one type of new social movement (like feminism and the campaigning of physically disabled people) which has opposed traditional authority.

- *Consumerism* In the British health care context consumerism has been an associated feature of an ideologically driven re-structuring of the welfare state. This has involved a separation of provider and purchaser functions and a policy emphasis on service provision having a triple source (public, private and voluntary sector). This shift has entailed one process of increased bureaucratization in the NHS (managerialism) and one anti-bureaucratic process (development of quasi-markets). Managerialism places a value upon consumer feedback to increase service efficiency and the development of quasi-markets encourages a shift of accountability and involvement, albeit indirectly, to 'consumers', (HMSO, 1990 and 1992). These reforms of the welfare state during the 1980s and 1990s were inherited in 1997 by the Labour government. The intention of the latter (from April 1st 1999) was to dismantle the internal market by healing the purchaser provider split, removing GP fundholding and introducing clinical governance.

It is relevant to note that the additive effect of the last two points is that user involvement was, until recently, encouraged by a Conservative central government and embraced by a previously emerging leftist service users' movement. However, this right-left pincer effect has not ensured that user involvement has had a straightforward passage into practice. The following constraints have reduced its full impact.

1 *Reinstitutionalisation.* The shift to community care and the elimination of the old asylum system has been incomplete. Most of the money spent on mental health services has remained hospital based. Acute psychiatric beds, day facilities on hospital sites, High Dependency Units, Regional Secure Units, the Special Hospital system and re-utilised asylum facilities between them absorb the bulk of mental health funds. Given this picture, it might be more accurate to describe recent mental health policy as being about reinstitutionalisation rather than deinstitutionalisation (Pilgrim and Rogers, 1994). This policy trend

places an emphasis upon *hospital* bricks and mortar and beds, and the preservation of older professional interests and practices, rather than on the citizenship of service users in genuine community settings.

2 *The resilience of bio-medical dominance.* Despite the disaffection expressed by users about bio-medical psychiatric theory and practice (Rogers, Pilgrim and Lacey, 1993) and the academic cogency of critiques of psychiatric positivism (Boyle, 1991; Johnstone, 1989; Bentall, 1990), bio-medical notions retain favour in central policy formation alongside a new administrative discourse. Accordingly, we find 'severe mental illness' appearing alongside 'severe and enduring mental health problems'. A medical discourse about epidemiology and diagnostic categories has remained powerful even within Department of Health documents reviewing *psychological interventions* collated by *psychologists* (NHSE, 1996).

3 *The uneven development of the service users' movement.* The development of a new social movement critical of bio-medical psychiatry was slow to develop in Britain compared to other countries (Rogers and Pilgrim, 1991 cf; Haafkens, Nijjhof and van der Poel 1986; Chamberlin, 1988). Moreover, within Britain there are local variations in the vitality of the users' movement. This can means that in some localities a user voice is virtually absent whereas in others user led services may have been established (Lindow, 1994).

4 *Social Care: the poor relation.* Despite the shift to community care within government policy, local authorities do not control the resources to ensure its optimal implementation. Mental health budgets remain under the dominant control of the NHS. Mental health problems, more than many others, implicate social and personal needs of users. These cut across agencies and thus impoverished, over-stretched and politically weakened local authorities are often not robust enough to respond fully to the concept of user involvement.

5 *Quasi-markets.* The emphasis upon consumerism, enshrined in *The Patient's Charter,* is highly misleading about health and welfare re-organisation in practice. Despite terms such as the 'internal market', the NHS in recent years has not been a market of goods for individual consumers to pick and choose from. It consists instead of service commissioners making proxy decisions on behalf of local populations. Moreover, true markets involve a range of goods and suppliers– what local commissioners are

usually faced with instead are monopoly suppliers. Such a situation severely limits the choices of local commissioners and is a barrier to choice at the individual patient or client level of service contact. This culminates in NHS patients often getting what they are given in their locality.

6 *Squaring the circle of voluntarism and coercive control.* Consumerism emphasises personal choice and the users' movement emphasises citizenship. Both of these are contradicted or negated by the powers delegated to service professionals under mental health legislation. Despite a slight liberalisation of mental health law in Britain when the 1983 Mental Health Act replaced that of 1959 (about inpatient voting rights), new professional constraints on patient liberty were also introduced (the nurse's holding power). Policy and legislative changes recently, such as supervision registers and supervised discharge, have marked a return to an emphasis within mental health work on the surveillance and coercive control of madness.

Mental health law is a relatively rare example of powers being delegated to ensure lawful detention without trial (in Britain the other two examples are powers under the Prevention of Terrorism Act and the National Assistance Act). This permits the involuntary detention of patients presenting with mental health problems who may be no immediate threat to others. The 1983 Act only requires the judgement that a person's mental health is in jeopardy to justify detention, as the civil sections of the Act do not mention 'danger'. Professional discretion is thus legally warranted about conduct which may fall short of demonstrable or proven dangerousness. This can be contrasted, in the field of physical health, to the case of the man in the Midlands in recent years who was HIV+ and boasted of having unprotected sex with a number of women. Health officials could find no legal grounds to control his conduct. More common examples of the differential treatment of psychiatric patients would include the continued liberty of speeding or drunken motorists and the social legitimacy ascribed to rock climbers, astronauts and racing car drivers. Another much more mundane example is that the dangerous habit of tobacco use is a proven threat to health and yet smokers do not have their liberty removed by agents of the state. Thus, dangerousness *per se* (to self or others) does not automatically lead to loss of liberty, it is the *way* in which a person is considered to be dangerous which determines such an outcome (Szasz, 1963). The peculiar powers of legal control over psychiatric patients means that, in practice, mental health law negates the principles of *The Patient's Charter.* (Despite this, the last government issued guidelines about the implications of this charter in mental health services.) Even when patients are not held formally under powers of the 1983 Act, they may still enter hospital under duress (Bean, 1986; Rogers, 1993) and the custom and practice required for coercive control inevitably colour the general professional ethos of mental health workers. This affects the confidence of service users in the commitment of staff to voluntarism and partnership—two key guiding principles of user involvement. Voluntarism and coercion are incompatible, as are partnership and paternalism.

7 *The political economy of user involvement.* The dominant interests in mental health services are underpinned by stable sources of economic power. The first of these relates to employment. Mental health workers are salaried by state, voluntary sector or private employers, with the first of these predominating. Second an indirect source of economic power resides in medical technology in health services generally. In the particular case of psychiatry, this mainly relates to the pharmaceutical industry, given that over 90% of people with a psychiatric diagnosis are prescribed psychotropic medication (Rogers, Pilgrim and Lacey, 1993). By contrast, psychiatric patients are overwhelmingly displaced from the labour process – most are unemployed and for all intents and purposes usually unemployable. This places most service users in a position of economic powerlessness. This powerlessness amplifies that accruing from their primary disability (their mental health problems) and the lack of social credibility associated with the role of psychiatric patient. To lose one's reason is to lose one's credibility as a human agent and citizen. Being poor then adds insult to this injury.

The group's activity considered in context
The gains and obstacles experienced by the participants in the study will now be discussed in the above context. The ten aggregate points outlined will be used as an interpretative framework.

1 *Deinstitutionalisation.* The possibility of this type of group existing is linked to this point. Most of the group, in years gone by, would have been long term residents of psychiatric hospitals. This group met in community settings and the participants lived in the community permanently or semi-permanently. This reflects the wider phenomenon of people with mental health problems joining

those with other forms of disabilities in campaigning to defend and extend their citizenship. As a consequence, a citizenship focus is evident in policy analyses of these campaigns (Pilgrim, Todhunter and Pearson, 1997; Barnes and Shardlow, 1997).

2 *The legitimacy of a bio-medical approach and the rise of the users' movement.* The relevance of this point in relation to this particular group is mainly about the facilitators not the service users. The latter had no track record of involvement in the user movement (see point 6 below). By contrast, the facilitators were clinical psychologists who over a number of years had identified problems with a blinkered biological approach to psychiatry, had studied the rise of the user movement and supported the principles of user empowerment and normalisation.

3 *Consumerism.* This policy development undoubtedly was a necessary, though not a sufficient, condition for this group to exist. The support given to it by its purchaser and provider funders reflected central government policy developments and expectations, despite the devolution of power and structural fragmentation of health and social services in recent years (quasi-marketisation). The local financial and political support for a group such as this would have been unheard of before the late 1980s in Britain.

4 *Reinstitutionalisation.* Whilst the group members lived permanently or semi-permanently in community settings, the local psychiatric unit set in a District General Hospital was a constant point of reference. All in the group had had contact of some sort with it and more than half in the group were either 'revolving door' patients or regular day hospital attenders (which was attached to the inpatient unit). The group noted a difference of emphasis between those who had only been outpatients and those who had had episodes of inpatient care.

5 *The resilience of bio-medical dominance.* This was apparent in the group in two main ways. First, many in the group simply internalised the idea that their skills, capacities and weaknesses as group members were a function of their mental illness. Second, the particular importance of their treating Consultant Psychiatrist was alluded to episodically. One member for example actually sought permission from his Consultant to attend the group. The idea that an illness framework held by psychiatric patients is an impediment to a sense of agency is not new. For example, Scott (1973) coined the term 'the treatment barrier' to describe the problems created for patients, relatives and professionals by an

adherence to a medical model which invalidates the personal agency of the first party on the list. This notion was invoked by Scott to account for obstacles to change which were separate from 'resistance' in psychotherapy. This internalisation of a biological psychiatric model shifted to some extent during the existence of the group. Some group members challenged others who resorted to illness as an explanation for inaction. Also some criticisms began to emerge about clinical regimes.

6 *The uneven development of the users' movement.* The clinical concerns just mentioned may have emerged earlier in the group had the locality had a stronger users' movement track record. This group had no history in this regard, although during the group several contacts were made with organisations such as UKAN (UK Advocacy Network), Survivors Speak Out and the Hearing Voices Network. With this has come a change of local consciousness about matters of concern to these national organisations. In the report given to the funders the group made very moderate demands for change upon current services and these tended to focus more on structural questions of service availability rather than criticisms of their treatment regime. This is beginning to change.

7 *Social care: the poor relation.* This had implications in the group in ways which were not immediately apparent. The accessibility of managers in the NHS was greater for the group than social services managers and the former had more flexibility of action than the latter. The group's existence was funded by health not social service money. Financial limits on social service facilities impinged in another way which alienated some of the group members. The group met for some of the time in a social service day centre. During that period the local authority has instituted a charging policy. This had provoked some centre attenders (which included some of the group members) into refusing to pay the charge. This in turn undermined the confidence of the group in the social service managers they contacted.

8 *Quasi-markets.* This feature like the last one also had a distal effect on the group in a number of ways. The group members never felt that they had a choice of services. Instead they accepted the position of monopoly supply in the locality from the statutory services but aspired to alter those services in a more suitable direction. Moreover, even when private facilities (a feature of the new 'mixed economy of welfare') were discussed, such as hostels and nursing homes, it was evident that the users had not chosen

these places of residence from a range of options but instead felt that they were channelled into these places on discharge. Indeed the item which was last on the hobby horse list was the complaint that local private residential facilities were of poor quality and did not enable people with mental health problems to make choices about their accommodation.

9 *Squaring the circle of voluntarism and social control.* Some of the group's members had been formally detained under the Mental Health Act and had experienced forced treatment and other coercive interventions such as seclusion. There was little discussion in the group about legal-ethical questions. The external constraint of legislation invoked no comment. Moreover, professional paternalism was viewed by some as benign and appropriate. However, the later discussion about clinical matters in the group included a desire to alter the seclusion policy at the local psychiatric unit and a need to find out why so many patients appeared to be 'zombies' on the wards there. The questions of legal control and professional paternalism are problematic in the context of user involvement for a number of reasons. User groups cannot unilaterally abolish mental health law and mixed views are held within such groups about such an eventuality. Psychiatric patients lack social credibility. Public prejudice, fuelled by selective media reporting, irrationally exaggerates the salience of their dangerousness (Philo, Secker, Platt, Henderson, McLaughlin and Burnside, 1994) and thus encourages a service culture which errs on the side of caution about the priority of patients' civil rights over public protection. The latter process in recent years has been formally reinforced by the introduction of politicians by further legal constraints on patient freedom (such as supervised discharge). These legal impositions have occurred during a phase of mental health policy which has not ensured the 'principle of reciprocity'. The latter notion is discussed by Eastman (1997), who notes that it is unjust for the state to impose restrictions on the liberty of psychiatric patients whilst at the same time failing to provide the resources to ensure effective and good quality care for them. This ethical failure of the state is beyond the immediate control of local users' groups or their collective national networks. Since Labour came into power in 1997, government commitment to users' rights has not been strong. In the policy document *Modernising Mental Health Services* (Department of Health 1998) public safety is emphasised as a priority. Moreover the government announced a 'root and branch'

review of the 1983 Mental Health Act. No prescriptions were made about this review *except* for the insistence that new legal powers should be implemented to ensure compulsory conveyancing of patients in the community to hospital who do not comply with their medication. This authoritarian cue suggests that the current government is arguably less committed to the civil liberties of people with mental health problems than their Conservative predecessors.

10 *The political economy of user involvement.* The economic realm is the final and ultimate constraint upon user involvement. All of the group members were unemployed and living on state benefits. Even a small attendance allowance (of £12 per session) was enthusiastically received but it caused the occasional flutter of concern about it affecting welfare rights. When users negotiated with salaried NHS and Social Service managers, they did so from a position of economic powerlessness which affected their style of negotiation: they had to access any meeting by public transport not by car; their clothes reflected their poor income and so could not match the props donned each morning by the managers they met; and no immediate formula was offered about the long term financing of user involvement by either purchasers or providers. These objective features of negotiating scenarios contained a range of subjective correlates about the confidence and self-esteem of people used to being marginalised and pathologised. An early review of progress of the users' movement in Britain noted that:

> *The dilemma for the users' movement is whether it can progress as a force for change without the more active support of sympathetic professionals, who have access to resources and power within the mental health system and other parts of the state. This issue of the movements' viability being closely linked to allying itself with the state, without being incorporated to its own detriment, extends essentially to the political economy of consumerism. Elsewhere, such as Australia, users' groups have secured permanent funding for their work from the state.* (Rogers and Pilgrim, 1991 p.147)

This comment about the users' movement, as an autonomous self-advocating new social movement, would seem to apply equally to user involvement initiatives triggered by sympathetic service mental health professionals and supported by short term finance from the local state. The ethical principle of reciprocity discussed by Eastman (1997) about treatment resources could apply equally to the state's obligation to provide stable financial support for user involvement. Without such a commitment, user involvement in any locality will be precarious and only as safe as its last piece of short term funding.

Confirmation of the importance of this final constraint can be found in the three main successful outcomes of this group. Local social service managers were only able to respond positively to the request for weekend opening because of their successful bid for funds from the Mental Illness Specific Grant. The local health authority was only able to establish a new paid mental health service advocate because of the residual money from a local asylum closure plan. The information booklet was only made possible because of the relatively small sums required from the health authority to support its production. These examples do not imply that all of the service developments desired by the group would be achieved readily by simply having access to more funds. Some of the changes would implicate complex clinical, legal, political and ideological shifts which would require more than money to occur. However, just as the *status quo* of mental health services cannot be maintained without finance, any changes in such services would also require stable financial backing.

References
Barnes, M. and Wistow, G. (1994a) Achieving a strategy for user involvement in Community Care. *Health and Social Care in the Community, 2*, 6, 347–356

Barnes, M and Wistow, G. (1994b) Learning to hear voices: listening to users of mental health services. *Journal of Mental Health, 3*, 525–540

Barnes, M. and Shardlow, P. (1997) From passive recipient to active citizen: participation in mental health user groups. *Journal of Mental Health, 6*, 289–300

Bean, P. (1986) *Mental Disorder and Legal Control.* Cambridge: Cambridge University Press

Bentall, R.P. (ed) (1990) *Reconstructing Schizophrenia.* London: Routledge

Boyle, M. (1991) *Schizophrenia: A scientific delusion?* London: Routledge

Chamberlin, J. (1988) *On Our Own.* London: MIND

Department of Health (1998) *Modernising Mental Health Services.* London: Department of Health

Eastman, N. (1997) The need to change mental health law. In T. Heller et al (eds) *Mental Health Matters: A reader.* London: Macmillan/Open University

HMSO (1990) *NHS and Community Care Act.* London: HMSO

HMSO (1992) Seeking Local Voices, in *Health of the Nation Mental Illness Handbook.* HMSO: London

Haafkens, J., Nijjhof, G. and van der Poel, E. (1986) Mental health care and the opposition movement in the Netherlands. *Social Science and Medicine, 22,* 185–192

Johnstone, L. (1989) *Users and Abusers of Psychiatry.* London: Routledge

Lindow, V. (1994) *Self Help Alternatives to Mental Health Services.* London: MIND

NHSE (1996) *NHS Psychotherapy Services in England.* London: Department of Health

Philo, G., Secker, J., Platt, S., Henderson, L., McLaughlin, G. and Burnside, J. (1994) The impact of the mass media on public images of mental illness: media content and audience belief. *Health Education Journal, 53,* 3, 282–290

Pilgrim, D. and Rogers, A. (1994) Something old, something new: Sociology and the organisation of psychiatry. *Sociology, 28,* 2, 521–538

Pilgrim, D., Todhunter, C. and Pearson, M. (1997) Accounting for disability: customer feedback or citizen complaints? *Disability and Society, 12,* 1, 3–15

Rogers, A. (1993) Coercion and voluntary admission: an examination of psychiatric patients' views. *Behavioural Sciences and the Law, 4,* 16–25

Rogers, A. and Pilgrim, D. (1991) 'Pulling down churches': accounting for the British Mental Health Users' Movement *Sociology of Health and Illness, 13,* 2, 129–148

Rogers, A. and Pilgrim, D. (1996) *Mental Health Policy in Britain: A critical introduction.* Basingstoke: Macmillan.

Rogers, A., Pilgrim, D. and Lacey, R. (1993) *Experiencing Psychiatry: Users' views of services.* Basingstoke: Macmillan

Scott, R.D. (1973) The treatment barrier. *Journal of Medical Psychology, 46,* 45–67

Szasz, T.S. (1963) *Law, Liberty and Psychiatry.* New York: Macmillan

Williams, J. and Lindley, P. (1996) Working with mental health service users to change mental health services. *Journal of Community and Applied Social Psychology, 6,* 1–14

CHAPTER 12

The service user/survivor movement

PETER CAMPBELL

A CTION AND PROTEST by people who use mental health services or who are seen and treated as mad/mentally ill has a long history. In the 1980s such action, which had previously been marginalised, was welcomed into the mainstream in the United Kingdom and resulted in the rapid growth of independent service user/survivor organisations, a growth that persists in the late 1990s. Although service users and survivors have produced much written material, no coherent historical account of the movement has yet been attempted.

This chapter is not such an attempt. Instead it tries to look at some (but not all) of the issues that are important to people involved in the movement: who do we think we are; what do we believe in; what are we trying to achieve? The movement has become so large and diverse that it is impossible to provide a comprehensive account in one chapter and what follows necessarily reflects a personal perspective. It is intended to reflect some of the achievements and dilemmas of a significant experiment in collective action as we embark on New Labour's 'Third Way' for mental health services.

Who are we?

All service user/survivor action is essentially a challenge to the perceived status of the diagnosed mentally ill in society. Like the vast majority of people whose distress has resulted in a mental illness diagnosis, activists have experienced the problems of role and identity that such a designation heralds. Questions like 'Who am I?' and 'What have I become?' have a particular resonance for members of the service user/survivor movement. There is a strong conviction commonly held by most people with a mental illness diagnosis that 'I am not what people say I am'. Activists are only different in that they demonstrate this belief publicly.

One aim of service user/survivor action in recent years has been to question a number of concepts used in mental health services. Another has been to confront the way in which mental health service users are described, both within the service system and in society as a whole. It has become reasonably clear that activists do not see themselves as, and do not want to be seen as: 'mad', 'psychos', 'schizos', 'nutters', 'loonies', 'mental patients', 'the mentally ill' etc. (Although, from time to time, small numbers may attempt to repossess and re-value some of this stigmatising terminology, e.g., 'mad', 'loony').

Nor do people want to be seen exclusively in terms of their diagnosis, regardless of whether they accept that medical classification of their problems is valid or not. So, although self-help and voluntary groups continue to exist around discrete diagnostic groupings and some of them have become or have always been service user/survivor-led organisations, there is nowadays little or no support for talking about people as 'schizophrenics', 'manic-depressives', 'the eating disordered', etc.

If it is clear how people do not wish to be described, it is not so certain how people really see themselves. Unsurprisingly, in view of lives spent in the shadow of psychiatric and other expert definitions, members of the service user/survivor movement have been reluctant to impose new terms, however positive, on each other. Self-definition, although sometimes inconvenient for activists and often exasperating for outsiders, has been well defended by the movement.

The last fifteen years has seen the emergence of a number of new terms to describe people with a mental illness diagnosis. These include: 'mental health service consumer', 'mental health service user', 'mental health service recipient', 'sufferer', 'member (of a service, day centre etc)', 'psychiatric survivor', 'mental health system survivor' and 'survivor of mental distress'. It could be argued that a number of these terms did not originate from the service user/survivor movement (only the terms recipient and survivor are rooted in the experience of activists) and that they now enjoy such wide currency that mental health service users may be adopting them without thought or even having them attached to them in much the same way as the old diagnosis-led terms. Although they do describe the nuances of relationships with the mental health services (the term 'recipient' was promoted as a counter to official use of 'consumer') none of them attempts to capture a rounded picture of the individual with a mental illness diagnosis in a wider social context.

Much has been made of the difference between the terms service user and survivor. The terms are now often linked together as in 'service user/ survivor action' as if to indicate that they are separate but closely associated. Although they clearly describe significantly different relations with services (service use is neutral, service survival is not; it is unlikely that social workers would call their clients survivors) they may not indicate profound ideological differences. For example, it is certainly an oversimplification to say that activists who call themselves service users are reformist while those who call themselves survivors are anti-psychiatric.

Almost all the terms outlined above focus on a relationship with mental health services. Although people with a mental illness diagnosis spend an increasing amount of time outside services, the focus of most service user/survivor activists still seems fixed on the service system. They appear to think of themselves as service users first and citizens second. In this respect, it is interesting to consider whether activists think they are disabled people and whether such a definition would open up their perceptions of themselves.

The disabled people's movement and the service user/survivor movement have not worked together very much in the last decade and there is still widespread ignorance and misunderstanding about the social model of disability that informs much of disabled people's action. Some service user/survivor activists question whether their distress is in any way an impairment, while others remember how denial of a disability has been a key part in their struggle to resist the medicalisation of their distress. Whatever may happen as society moves to a greater acceptance of civil rights for disabled people, it is currently clear that, while recognising that they may in a sense be disabled people, most activists would not choose this term as a primary self-definition.

As we approach the next century, the position of the diagnosed mentally ill is uncertain. Although we have made it clear what we do not want to be and had that partially accepted, it is by no means clear what we will be allowed to become and unfortunately we are confined by what society will allow us. Consumer may be better than mental patient but it is not the designation many activists are seeking. Most significantly, society is still deciding what sort of citizens community mental patients can be. As Lewis, Shadish and Lurigio (1989) have commented: 'Mental patients may be more of a mystery today, living among us, than they were when hidden away in the asylum. We do not know them, because they are neither outside society in the world of exclusion, nor are they full citizens, individuals who are like the rest of us. Being neither other nor self, they are a new kind of social construction'. In the coming struggle to engineer a social status founded on positive models of difference, people with a mental illness diagnosis are going to need action as well as words.

What do we believe in?

Negative personal experience of mental health services is a major stimulus for service user/survivor action. In the mid 1980s, activists were often criticised for having nothing positive to offer (for example following the National MIND Conference in Hammersmith, Autumn 1986). But even today, when the positive contribution of service user/survivor organisations can hardly be questioned, it remains true that shared memories of personal mistreatment at the hands of mental health workers are powerful cohesive elements in the movement. Legends of oppression met and overcome are important parts of the service user/survivor culture.

Although activists may share personal experiences of the failures of services, this does not necessarily imply a common analysis of what has gone wrong. For example, it is often suggested that the movement is opposed to the medical model. While this may be true in a general sense, the statement conceals a number of different positions. Some activists base their opposition on their judgement that there is insufficient evidence to support the proposition that the problems psychiatry addresses are illnesses – in short that psychiatry is based on false premises. Others oppose the medical model not because it is a false model but because of what it leads to – the dominance of psychiatry, the absence of holistic approaches and, most important of all, care and treatment that doesn't work. In practice, these two groups of activists are likely to be working together. The overlaps in their beliefs seem more important than the differences.

The movement's loosely defined opposition to the medical model may help explain another supposed belief of the movement, or at least a faction within it: the belief in anti-psychiatry. It is actually very difficult to assess the true contribution of anti-psychiatry to the service user/ survivor movement. This is partly because the term is used in such a perorative way by powerful people in mental health services that few activists want to get lumbered with it. The label of anti-psychiatry attached to any contribution to the mental health debate nowadays is an effective guarantee of marginalisation. At the same time, whereas in the early and mid 1980s numerous people in the service user/survivor movement had personal contact with R. D. Laing and his supporters, that inspiration has dissipated in the 1990s, anti-psychiatry texts are seldom referred to and other 'isms' have a greater impact. It would be difficult to argue that all or parts of the movement are advancing an anti-psychiatric plan. Nevertheless, in a spiritual rather than a programmatic sense, it could be said that service user/survivor action is inherently anti-psychiatric.

Feelings of opposition to numerous attitudes and practices in society and within mental health services provide a very significant bond throughout the service user/survivor movement. Nevertheless, the movement also shares important positive beliefs. Pre-eminent among these is the belief in self-advocacy – the possibility and desirability of people speaking out and acting for themselves. It could be argued that the principle of self advocacy underlies the entire project of service user/survivor action and that the way it has been interpreted by action groups over the last fifteen years has given the movement many of the particular characteristics it now displays. For example, Survivors Speak Out, founded in 1986 as a national networking organisation for the emerging movement, has rarely campaigned on specific issues (the Mental Health Act being the major exception), but promoted the idea and practice of self-advocacy. When groups were offered support, this was not conditional on accepting a particular programme or platform. Action of any kind was more important than channelling action in a particular direction. People could set their own priorities. The value of groups having manifestos or platforms of action, which had been popular in the early 1980s, became less obvious. A belief in self-advocacy, combined with a reluctance to tell other service users and survivors what to believe in and a distaste for replacing psychiatric orthodoxy with a new orthodoxy, has encouraged a movement that is more diverse and less coherent than it might otherwise have been.

A number of positive beliefs are clustered around the central belief in self-advocacy. These include: belief in the essential competence of people with a mental illness diagnosis; belief in the value of self-help and collective action; belief in the value and possibility of self-organisation by service users and survivors; belief that people with a mental illness diagnosis may have special expertise to offer society as a result of their personal experience. All of the above inform and inspire action by the movement yet have won (at best) only partial acceptance in most parts of society. The basic proposition, towards which all these beliefs are pointing, that people with a mental illness diagnosis have a contribution to make, *because of rather than in spite of* their life experiences, remains highly controversial.

Belief in civil rights for people with a mental illness diagnosis is inherent in service user/survivor action. Yet, in actuality, this belief seems to have played a secondary role in the movement, except in regard to the Mental Health Act. The focus has more often been on consumer/ patients' rights and this has resulted in the production of charters for users of mental health services. These emphasise the qualities many service user/survivor activists expect to be built into all services. For example, service users should have a right to: personal dignity and respect; information; accessible services; participation and involvement; choice; advocacy; confidentiality; complaints procedures; the least restrictive, least harmful treatment available (Mental Health Task Force User Group 1994). Although charters of this kind have limitations and do not reveal some of the more divisive concerns within the movement (e.g. around compulsion or the value of particular treatments), they do illustrate the consensual and pragmatic nature of much service user/ survivor action in the last fifteen years, when doing something, even doing anything, has seemed more important than standing on principle.

Evidence, understandings, expertise. What is the contribution of the diagnosed mentally ill?

The changing position of persons with a mental illness diagnosis within mental health services is partly founded on a greater recognition of their rights e.g., rights to information, to independent advocacy, to be fully involved in their own care and treatment. But it is also based on a new acceptance that service users have a contribution to make in creating more effective services. In the light of the last 150 years of psychiatry, this is an extremely novel idea. It is not surprising therefore that some elements in the service user/survivor movement have taken the proposition much further than was originally intended and have begun to claim a role in areas not previously contemplated.

Evidence from service users about what it is like to use mental health services is now widely accepted as a necessary part of planning and managing services. Nevertheless, some types of evidence are more acceptable than others. Concerns about representativeness continue to hover around evidence given by service users, although those who control the process rarely define their criteria and prefer to play fast and loose with mechanisms that most people acknowledge can never provide representativeness. At the same time, repeated unspecific warnings from leading mental health professionals about 'the professional user' make it clear that it is still not legitimate for service users/survivors to self-organise like other stakeholders in the field. What many service providers seem to hanker after is raw evidence, uncontaminated by reflection, that they can work upon unimpeded.

Accepting the idea of someone with a mental illness diagnosis as a consumer of services able to reflect on such consumption is one thing. Accepting that person as an agent able to reflect on their mental distress and to provide valuable understandings of it is quite another. It is therefore hardly surprising that the increasing tendency for elements in the service user/survivor to move from offering evidence to offering understandings and to switch from the nature of services to the nature of distress has not been universally welcomed. Even so, both the National Self-Harm Network, focusing on self-harm, and the Hearing Voices Network, focusing on auditory hallucinations, have already achieved a degree of success in promoting new understandings and approaches rooted in direct experience. It is too soon to be certain what status such material will secure in a mental health debate still dominated by professionals. Nevertheless, it is clear that it is a level of debate to which many activists seek greater access. For them, re-valuing personal experience is just as important as re-shaping health services.

Implicit in the development of new understandings of distress is the possibility of new ways of coping. Thus, the work of the Hearing Voices Network and the National Self-harm Network both contain strong elements of practical self-help and self-management. At the same time, there are considerable overlaps between the ideology of self-advocacy and the ideology of self-help and most service user/survivor groups, although action oriented, are in practice a combination of action and support. By daily example of this kind, as much as by deliberate argument, the service user/survivor movement has been providing a critique of traditional professional (expert)-patient (recipient) relationships and proposing alternatives based on the values of empathy, exchange and mutuality. Central to such developments is the proposition that people with a mental illness diagnosis can be providers as well as recipients of care.

Employing people who use mental health services as a result of, rather than in spite of, such experience is a relatively new phenomenon in mental health services. Until recently it almost always occurred in the voluntary sector and in posts somewhat removed from the direct provision of care e.g. advocacy. It could be argued that what was often being valued was experience of using the service system rather than experience of distress. Nevertheless, the Pathfinder NHS Trust in South London gave a pointer to the way things might be going with its 1997 announcement that they will actively seek to recruit people with mental health problems and aim to ensure that 10% of its nursing workforce has experienced such problems. It remains to be seen how many trusts will follow this example.

In the meantime, it is unclear what health and social work professions really feel about people with a mental illness diagnosis joining their number. Even in professions that claim to be empowering clients/patients with mental health problems, colleagues who succumb to the self-same problem often endure clear discrimination. Although it is possible for someone with a mental illness diagnosis to teach nurses, and this is in fact encouraged by the English National Board, such a diagnosis would be a major obstacle if they wanted to train to be a nurse. The Clothier Report (1994) suggested: 'Further consideration should be given to proposals that any nursing applicant with excessive absence through sickness, excessive use of counselling or medical facilities, or self-harming behaviour such as attempted suicide, self-laceration or eating disorder, should not be accepted for training until they have shown the ability to live without professional support and have been in stable employment for at least two years.' Such a sweeping disqualification when coupled with the evident discrimination experienced by nurses who succumb to distress, suggests that in one caring profession at least, the revaluation of these personal experiences is distinctly limited.

It is very much in the interests of the service user/survivor movement to emphasise the positive contribution or potential contribution of people with a mental illness diagnosis. This is a direct way of building our self-esteem and challenging society's preconceptions about our role and capacities. Unfortunately, it is also very much in the interests of those who run the mental health system, including the caring professions, to maintain clear limits on our contribution. Too wide a challenge to their expertise and authority could bring the system down. As a result, it would be hard to claim that the move away from the idea of the individual as mental patient has gone further than the idea of mental patient as consumer or service user. Indeed these are the phrases of today's official language. These phrases give room for the provision of evidence of service use and consumption. They do not recognise understandings of distress or the expertise that can be rooted there. To advance a programme with such ambitions, service user/survivor groups may have to look beyond the service system.

The 1990s and beyond: achievements and challenges

The service user/survivor movement can point to a number of successes in the last ten years. Not least of these is the current recognition that mental health service users have a legitimate place in debate about mental health. It should not be forgotten that in the early 1980s service users were not involved in the planning and monitoring of services let alone in wider areas of the mental health system. There were less than a dozen independent service user/survivor groups. People with a mental illness diagnosis were on the outside. They could hardly even claim a place on the fringes of significant action.

That we have moved appreciably from the situation of the early 1980s to the current position where it is necessary, either by law or custom, to involve service users cannot be credited to the service user/survivor movement alone. Indeed, it can be argued that the speed and completeness of the victory of ideas about 'user involvement' owes more to changes within national government and the health and social services establishment than to pressure from grassroots action groups. Despite this, it remains true that the character of the debate about community mental health care has been heavily influenced by the development of hundreds of independent local service user/survivor action groups. Official enthusiasm for service user involvement need not inevitably lead to widescale growth of independent groups. The historical evidence suggests it would have been possible for service user involvement to have been provided largely, if not exclusively, around large organisations like MIND or the National Schizophrenia Fellowship. This has not happened. Instead, service user involvement is closely linked to a network of independent local action groups. Thus service user involvement has been mirrored by self-organisation.

Although the position of service users as legitimate stakeholders may no longer be subject to open challenge, the question of service user credibility remains open to more debate. As indicated earlier, there are some areas where the contribution of people with a mental illness diagnosis is more acceptable than others. At the same time, concerns within service user/survivor groups regarding tokenism have not decreased noticeably during the 1990s. A review of mental health service user involvement with Social Services following the NHS and Community Care Act found an absence of coherent departmental strategies for developing user involvement. Most tellingly, even ten years after involvement became a significant issue, it found widespread confusion about its meaning and purpose (Bowl 1996). As we approach the end of the 1990s, it seems likely that both service users and service providers have major concerns about the quality of involvement.

The greater part of activity in the service user/survivor movement has been directed to effecting changes within mental health services. The area where there has been the most visible progress has been in relation to extending service users' influence over their day to day life in services and to the development of independent advocacy. Once again, it is worth remembering that in the early 1980s there was little or no mental health advocacy. Although there is still no clear-cut legal right to advocacy and the availability and quality of independent advocacy services varies greatly from area to area, there can be little doubt that advocacy is now seen as a necessary element of high quality community mental health services and that service users increasingly expect to have access to, and to use, an advocate during their journey through services. This move towards advocacy, while certainly reflecting the general ethos of user/consumer-led services that has grown in the last twenty years, owes a great deal to the activity of service user/survivor organisations. They have not only made the provision of independent advocacy a prominent item in their overall demands but have often been involved in establishing and running local advocacy projects. A significant portion of the existing expertise in mental health advocacy in the United Kingdom now rests in the hands of service users and survivors.

Alongside the development of advocacy services, the service user/survivor movement has also achieved some success in other attempts to increase individual control over care and treatment. Crisis cards that assist people in crisis to contact an advocate originated within the movement. Advance directives, legal instruments that may give people a powerful say in their future treatment, were first championed by service users and survivors. Equally, a number of local groups (notably in London and Nottingham) have involved themselves in developing better information packages for service users. Since the introduction of the Care Programme Approach, one or two publications have appeared that enable the individual to 'write their own care plan' (e.g. Leader, 1995).

Increasing individual control through improving the provision of advocacy and information has been a profitable area for service user/survivor enterprise. More direct attempts to change care and treatment practice have been less successful. Although it has rarely been clear how far any particular service user/survivor group would go in restricting compulsory detention or compulsory treatment, the movement as a whole has been united in opposition to any extension of compulsion. In this respect, the last fifteen years have not been a story of success but of a rearguard action in alliance with many other mental health groups, culminating in a small but significant extension of compulsory powers in aftercare under supervision. The autumn 1998 press release by the Health Minister, Paul Boateng, announcing the creation of an expert group to advise on changes to the Mental Act with its statement that 'the law must make it clear that non-compliance with agreed treatment programmes is not an option' is clear confirmation that two of the movement's strongest messages – the essential competence of service users and the undesirability of compulsion – have made little impact.

In the same way, it is difficult to argue that service user/survivor groups have significantly affected the practice of ECT or drug treatment, the two mainstays of mental health care. Although overuse of psychiatric drugs has been a common complaint, the service user/survivor movement, perhaps inhibited by the fact that so many of its members take medication, has not yet developed a clear and assertive position on drug treatments. It is an indication of the movement's comparative powerlessness that the recent increase in openness about the negative effects of the anti-psychotics and anti-depressants of the last 30 years was brought about by the arrival of new and supposedly 'cleaner' drugs not by pressure from campaigning groups.

Compared to medication, campaigns against ECT have always been more possible and there has been renewed enthusiasm for direct action on this issue in recent years. Even so, despite evidence of a reservoir of concern among the public over ECT and the fact that a major voluntary organisation like MIND has become much more clearly opposed to aspects of the treatment over the last decade, very little has changed. Even, or perhaps especially, on controversial issues, alliances of service users/survivors, voluntary groups and mental health workers do not seem to be enough to make an effective challenge.

Not that the desire of the service user/survivor movement for confrontation should be overemphasised. However effective the challenge has been, it has almost always been conducted in moderate tones. Involvement in the training and education of mental health workers is a good example of the willingness to attempt change through collaboration. Work of this kind is a particular feature of action in this country compared to others with well-developed movements. Although many activists value educational activities, it is very difficult to assess how much impact it is having. It could be that it has done more to shape the approach and outlook of service user/survivor organisations than it has to change the nature of services. Nevertheless, professional organisations like the Central Council for the Education and Training of Social Workers (CCETSW) and English National Board (ENB) now require the involvement of service users in their programmes and there is the possibility for contributions to move beyond anecdote to analysis. If the collaborational model of action that has predominated within the service user/survivor movement continues, involvement in training and education may increase. It is non-confrontational and attractive to funders.

Any review of the service user/survivor movement must note the practical difficulties of action and organisation. There may now be hundreds of local groups, but many of these are small and suffer from the insecurity of inadequate or short-term funding. The need to learn new skills for running a group or to adapt to and find support for key members going through distress poses a continuing challenge. At the same time, there now appears to be an imbalance between local and national groups. The movement has characteristically been focussed on local activities and local groups have frequently been better funded than their national counterparts. But it could now be argued that there are too many national networking groups, that none of them are sufficiently strong and that their work overlaps too much. As the movement continues to grow and diversify, there is an increased danger of fragmentation.

A strong, representative voice at national level something the movement has hitherto avoided or been unable to create could be a necessity for continued success in the next decade.

One challenge for the movement is organisational to create and maintain effective action groups. Another challenge is to do with priorities and direction. It is one of the ironies of the last fifteen years of action that, although the position of the diagnosed mentally ill within services has improved, their position in society has not altered radically and in some respects may even have deteriorated. Arguments in support of the positive contribution of service users and survivors that have made limited headway within services have had a minimal impact on the wider community. Here, the idea of the 'mentally ill' as burden or threat, promoted by the Zito Trust – Schizophrenia A National Emergency (SANE) 'You don't have to be mentally-ill to suffer from mental illness' – has ascendancy. If the long-term liberation implicit in community care is ever to be realised, service user/survivor groups will have to address this discrepancy and do more to challenge social attitudes and practices.

This will not be easy. It has been both a blessing and a curse that service user/survivor action in the United Kingdom was engulfed so quickly in service-led enthusiasm for user involvement. One result has been that activists seem to see themselves as service users rather than citizens and have only been peripherally involved in civil rights campaigns. Another consequence has been that, although action groups have become quite accustomed and skilled at working with mental health professionals, they have limited experience of working with other groups and are not used to presenting their case to the public.

The challenge for the service user/survivor movement in the next few years is whether to take on a broader agenda – civil rights, access to employment, revised social understandings of distress – or whether to confine its energies to what goes on within mental health services an area where, despite the gains of the last fifteen years, there is still much to be done. This dilemma may not need an 'either/or' response. It is quite possible for groups and individuals to work in a number of areas. But any attempt at broader social change will require new skills and, in particular, new alliances with other oppressed and disadvantaged groups: disabled people, the poor, black and ethnic groups.

At a time when government and the media are focusing on the safety and social control aspects of mental health services and psychiatry is pursuing the neurochemical origins of distress, there is a real danger that people with a mental illness diagnosis will be separated out as a special group among the marginalised. Emphasising the common nature and origins of our common experience through common action on social issues could be both useful and necessary. While championing the positive acceptance of difference, we should do more to demonstrate our humanity.

The service user/survivor could never be accused of a lack of energy. Yet much of its work has been done in tandem with agencies that have their own very powerful agendas. What is increasingly needed is a coherent, overall vision and sense of direction for the movement and a clearer exposition of the ideas and values that hold service user/survivor organisations together; a vision that encompasses a social reconfiguration of 'mental illness' as well as the reform of mental health services.

References

Bowl, R.(1996) Involving service users in mental health services: Social Services Departments and the NHS and Community Care Act 1990. *Journal of Mental Health*, 5 (3), 287 303

Department of Health (1994) *The Allitt Inquiry: Report of the Independent Inquiry relating to the Deaths and Injuries on the Children's Ward at Grantham and Kesteven General Hospital During the Period February to April 1991.* London: DoH

Leader, A. (1995) *Direct power: A resource pack for people who want to develop their own care plans and support networks.* London: Community Support Network/Brixton Community Sanctuary/ Pavilion Publishing/MIND

Lewis, D., Shadish, W. and Lurigio, A. (1989) Policies of inclusion and the mentally ill: long term care in a new environment. *Journal of Social Issues*, 45 (3) 173–86

Mental Health Task Force User Group (1994) Appendix 1. *Guidelines for a Local Charter for Users of Mental Health services.* London: HMSO

For further information you can contact:

National Self-Harm Network
HSHN
PO Box 16190
London
NW1 3WW

Hearing Voices Network
c/o Creative Support
5th Floor
Dale House
35 Dale Street
Manchester
M1 2HF

United Kingdom Advocacy Network (UKAN)
Volserve House
14-18   West Bar Green
Sheffield
S1 2DA

MindLink
MIND
Granta House
15-19 Broadway
Stratford
London
E15 4BQ

ECT Anonymous
14 Western Avenue
Riddlesden
Keighley
West Yorkshire
BD2O 5DJ

CHAPTER 13

Survivor controlled alternatives to psychiatric services

VIVIEN LINDOW

THIS CHAPTER IS about alternatives to psychiatric services set up and run by people who have received these services and who want something different. It is not about alternative or complementary therapies, which is a different subject also of great interest to many psychiatric system survivors.

Other chapters make it clear why people who have experienced psychiatry as oppressive and harmful want alternative supports for their lives. In stating that current ideas about so called mental illness are an unhelpful way to categorise our expressions of grief and distress, we do not deny that we need help and back-up. As with other oppressed groups, helping and supporting each other has proved one route of satisfaction and a better future for many psychiatric system survivors, world-wide.

The self-help movement of people who have been labelled by psychiatry has a long history, much of it hidden. This has involved many different activities, including campaigning for better conditions in the psychiatric system, setting up alternative support and cultural projects, re-valuing the meaning of our experiences, and self-help personal growth activities.

This last category, of personal growth activities, often does not have a political, 'change the psychiatric system', aspect. Instead, people who have problems in common meet together to share their experiences and find ways to tackle their difficulties. The strongest vein has been in the field of substance dependence. One major movement has been that of the twelve step groups, starting in 1935 with Alcoholics Anonymous in the USA. Nowadays there are many and varied self-help personal growth groups.

Often these groups are almost hidden from the mainstream psychiatric system, and they receive little attention in the professional literature. This is not surprising as they frequently eschew professional intervention, and in the case of twelve step groups are entirely self-supporting so do not answer to funding organisations. Those that are most successful tend to have a great emphasis on direct democracy, being organised by and answerable to their day-to-day membership. One feature of all self-help and survivor run alternatives is that they have to attract members: if people do not like them they vote with their feet.

Of course, the distinction between political and personal change groups is not absolute: some user and survivor organisations contain aspects of both. The Hearing Voices movement, for example, in Great Britain has taken the form of groups of people who hear voices meeting in an expanding network of local groups. At the same time, some leaders in the movement and some professional people have banded together to attempt to influence the way voice hearers are responded to within the psychiatric system. The National Self-Harm Network has similar, dual aims of people who harm themselves meeting for information exchange and to influence professional practice (Dace, et. al., 1998).

One feature of the more political groups of mental health system survivors, is a civil rights theme that demands that society accept us as we are, extending tolerance and ending discrimination, expressed thus in one project:

> *We have ordinary human needs and McMurphy's does not attempt to professionalise these – i.e. turn our need for friendship and support into social work.* (McMurphy's Review, 1997)

Described in this chapter are alternative projects to orthodox statutory and voluntary sector services that provide support for community living. Examples are given from the world-wide movement, as far as known to the writer. We have grown parallel to the liberation movements of women and Black people, and other oppressed groups in societies. There are many lessons for us to learn from the longer established social movements of women and Black people. In a situation where psychiatry in many countries is again extending its control by forcibly medicating us outside hospitals, we need the inspiration and support of these other communities. This is more so because the more oppressed groups in society fare even worse in the psychiatric system than more privileged citizens.

A prime activity, a duty even, of psychiatric system survivors is what, in the heady earlier days of the women's movement, was called 'consciousness raising'. By this I refer to the need to continue to tell each other our stories so we know what we have in common, and that it is possible to rise above the oppression experienced as a psychiatric patient. I will never forget the overwhelming relief I felt when I first read an account of someone else who had to grieve and become angry about the inappropriate and sometimes downright damaging reactions of the system to our distress and emotional pain. After such sharing we move from grief into action together to provide our own support systems and to campaign to change psychiatry and the societies that endorse the inhumane aspects of the 'mental health' system.

The survivor movement started a decade and more earlier in some countries than in the UK, notably in Japan, the Netherlands and in North America.

Much of the documentation available is from the USA, where there is this longer history of 'client controlled programmes'. There are three key pioneering books on the subject. Judi Chamberlin's *On Our Own* was first published in the USA in 1977. I would also like to acknowledge my debt to *Reaching Across: Mental health clients helping each other* edited by Sally Zinman, Howie the Harp and Su Budd (1987). Their title celebrates the equality that survivor-controlled alternatives strive for; we reach across to each other, not up or down. In 1994 Sally Zinman and Howie the Harp edited *Reaching Across II: Maintaining our roots/The challenge of growth.* They wrote this because the advice to groups in the first volume was well received, but as projects grew and became more accepted, there was a need to treat more technical subjects such as equal opportunities, employing workers and fundraising, while continuing the philosophical work of the earlier volume.

In this chapter I use the term 'survivor' to mean current and former users of the psychiatric system and of mainstream mental health services provided by the voluntary and statutory sectors. There are many terms, in the USA 'consumer' and 'patient' are used, in Japan the term can be translated as 'psychiatrically disabled people'. I wonder if that implies 'disabled by psychiatry'? Howie the Harp, the USA pioneer, preferred 'crazy folk'. I also tend to use the term 'psychiatric system' more often than the term 'mental health system', as I find it more psychiatric than mentally healthy.

In setting up alternatives, one difficulty that survivors do find is the tension between the need to advocate for our peers within the psychiatric system, and the energy it takes to set up and run alternatives. Most survivors engaged in providing alternatives find that it is essential to keep in touch with the civil rights needs of current mental health system service users. Integrating these activities with survivor-run alternatives is seen as essential to prevent the alternative projects moving towards the norm of voluntary sector provision, the problem of co-option that will be discussed later in this chapter.

A paradox of user-controlled services is that because out-of-control behaviour tends to be much less evident in these projects, critics say that they only cater for less severely impaired people. In fact, it is extremely unlikely that people with minimal difficulties with living will take part in these projects. They are hard work, and the dedication needed to start and continue to support user-controlled services is frequently motivated from long and unprofitable experience of mainstream services. The stigma imposed by society also remains truly crushing and those people who can tend to move out into situations that enable them to shed the psychiatric label.

Some survivor-controlled alternatives

What kinds of service do people set up when they feel that mainstream services have failed them? By far the most numerous projects world-wide are clubs and drop-ins. In the UK, these often start because existing day services don't cover the times that survivors find most helpful. Oxford Survivors started like this in premises run by a local Mind drop-in, and then moved to their own independent centre (Lindow, 1994a, gives more details about self-help alternatives).

In Sweden, the government has supported the development of an autonomous survivor movement with funds, particularly to enable survivors to be paid for the work they do in providing community projects. As a result, user controlled clubs are commonplace, and can open as needed. Sometimes the club is a flat in a residential area, sometimes it is open for 24 hours, seven days a week.

An early UK self-help alternative to mental health services is McMurphy's in Sheffield, already mentioned, set up in 1986 (moving into their building in 1988) by young people in residential services discontented with current day provision. They named their project after the character McMurphy in *One Flew Over the Cuckoo's Nest*, who also expressed his dissatisfaction with existing psychiatric provision, with less happy results for him. Taking over a near-derelict building, they refurbished it by their own labour into a clubhouse with a catering-standard kitchen. In their early years they encountered difficulty attracting sufficient women members to fulfil their equal opportunities aspirations. Quotas on the management group and the banning of pornography including some tabloid newspapers failed to attract women without further action. The fitting out of a separate women's area has helped to overcome this problem. Providing a safe psychological space for all people who encounter the psychiatric system often leads to the need for people to meet in separate anti-oppressive groupings as well as together.

McMurphy's has survived with difficulties caused by regular funding crises, in particular paying for workers. This uncertainty and under-funding is typical of user-controlled services, unlike the statutory sector. Here is a quotation from the newsletter of a user controlled group in Newcastle:

> *Since the beginning of Lifeboat it has felt that unlike other charities we have had to justify ourselves. The statutory services far from helping and supporting us have given each crumb of aid with calculated grudge.* (Boat on the Tyne, 1998)

Another pioneer project that has experienced funding difficulty is the Black Women's Mental Health Project in Stonebridge, North London. As one of their founders, Angela Linton-Abulu (1998), has written, 'Black users and survivors suffer the most pain, their voices are heard the least, if they are heard at all'. When these survivors found that women from black communities were being denied good practices in local services, they took matters into their own hands and set up a drop-in and advice and information line. Their experience of statutory services was that they were inadequate and did not make mental health services safe or welcoming for women. Issues such as racial harassment and sexual exploitation of Black women was not even on their agendas.

The Black Women's Project has faced opposition from many people. Mental health workers have behaved as though threatened when the women were seen as doing more for themselves, and saw the empathy shown by survivor volunteers in the project as 'unprofessional'. Even some Black workers have shown these attitudes. White survivors are also among those who have opposed this group, on the grounds of competition for funding. Since this occurred even when not in direct funding competition, it underlines the need for predominately white survivor groups to ensure that they receive anti-racist training. Black women survivors, their families and the local community, on the other hand, have been very supportive.

Once the Black Women's Project had established its drop-in and advice line, after countless hours of unpaid work and unsuccessful funding applications, the Project nonetheless decided to reach out further, to Black women in hospital. They were determined not to be stopped, and eventually in 1998 received funding for one worker. In reaching out to women in the statutory sector, they have followed the pattern that other projects have found essential: to combine self-support with an advocacy and campaigning edge that keeps them in touch with the psychiatric system. Part of their vision is:

> . . . to enable, support and encourage all Black Women
> and women who define themselves as being Black in this
> society, in demanding for themselves collectively, good
> practices in mental health. (Black Women, 1998)

This dual function of support and campaigning is equally a part of the Japanese survivor movement. They have a longer history of twentieth century survivor-controlled projects than in the UK, reflecting the even greater social discrimination that they still experience. Starting as mutual support groups, often meeting to eat together, some Japanese groups have developed into work projects in a way familiar in other countries, including New Zealand, Canada, USA, Italy as well as here.

The Sumirekai group on the island of Hokkaido in Japan is named after a small insignificant flower that massed together in a bunch is very beautiful. This group started as early as 1970 for friendship, to decrease the isolation felt by people discharged from psychiatric hospitals. They started a monthly newsletter and gradually expanded, having 24 clubs in 1994 (Lindow, 1994b). They also have a co-operative workshop which processes paper, trains cooks and provides a cheap meal for about 30 people a day. There are 40 workshop places, and other members can visit as they want. Like survivor clubs world-wide, they also go on sports and leisure outings.

Setting up businesses is certainly a growing activity to enable psychiatric system survivors get into work and remain in control. In New York a survivor controlled business development and assistance agency, INCube Inc., has been funded to help people to set up 'consumer-run' businesses of many kinds (Schwarz, 1998).

The co-operative structure remains a popular and successful one for both work and housing projects. Another pioneering work project, in the USA, is the Wyman Way co-operative. Started in 1985, it was modelled on co-operatives in northern Italy that followed the closing of Italian asylums after their liberal mental health legislation in 1978. Wyman Way runs a small building and landscaping business, and aims to be self-supporting. It is worker owned and managed on non-profit lines, and obtains grants to enable it to train new workers in useful skills.

While some workers at Wyman Way move to open employment, this is not the be-all and end-all of the business. It has the flexibility to enable some workers to do shorter hours to fit in with the benefits system, a problem for survivors trying to get back to work in many countries. These are quotations from workers at the Wyman Way co-op.

• *Owning something means that you belong to something and it means a lot to all of us that we belong somewhere besides a hospital, or a day treatment facility.*
• *I have been with the Co-op going on six and a half years and I have seen a lot of changes with each of the employees. Some have gotten their self-esteem back, some have gained more self control, some have found the motivation to at least become active.*
• *We become more than a team, we become a family of friends.*
• *What I like the most about my work in the Co-op is acceptance for who I am. They only tend to push you in a positive direction and in what your capabilities are.*

As the work has expanded, the Co-op has bought necessary tools and machinery, such as lawn mowers and a van. They have a promotion structure, and the workers decide as a group matters of policy and which contracts to pursue and accept. Membership is for life. Members can be temporarily suspended if they are unable to work, but they cannot be fired.

The Co-op's personnel policies have been developed to help

with trouble-shooting of the kind needed in all businesses. All job descriptions at Wyman Way Co-op contain the wording:

> *The employed member will perform these duties in a manner which is warm, friendly, caring, flexible, part of a team and committed to change and the financial independence of the Co-op.*

They found that at first some mental health workers in the surrounding community found it difficult to let go of their old role. This changed as the Co-op developed.

Another survivor-run company, this time not a co-op, is Fresh Start Cleaning and Maintenance, a user-controlled company in Toronto, Canada founded in 1989. Their Internet contact point (http://www.freshstartclean.com) tells us:

> *With a wide roster of clients ranging from public to private sector, offices to lawn care, Fresh Start has established itself as a can-do company, providing over two hundred hours a week of work to over forty employees. All revenue is put back into the company to provide training, cleaning supplies, wages, site expenses, and social events.*

They also tell potential employers some of the advantages to the community of their company (in addition to getting the work done):

> *So we come to work for Fresh Start. Now, do you want to know what we give back? Disability income previously collected by some of us... Oh, and the average hospital stay prior to Fresh Start is 49 days a year. Six months after coming on board that number and the dollars associated to that number drops to an average four days a year. This is giving back in a big way!*

These user-controlled projects show some of the potential of work schemes. In the UK co-operatives are unfashionable, but many survivors have set up small businesses and social firms or set up as sole traders. A popular option is working as independent consultants and trainers to assist mental health services to change at both management and mental health worker levels. There is one UK co-op known to this writer, the Distress Awareness Training Agency in Greater Manchester, England, a small group of survivor-workers who have banded together as trainers.

Survivors are also working in many cultural activities. Artists, play and other writers, poets and performers are banding together or working separately to express themselves as survivors. Survivors' Poetry is perhaps the most organised network of creative writers who work with their common experiences of the psychiatric system, with groups in various places in England and Wales and several publications under their belt.

Attempts to change media representations of 'crazy folk' are also of great interest to survivors and can provide work opportunities. In Vermont, USA, White Light Communications is a television production company operated by ex-patients. As well as creating a demand for their programmes on the television networks, they have produced many tapes featuring early leaders passing on their experience of the survivor movement and self-help.

Two other major kinds of user-controlled project can be found: reaching out to homeless survivors, and providing various forms of housing providing a choice between communal and individual living spaces. Survivor-run outreach projects are often based on the disabled people's Independent Living model. A pioneer in this is the Oakland Independence Support Center (OISC), in California, USA, which employs survivors, many of whom have been homeless, to meet support and survival needs of local homeless people.

Housing needs are met in as various ways as businesses. In Sweden, a survivor group took over the lease of a whole apartment block to provide housing for people who want to live in a situation safe from discrimination by immediate neighbours. One of Auckland Survivors' earliest activities was to provide emergency housing for people experiencing a mental health crisis.

A non-medical refuge or asylum in a mental health crisis is one of the most frequently sought alternatives for people who have not been well served by the psychiatric system. What is talked about is not just crisis housing, but a safe place with support as needed. This is an area that presents a direct challenge to the profession of psychiatry, and has proved remarkably difficult for system survivors to set up as alternatives. Not only is a user-run crisis house frequently opposed or marginalised as a priority by mental health workers, but it needs more funding than most alternative projects because providing safety and support needs workers.

Much has been said and written by survivors about the variety of supports that people need in times of crises (for example, Lindow,

1996). Statutory services in many places in the UK have moved towards giving access to community support on the medical model to prevent hospital admission. But for those people who want an alternative non-medical refuge away from home, little is happening here or in most other parts of the world. Jan Wallcraft (1996) has written:

> *A radical survivor-led model would build upwards from the expressed needs of people in crisis or those who have survived crises, rather than downwards from legal requirements and state policy.*

Because survivor run crisis houses are as rare as hen's teeth, I will here describe a project that has been developed in Birmingham on a 'user-led' basis. The term 'user led' is best met with an open-minded suspicion. Often (as in this example) it does describe a genuine move to put service users in charge of what happens to them, but equally often it describes tokenism and mental health workers wishing to be politically correct without actually changing what they do. At Skallagrigg, started in December 1997, the workers – who have themselves experienced mental health crises – provide a holistic approach to recovery and an alternative to hospital admission. Working closely with the local Home Treatment Team, people can choose to go to Skallagrigg rather than be admitted to hospital.

Once people are at Skallagrigg, the workers help people to look at the causes of their crisis, be they practical such as benefits or housing problems, or emotional such as abuse or other relationship difficulties. This sensible and humane procedure is seen as challenging by some mental health professionals, while others, including the Home Treatment Team, have been interested in how quickly most people come out of their crisis and have sought to learn from this approach. A major ethic of the house is respect for other people, by both staff and residents. The Home Treatment Team continues to provide medical care as needed, and people have the choice to take medication. Some complementary therapies are also available.

Planning and running survivor-controlled alternatives
It has not been possible to give a tidy or anything like a full picture of the development of user-controlled projects: it has been a fast development, often by groups of people unaware of developments

elsewhere. With resources grudgingly given people have been inventive and resourceful. The next part of this chapter shares information from existing projects about setting up and running user-controlled alternatives to mainstream provision. They are presented here, of course, as suggestions only.

Sufficient planning is one essential key to a successful project. People have to be attracted to take part in the planning; decisions have to be made about the scope of the project and how to get the necessary work done. Many things must be sorted out even before money can be applied for. When funding is gained, there are still many preparations to be made before a project starts: the extent of all this preparation depends of course on the scope and size of the alternative.

The planning stage throws up many of the issues that have to be attended to throughout the life of the project. In considering whom the project will serve, equal opportunities have to be brought into action. The planning group needs to reflect the whole community of survivors to be served. One good start is always to hold your planning meetings in a wheelchair accessible place, safe (psychologically and physically) for women and people of minority ethnic communities to travel to. As soon as you can, get a small fund to reimburse people's travel expenses. If your planning process recognises the oppressions of marginalisation and poverty, your project is more likely to do the same.

The planning stage needs to include attention to how decisions will be made in the project. Attention to core values at an early stage can be part of this process: alternatives usually have equal opportunities and member satisfaction as paramount values. Spell out the respect of everyone in the project as equals: management group and members, workers, residents or whoever the project is for. Go on from there to find the most inclusive way of making decisions.

The decision-making structure of your new organisation will determine whether it is controlled by its users or it clones existing statutory and voluntary sector services. This is the greatest danger for survivor-controlled organisations, known as co-option or 'provideritis', that is, becoming like existing providers. Joseph Yaskin (1992) writes about provideritis:

Think of this problem as a potentially fatal disease – something like cancer – that can be controlled with early detection and intervention. To fight provideritis successfully,

*it is important to understand its causes and symptoms. The
primary causes of provideritis in a consumer group are the
pressures and demands that come from outside.*

*All user/survivor groups recognise the calls from outside
that ask us to dance to other providers' agendas, diverting
us from what we set out to do. 'User involvement' is one
main culprit in the UK. In setting up alternatives, negotiation
of absolute independence and confidentiality from the
outset will help to guard against co-option by the values
and demands of 'the system'.*

Survivors sometimes unwittingly assume that the way other services
are organised is the 'correct' way to do it, without analysing the
basis of the power differences that traditional organisation
structures promote. The earlier part of the chapter described some
co-operatives. This is a legal structure for a company in the UK,
and does not prevent different people from taking on different roles.
If adopting a management committee structure common in the
voluntary sector, consider whether you really want to be a charity,
with its echoes of paternalism of old. It does prevent people from
being paid for taking on management roles. The statutory sector
can equally fund not-for-profit social firms and companies. If you
do have a management group, many projects have found it best to
ensure that it takes the minimum of decisions, leaving as much as
possible to membership meetings.

Two of the projects mentioned earlier have made special
arrangements to ensure participation in management by particular
groups. McMurphy's elects a 60:40 ratio of women to men to its
management group. I will describe the management of Oakland
Independence Support Center (OISC) in a little more detail to
illustrate some principles of management adopted by one successful
survivor-run project. The Board of Directors has powers to establish
policy, hire and fire permanent staff and various other functions. It
is made up of at least 60% day-to-day members of the project, and
at least 60% members of minority ethnic communities (to reflect its
surrounding community). Those members who are not survivors
are key community people, not mental health workers. Half of the
members of the board are elected each year for a two-year term,
thus ensuring both continuity and accountability.

Four elected officers of OISC – Chairperson, Vice-Chairperson,
Secretary and Treasurer – are elected annually and are not eligible
to serve for more than two consecutive one-year terms. Elections

take place at the annual general membership meetings. Any five members can call a General Membership Meeting for other major decisions.

The management of OISC illustrates not only some aspects of equal opportunities in action, but the principles of rotation of power by having time-limited terms of office and as much direct, face to face, democracy as an organisation with 15 workers can include. Membership meetings tend to be a key feature of survivor-run organisations. They enable people to take part in as much of the running of the project as possible. Transparency and power-sharing are essential, the more so when salaried workers are employed. By transparency, I mean not keeping information and decisions in the hands of a few. Auckland Survivors, for example, keep their accounts in detail on a wall passed by drop-in members. Direct democracy is a slow way of making decisions, and sometimes the membership has to mandate others to do work, such as staff appointment or management, on its behalf. If the organisation is too complex for all decisions to be made at membership meetings, the membership can regularly appoint those people who do make the decisions.

With so much depending on membership meetings, attention needs to be paid to recruiting and involving new members. New members are the lifeblood of survivor organisations: they need to be welcomed and encouraged to take part. It has been found that this needs to be the subject of constant attention, identifying existing members who will answer questions and make new members feel comfortable, providing written and tape-recorded information about the project, ensuring that the new member knows that his or her voice or sign language is equal to everyone else's.

Before coming to the crucial questions arising from becoming employers, a word or two about leadership. Without leaders, nothing happens in human groups. Leadership in survivor groups is essential, but the style of leadership has to be inclusive and participative, involving as many people as possible in activities and power-sharing on every possible occasion. As with membership of management groups, it is also essential that informal leadership rotates if a project is not to become dependent on one person and move away from being member-run. The wise leader allows him or herself lots of time out, so that everyone (including the leader) knows that they are not indispensable. It can be surprising for someone who has lost all confidence while in the psychiatric system to find themselves a leader. It is a welcome surprise, to be shared around.

Many survivor-controlled projects have evolved from small

self-help groups. When a decision is made to expand to provide a service beyond mutual support or activist meetings, the issue of getting the work done arises. Having decided on a structure that brings maximum direct democracy, a group has then to grapple with the introduction of a hierarchy, with a paid worker or workers having power arising from a salaried position and access to most information in the project.

If the project is small-scale, one solution to this issue is to have co-workers: in the USA there are examples of two to six workers (variously named facilitators, co-ordinators or administrators) sharing the tasks. This can help people to retain their benefits status as well as prevent domination of the project by one individual.

The disadvantages of sharing the work in this way include lack of continuity in getting necessary tasks done, and the need to provide a living wage when individuals are able to contribute much time to a project. It is not good practice for survivors to exploit each other, and the provision of paid posts in our own projects is one way in which people are empowered. However, when a project becomes much bigger, co-management by two or more people can help flatten the hierarchy and at the same time assist leaders by sharing the responsibility.

One common feature in the USA survivor controlled projects is the provision of a number of hourly paid tasks. These are usually carried out by members who have shown their involvement in the project as unpaid workers (volunteers), and are sometimes time-limited. Having (say) the cleaning or the representation on a district committee job as a rotating post enables many people to be empowered over time, prevents 'ownership' of something communal and shares the scarce resource of paid jobs.

Sometimes these hourly rate jobs come up for periodic election, or else a volunteer can 'earn' a paid position by length of unpaid service. Whatever the mechanism, these tasks should not be in the 'gift' of one individual or problems of power are sure to arise. Who holds paid posts must be decided fairly by the members or a group of member representatives.

For all workers, paid and unpaid, provision needs to be made to ensure that conditions of work are fair and pleasant. Training and conference opportunities are one aspect of this. Unpaid workers might be able to become formal trainees, with recognised completion of a training period and provision of references for employment. In the USA, this provides a gradual route to employment for many members of client-controlled projects. The Berkeley Drop-In Center in California has other good ideas. They have 'volunteer of the month' awards and volunteer appreciation dinners. Projects that rely on much unpaid help still need to obtain reasonable finance to support a volunteer programme, including paid people responsible for facilitating members in unpaid work. The unpaid work of members is a valuable resource, and this needs to be openly recognised, with regular thanks given.

Lack of preparation for becoming an employer has been a difficulty in many survivor groups in the UK. Much preparation and continuing ongoing support by the management group or co-operative are essential. A whole raft of policies need to be worked out, employment contracts (work conditions, holidays, sickness, disciplinary and grievance processes etc.) prepared and equal opportunities recruitment procedures carried out. How the worker is to be supported and managed needs to be clear and in place.

It is clear that in fundraising for a survivor-controlled project, funding for training for the people who are setting up the project is a first call. It is not possible here to go into the sources of funding in the UK for such projects. It is my personal view that it is better to try to engage the local statutory sector from the beginning if at all possible in order to attract continuous funding. Challenge their stereotypes and if you can, find ways for them to get to know you and the vision of your group. They might fund an initial survey to demonstrate need, and once you have attracted their interest and shown your competence they are more likely to offer continuing funding.

Fundraising is never easy. It is the time to blow your trumpets. Whatever experiences and skills your planning group members have – be they plumbing, language skills, computer wizardry, management or whatever – be sure to mention them to potential funders. If possible, demonstrate from other places that a project like yours is a viable option. Tell them about your group's achievements so far (known as your 'track record'). Maybe you can attract a potential funder to visit a successful survivor-run project in another town with you: the United Kingdom Advocacy Network (UKAN) may be able to put you in touch with other groups.

We have the vision (we're particularly good at visions). Successful survivor-run projects are in place. For those of us who are not helped by mainstream services, or who want something extra alongside 'community care', we can go forward together in providing more alternatives.

References

Black Women – Our News Insight Issue 1, Spring 1998,

Boat on the Tyne, (1998), Volume 2, Issue 28, 2

Chamberlin, J. (1977) *On Our Own: Patient controlled alternatives to the mental health system.* Hawthorn: New York. UK edition published by Mind Publications in 1988

Dace, E., Faulkner, A., Frost, M., Parker, K., Pembroke, L. and Smith, A. (1998) *The Hurt Yourself Less Workbook* The National Self-Harm Network, P O Box 16190, London NW1 3WW

Lindow, V. (1994a) *Self-Help Alternatives to Mental Health Services.* London: Mind Publications

Lindow, V. (1994b) The Japanese psychiatric system survivor movement, *Changes* 12:2, 141–4

Lindow, V. (1996) *A Special Place for People in a Special State of Being: A conference report on crisis care in mental health.* Bristol Survivors' Network

Linton-Abulu, A. (1998) *Sisters of the Yam.* Summer, Issue 2

McMurphy's Review (1997) Sheffield

Schwarz, G. (1998) INCube Inc. and the TAP Programme – an innovative programme for consumer-run business development in New York City. *A Life In the Day* 2:3, 6-11, Pavilion Publishing

Wallcraft, J. (1996) Some models of asylum and help in times of crisis. In D. Tomlinson and J. Carrier (eds.) *Asylum in the Community.* 187-206

Yaskin, J. (1992) *Nuts and Bolts: A technical assistance guide for mental health consumer/survivor self-help groups.* National Mental Health Consumer Self-Help Clearinghouse/Project SHARE

Zinman, S., Harp, H. T. and Budd, S. (1987) *Reaching Across: Mental health clients helping each other.* California Network of Mental Health Clients

Zinman, S. and Harp, H. T. (1994) *Reaching Across II: Maintaining our roots/The challenge of growth.* California Network of Mental Health Clients

Groups and projects mentioned in the text

Black Women's Mental Health Project, London (0181 961 6324)

Hearing Voices Network c/o Creative Support, Dale House, 35 Dale Street, Manchester M1 2HF tel (0161 228 3896)

Skallagrigg is run by Change c/o IMHN, 71 Fentham Road, Erdington, Birmingham B23 6AL

Survivors' Poetry, 34 Osnaburgh Street, London NW1 3ND.

UKAN (United Kingdom Advocacy Network). 14-18 West Bar Green, Sheffield S1 2DA (0114 272 8171)

White Light Communications, Seven Kilburn Street, Burlington, Vermont 05401, USA

CHAPTER 14

The duty of community care: The Wokingham MIND crisis house

PAM JENKINSON

I AM A RADICAL SEPARATIST. I have never worked within the professional mental health system so although I have been involved in mental health for close on forty years my view of the system is that of an outsider looking in. I dislike what I see. Most of what I see is about power and control, about ambition and professional career advancement, about medical domination; very little is about mental health. So I have no desire to be involved in the system. I would not use their services if I were the person in mental distress. I cannot change them but I can do the other thing – offer something better outside the system.

Colonisation of the voluntary sector by mental health professionals is rife. Probably a majority of voluntary organisations employ professional staff, adopt professional procedures and are in fact part of the professional mental health system in all but name. The result is that the user has no real alternative or choice of service. That is not the case in the Wokingham MIND Crisis House. When a group of users and carers got together to set up the Wokingham and District Branch of MIND in 1988 they asked me to head up the organisation and I agreed to do so provided that it was to be genuinely voluntary, separatist, and banned professionals. Everyone agreed and these principles were enshrined in the Constitution. So when we opened the Crisis House in 1991 the foundations of a genuine alternative to the system had already been laid.

Image and reality
The young members of Wokingham MIND laugh at my image. They

tell me that radical separatists starve in garrets and have their hair standing up in spikes. To have the right image I should discard my Liberty prints and wear a tee shirt with a picture of Che Guevara. In all the hilarity these young people miss the point. Many system services have a radical *image*. Judi Chamberlin's therapist in his jeans and boots sitting on the floor appeared radical but he still had power over her life (Chamberlin 1988). If it were about the way you do your hair then I am currently trying to get mine like Ingrid Bergman's in 'Casablanca'. Politics are not about *appearance*; they are about *power*. Colonisation, the actual process of what happens, is always the same whether you are looking globally at Cuba and the Congo or locally at mental health. Colonisation occurs when one group of people invades the territory of another group of people and takes over its resources for its own use. The invaders always think that they are superior to and know better than the invaded. Sometimes colonisation has been internalised in their thinking so that they see themselves as genuinely conferring benefit upon those whom they invade. The invaders bring their own culture with them and stamp out the culture of the invaded, seeing them in metaphorical terms as naked savages; but the invaded group do not want to be colonised and prefer and value their own culture. That is precisely my position in relation to the mental health system and I believe it to be the position of most survivors. So how do you keep your radical separatist crisis house safe from invaders? Firstly, you must have someone with a long-term commitment; then they must know the game; finally you need an artist. The local psychiatric system seethes impotently because I have convinced the local politicians that the crisis house is 'mother and apple pie': psychologists will agree that if people have it firmly fixed in their perceptions that a thing is *quaint*, then they will have the greatest difficulty in perceiving it to be radically political.

An alternative service
Before setting up Wokingham MIND in 1988 I had been involved briefly with another local mental health association in which I observed the process of colonisation. The experience was useful because it taught me how to protect Wokingham MIND and prevent something similar from happening there. So what actually happens? How do they do it? In the very early days of the formation of a voluntary organisation the founding group of users and carers is usually left alone by the professional services to see whether they can make anything happen. It is when a potentially valuable

resource is created that the invaders move in. Their strategy is to get onto the Steering Committee, formerly the interest group, and assume all the powerful positions for themselves without needing any democratic process of election. They are giving you professional support, for which you are expected to be grateful. Everything then follows in logical progression from that main act of invasion. It is not long before you have the low-paid, low-grade social services employee in post, bossing about the volunteers and oppressing the users. A day centre will inevitably follow with its identical orange plastic chairs that you stick to in hot weather and which inflict agony upon the arthritic since they are all of a uniform lowness. You will get your office with its secret files from which users are banned and you will suffer dehydration since your cups of tea will be rationed, even though medication is known to make you thirsty. The Community Psychiatric Nurses will move in with their injections and you will have in the community a mental hospital in all but name. The professionals will get their hands on your charity number and thus obtain access to sources of funding not otherwise available to statutory bodies. It is therefore in those very early days that one must get it established in the Constitution that professionals are banned.

Constitutions can only be changed legally by a majority vote of members at a general meeting of the association. If you ban professionals from the beginning all your members will be users and carers and will have no motivation to vote for change to allow professional infiltration. It is, however, no good having separatist constitutions, if you cannot provide a service which is better than that offered by the mental health system. What then do users and carers want? Ask any user. They want a crisis house. many hate the mental hospitals. When one has been around in mental health for nearly forty years, one has spoken with a lot of people. They all say the same thing: 'When I started having problems I just needed a place to go to. I only ended up in the hospital because I could not get away from my situation.' Just listen and they will tell you. 'I needed a sanctuary. I needed a crisis house. I needed somewhere to go where I could sort out my problems in peace with some helpful people around to support me'. We say that the Wokingham Crisis House started in 1991. It didn't. It started in 1963 when I first experienced that emotion of having nowhere to run to in crisis. I fully believe that it was the strongest negative emotion I have ever experienced in my life. So you win but not without a fight. Our Vice President in disagreement with me some years ago said 'I am tired of being dominated by one person's ideas. You are a dominating, overpowering woman!' to which I replied, 'They always are, the ones that defy the system!' And then we, the best of friends, started rolling around with laughter. It is true. Shy little flowers in hedge and dyke that hide themselves away are there to make the world pretty, not to change the face of society and even less the face of psychiatry.

Mental hospitals and mental health system facilities

Certain things are just plain physically wrong with these and are easy to rectify. Mental hospitals are remote. The Wokingham MIND crisis house is in the heart of the community. System facilities are either dirty and depressing or cold and clinical. The crisis house is clean, warm, cosy and cheerful. One of our guests commented, 'This place has gone to such lengths to look normal that it has ended up looking abnormal'. I know what she meant. The environment that we have created is essentially a contrived environment, contrived to make users feel safe and to bemuse the authorities. 'It's just like home' they say. But actually the crisis house is not like a typical home at the end of the twentieth century. The crisis house is Victorian and the decor and furniture take one back to a gentler and less frantic age. It is like grandmother's house. It is old fashioned and solid. There is a lot of pretty china on display. There are crystal decanters with sherry and whisky on offer as well as tea. It is a nice comfortable club where you can put your feet up and read the paper, smoke your pipe and play cards. In the old mental hospitals patients have to share washing facilities but our sanctuary bedrooms have en-suite facilities. Our chests of drawers are lined with lavender scented paper and we use scented soap and Andrex tissues instead of the institutional stuff that one gets in system facilities. I have tried in the crisis house to provide something for every taste and this also results in a slightly contrived look because individual homes tend to look consistent whereas the crisis house covers a number of decades and tastes. We always iron the bed linen very carefully and, while not strictly necessary, users report it as being nice to have everything so perfect. While it is not a hospital, the crisis house is not a conventional home either. It is designed to improve mental health and people in mental distress need to feel *more* secure, *more* comfortable, *more* relaxed than the person who is not in a state of distress.

'To create a place like this you need someone who loves it' said a user years ago. I agree, but the obverse of that coin is that you also need someone who *hates* the mental health system. Not everything wrong with the system is physical and easy to correct. A crisis house must also eliminate hierarchy and oppression. Conventional mental health services are strictly hierarchical with the medics on top and the users at the bottom. Other mental health professionals fit in somewhere under the doctors and above the users and carers. *All* professionals are banned from the crisis house, so either a user or a carer is all one can be.

Running the house

Wokingham MIND is run by an elected executive committee of twelve people half of whom are users and half carers. I run the crisis house on a day-to-day basis but I have no power and my position on the committee is ex officio (as President) without a vote. The Committee can and has over-ruled me on occasions and has, for instance, ordered tightening up on political correctness particularly with regard to anti-racism and anti-sexism in the association. The crisis house has rules. So did all communities that were ever colonised. Our rules are not the same as the rules adopted by the professional services. They are rules which are important to and agreed by us. We have, for instance, no rule of confidentiality. This is the sacred cow of the medical profession adopted largely to enhance their power and to cover up their incompetence. Before you can persuade us to adopt it, you have to persuade us to value it. We do not value secrecy. We value openness.

Getting your hands on a house

All kinds of premises can be suitable for development as crisis houses (Jenkinson 1995). Each group of survivors needs to take any local opportunity offered. Once Wokingham MIND was formed, it was not long before we heard rumours that the local mental health team, housed at Station House, would be moving out to a new unit at the hospital and that MIND would be offered Station House as a base. I have no doubt at this stage in the proceedings that the local psychiatric establishment had its own agenda for our future development very much on the lines I have described. But before we took over the house we had already established a drop-in and thus a core group of crisis workers and befrienders, so that as soon as we got the keys to Station House in April 1991 we were ready to set up the crisis house immediately.

Bureaucrats are inefficient. We had been going for three months before an indignant social worker from the local mental health team came down to see us, hoping to overturn our work. He told me that I was stupid to think that I could run a crisis house without professional support. Crisis intervention, he claimed, is a very highly skilled area of work. He was the perfect example of the colonising professional, thinking that he knew better than the volunteer. What also struck me was that he was genuinely worried. He had internalised colonisation into a belief that survivors, the naked savages, should not be let loose on society. 'You will have suicides', he said. 'You will be accused of sexual abuse. The hospitals will dump people on you and you will not be able to cope. You are trying to run this place with no professional support at all'. This social worker held the view that 'professional' equals 'magic'.

But there is no magic in mental health. Crisis intervention is not a highly skilled area of work. The only thing that medical professionals can do that we cannot, is prescribe drugs, and non-medical professionals have nothing at their disposal that we do not have. Being a mental health professional is not a skill like being a plumber or being a dentist. Instead it is about participating in a system and keeping the system going. It is composed of going to meetings and whispering secrets, of writing reports and keeping files intact, of seeing the relevant number of people on the relevant day. I have no doubt that there are nice people as well as nasty ones working in the mental health system, but these nice people are tied up in it. They are not allowed to respond spontaneously to their 'clients' or to free those 'clients', from the chains of oppression. By contrast, we, being ordinary members of the community, are free to identify the needs of our fellow human beings and to do all within our power to meet those needs and to help them to enjoy happier and more fulfilling lives.

This professional view of survivors as being stupid and incompetent is a necessary part of the mental health system. The system is founded upon a false concept and everything that it does emanates from this preposterous falsity. The concept is that you have two groups of people – the sane and the insane. Psychiatric reports also emphasise success and failure in terms of the employed and the unemployed, the married and the unmarried, the educated and the uneducated, the qualified and the unqualified, the straight and the gay, the white and the black, the well and the sick, the important and the unimportant, and so, ultimately, the powerful and the powerless.

Wokingham MIND is radical because it debunks this concept. Instead we see each individual as a unique individual with a mixture of strengths and weaknesses but all people are seen as being of equal value.

The rules

Our rules are: no abuse of alcohol, no abuse of drugs, no violence, no stealing, no abuse of the premises, no smoking except in the smoking room, no sexual harassment, no racial harassment, no disturbing the peaceful enjoyment of others, no intervention by professionals without the permission of the MIND Executive Committee.

Attempted assaults on our autonomy from outside have been quite naive. There was, for instance, the Consultant Psychiatrist who tried to undermine our crisis house by criticising our lack of confidentiality. He thought he was God, but I thought that he was an idiot, not least by failing to see what we were about. Our role is not professional. We are *community* care and the community is not confidential. It is based upon Mrs Smith meeting Mrs Jones in the High Street and telling her that Mr Brown has had a fall and needs someone to get his shopping. It is dependent upon everyone knowing how everyone else is. The mental health system is quite naively authoritarian and this particular psychiatrist, unrealistically dictatorial. They say that we freak out! Fancy thinking that, just because you have studied medical science and have an employed position in the National Health Service paid from public funds, you can dictate the activities of ordinary members of the community who are involved in charitable work and, as such, are unpaid, and not under your auspices. Talk about having fixed false beliefs. This shrink was surprised to see us defend our territory and to see that we did not share his opinions nor hold him in awe. A lot of psychiatry is rubbish. So is a lot of social work. What *we* believe in is self-help and taking responsibility for one's own life.

Drugs

Not everyone in the crisis house is in sweet and harmonious agreement and it would be a very unhealthy and inhuman place if they were. Some members believe that one can differentiate between the nice clean drugs that the doctor gives you and the nasty dirty drugs that you buy on the street – approving of the former and disapproving of the latter. After forty years in mental health ,seeing numerous individuals who could otherwise have led quality lives spending them instead doped up to the eyeballs and waiting in vain for the mental health system to solve their problems, I do not agree with this position. The only person who is going to sort out an individual's life is the person him or herself with support from friends. Drugs from the doctor may help as a crutch but they are not a cure for mental or existential problems. When it comes to recreational drugs, then alcohol and nicotine are every bit as much drugs as are cannabis, cocaine, morphine and amphetamine. Which of them any individual prefers is a matter of indifference to me and I am not concerned if our members use them provided that their resultant behaviour does not distress other people. This is where the professional's position is so different from the survivor's. The professional feels an obligation to intervene in the behaviour of others. I do not. The MIND Executive Committee over-rule me on this issue with a corporate view that my attitude is too permissive and that illegal substances must not be used in the crisis house. The issue raises its head regularly since I fail consistently to intervene if anyone is using drugs but not bothering other people.

Drugs procedures

The crisis house has procedures about the drugs prescribed to guests staying with us. A majority of guests have prescribed drugs and administer their own unless they are in absolute crisis with confusion or suicidal feelings. Guests in absolute crisis have a MIND crisis worker staying overnight with them and this person assumes responsibility for the guest's drugs until the immediate crisis is resolved. It is a credit to Wokingham MIND that in all our years of existence, having accommodated about one hundred and fifty people in crisis, we have never had a suicide, an overdose, any self-harm, any violence or any other seriously untoward incident on our premises.

Because the crisis house is a self-help facility and has no authority figures, individual guests may take or not take prescribed drugs as they choose. Apart from the interventions described on behalf of the suicidal, we do not intervene with guests, unless invited. If requested, we would provide an individual wishing to reduce or come off psychiatric drugs with literature and support for the process, but no pressure is put upon any individual to do this. We do not take an ideological stand, either pro or anti psychiatric drugs, but leave individuals to make their own decisions about what they wish to do in this as in all other areas. We have an excellent mental health library of two hundred and fifty books, tapes and videos. This is run by a user. The library includes all MIND' s own publications on psychiatric drugs, books on drug withdrawal, research papers and books by protagonists such as Dr Peter Breggin (1991) which argue against the use of drugs in all circumstances. We aim to provide users and carers with up-to-date information so that they can make informed decisions.

So if you have banned professionals and have no paid workers who are all these people who act as befrienders, crisis workers and drivers and form the committee that runs MIND? The answer is that they are users and carers who use our services. Some have been with us from the beginning and others are new to our crisis house. Do you have problems if you get a user or carer who is also a professional? The answer is 'Yes!' and it keeps one on one's toes because such people could become 'the enemy within'. You have to be very firm that you will *never* work their way; you are not even trying to. You can't ban them because they need you so you just fail to do what they expect – forever.

Guests' experiences of the system

Even users who are also professionals do not have good experiences of the mental health system. They don't think that the system is good; they just don't have the confidence to defy it. Users who are not professionals think that it is crap. Take current guests, Janey and Rob, as examples. Rob was referred to us in absolute crisis after taking a very severe overdose that nearly killed him. He suffered severe depression and dependence upon alcohol when he lost his job due to poor physical health and was then rejected by his wife. Rob was referred to the local system-run day centre for the mentally ill and was admitted to the mental hospital frequently when he overdosed. None of these facilities benefited him because they did not address his fundamental problems. At the day centre he met Janey and started to form a relationship. Janey had been sexually and physically abused all her life and, most recently, in her marriage. The mental health system treated her anxiety and depression with drugs and did nothing to ameliorate her condition because she was still living in the abusive situation. When Rob was admitted to the crisis house, Janey asked to stay with him and we agreed immediately because our guests are free to have staying with them anyone of their choice.

The mental health system doesn't want people to return to normality because this threatens both their livelihood and their superior status. Allowing Rob and Janey to stay together caused quite a fluttering in the dovecotes. Professionals are non judgmental and objective, until such a situation actually occurs, then objectivity goes out of the window and threat to self flies in.

In the crisis house Rob and Janey are *working* on their problems and planning a future. The system was no good to them because it treated unhappiness as an illness and left them trapped in unliveable situations. The crisis house offers stepping stones to a new life because it provides guests with the time and the space to consider past mistakes and to move on to a new life in which such mistakes are avoided.

Pete's experience also illustrates the system's desire to keep people sick. Pete came to us in 1990, referred by a psychiatrist. He suffered from anxiety and agoraphobia. He had attended a therapeutic community and a day hospital, to no effect. He told me that he was bisexual, but I did not believe him. Pete was not bisexual, he was a homosexual who had been forced to be what the system calls 'normal' and had, as a result, become 'ill'.

For years I made no attempt to intervene in Pete's situation because he did not ask me to. Our policy is non-interventionist. When he asked for help, I gave it to him. Pete at that time was living with his ageing parents who did not like his homosexuality and kept it firmly under control. He occupied a tiny bedroom with a little two-foot-six bed – suitable for a child of ten! I put Pete in touch with a gay socialising group to help him find a partner. His new partner also lived within restrictions, but this time within the mental health system itself. He lived in an 'aftercare' hostel whose residents occupied single rooms equipped with a single bed, no en-suite facilities, no facilities for making drinks for guests, and everything designed to deter them from forming relationships and getting back to normal. 'They want to keep us sick' was the comment they made. Pete and Ken were guests in our double sanctuary until I found them a council flat where they could live together in a proper relationship. In due course we celebrated their wedding. A happier couple would be hard to find.

Some system services are so awful that 'outrageous' is the only term one can apply to them. Another gay man we helped also attended the local day hospital for the mentally ill. This thirty four-year-old man joined a group to help with his manic depression. The nurse in charge said, 'Today I am going to play some music and you can choose to be fairies, giants or wizards. When the music stops, fairies become giants and giants become wizards'. This man chose to be a fairy, flew away and never returned.

Community care

When community care is reclaimed from professional colonisation by a radical separatist mental health association, then it becomes like an extended family. Such families were once common in our culture and still are in some ethnic minorities. In an extended family there are always plenty of people about. There is always an auntie to mind the baby, an uncle to do odd jobs, a young man with a car to give you a lift to hospital, someone who will bake you a cake, someone who will style your hair, etc. Everyone is interdependent. But the level of emotion in it all is generally less intense than that in a nuclear family. This is why extended families like the Wokingham crisis house are so successful in providing care for people in distress. Many mental health problems are connected with the high level of emotion that prevails in nuclear families and also with the restricted space in such homes. Look at Pete, for instance, crushed up in his two foot six bed in a broom cupboard wasting his life in lonely frustration in order not to cause embarrassment to his ageing parents.

Terry, an eighteen-year-old, came to us in crisis because his abuse of drugs and alcohol had become intolerable to his family. It transpired that he lived with his mother, her new partner, and five of her six children, age ranges six to twenty, in a little three-bedroom house. No wonder there was friction. My partner and I occupy a house, which has four bedrooms, and three bathrooms just for the two of us. We do not consider it to be over large. The idea that one can place an eighteen-year-old in a little bedroom with a ten-year-old and an eight-year-old and expect healthy development to take place is madness. People need space, privacy, the opportunity to express personality, the opportunity to conduct a sexual relationship, the opportunity to have people around them and also to be on their own when they want to. The Wokingham crisis house is designed to provide all this and when one does not provide it, one gets mental ill health.

Another example is Ryan. To his family, Ryan, a man with a diagnosis of schizophrenia, presents a huge problem. When he tries living with his sisters who have children his behaviour makes for difficulties. Ryan needs a neutral ambience. Staying in one of our sanctuaries he can stare into space if he wants to, wander around if he wants to, and we are not in the least bothered.

It occurs to me that the mental health system either isolates people in lonely flats or crushes them up in high expressed emotion families or overcrowded hospital wards and hostels. How about the idea of giving people both space *and* company? The same is true of privacy. In our local mental hospital women have to walk through the male patients' toilets to get to the showers. Surely it is obvious that male and female patients should have separate and private facilities. The Consultant Psychiatrist who tried to undermine our crisis house did not know that from time to time I visit his hospital. 'Instead of interfering with us', I told him, 'get something done about your hospital. On my last visit I walked through a ward and was concerned to see a naked female patient sitting up in bed with the curtains hanging in tatters about her and no nurse to be seen!'

He thought 'Of all the gin joints, in all the towns, in all the world she walked into mine!' The fundamental things apply. If they are the professional experts and we the bungling amateurs then why are *our* services so much better than *their*?

Top Ten Tips for setting up a crisis house

1 Ban professionals not only from your association but *legally* in its Constitution so that not only can they not get in, but that they can *never* get in. If you don't do this you won't get a crisis house, you will get a hospital masquerading as one.
2 Get together a group of survivors and carers who have a long term commitment to mental health. Establish a drop-in so that when you get your crisis house you have the people power to get going immediately, before the local mental health system has a chance to realise what you are doing.
3 By hook or by crook get your hands on a house. Every community presents the opportunity. You have to take your chance when it comes.
4 Make the house beautiful. It is no good being radical and separatist if you end up providing the same crap that the system provides.
5 Establish some sensible house rules, which will eliminate all anti social behaviour, and see that these are applied rigorously.
6 Avoid all contact with the local mental health system. Never go to their meetings and do not respond to their offers of help or involvement. You are much more difficult to control if you are not there.
7 Get a good relationship with the local community including its elected representatives; councillors, MPs etc. The mental health system can then seethe with rage but they cannot close you down.
8 Be very careful when accepting guests into the crisis house. If an individual is far too violent to be there, you won't do the person

any good and you will also undermine the project.

9 Keep a drop-in going at the crisis house so that you always have to hand a group of sympathetic people who can help guests in crisis in any way necessary.

10 Win all the prizes! Once you have seven national awards as we have, I don't say you are safe – you are never that, but the system will have a job to demonstrate that you are ineffective or incompetent.

References

Breggin, P., (1991) *Toxic Psychiatry.* New York: St Martin's Press

Chamberlin, J., (1988) *On Our Own.* London: MIND Publications

Jenkinson, P., (1995) Setting up a sanctuary. *Changes: An International Journal of Psychology and Psychotherapy, 13,* 2, 139–44

CHAPTER 15

Promoting community resources

JANET BOSTOCK, VALERIE NOBLE AND RACHEL WINTER

CONVENTIONAL NHS mental health services are likely to offer medication, individual or group support, some opportunities for therapy, social services and, occasionally, specialist advice on welfare rights and employment/training. It is usually assumed that taking prescribed medication is well-advised, and that talking about problems with a professional is helpful. Services tend to be separated between social, psychiatric or mental health, and physical health. In our experience, NHS agencies offering formal psychotherapy suggest that their services are not suitable for people in socially unstable situations. Informal supportive counselling is offered to some people who are given a psychiatric diagnosis and considered to warrant the involvement of mental health teams.

Despite the academic, medical culture which pervades training in the mental health professions, a neutral, scientific or objective stance on the understanding of people's mental health needs is an elusive notion. Much of the literature on mental health and psychotherapeutic approaches will assume the authors' disinterest in the defining of what may or may not help people. Yet all the professional approaches to the 'treatment' or resolution of psychological suffering are inevitably steeped in their own dedication to safeguard their professional place and to survive economically. Thus all psychiatric and psychotherapeutic approaches to mental health services have interests which are wider than those of the people who use the services as clients. These interests may or may not be congruent.

The acknowledgement of our self-interest as professionals is hopefully a first step in developing a reflexive, critical, and open-minded approach to helping people overcome their difficulties, and to ensure that our needs do not interfere with those of our clients. Clinical psychologists, for example, often have intellectual and status interests (and perhaps some have a yearning to count and measure!) that are well-served by their professional practice. Some also appear to have medical affiliations which mean that much mainstream conceptualisation of psychological distress is influenced by diagnostic categories and randomised controlled trial methodology that can seem remote from people's actual, everyday experiences.

We can, for instance, read about 'agoraphobic women' in a way that focuses on symptom measures and treatment techniques. These accounts do not give an impression of why these women are fearful of certain public places, why many of them do not complete the treatment offered to them, the details of their current circumstances, or what distinguishes those who make greater progress. (Hutchings et al, 1997). Yet such factors as the quality of close relationships (Dalgard et al, 1996), histories of domestic violence, and the financial viability of a woman's independence are empirically and experientially known to be vital (Sanford and Donovan, 1993).

While counselling is often highly conscious of issues of political identity such as race, there is a tendency for these to be diminished to micro-environmental influences on the therapeutic relationship, rather than added into broad socially sensitive formulations to inform ideas for interventions. Relationships are clearly important sources of understanding, support or pain. But a multi-faceted approach to mental health needs to consider the impact of wider environmental factors such as the safety of a neighbourhood and opportunities for education on a person's past and current functioning.

A psychologist, counsellor or therapist usually has some particular theoretical orientation about understanding the causes of emotional distress and ways of resolving these, but the manner in which this knowledge is shared is important. For instance, a traditional Rogerian approach of minimal prompts from the therapist may be quite alien and mystifying to some people. Many schools of counselling and psychotherapy advocate an adherence to a particular model of therapy, and to match clients' attributes to the array of approaches available, rather than adapting a therapeutic approach according to the style and preferences of the client.

Another assumption of talking treatments is that talking or disclosure, emotional expression, and a therapeutic relationship are fundamentally helpful. Long-term counselling is often uncritically considered well-advised for people with complex or long histories of distress, without an understanding of how the scope for relief from psychological suffering is contingent on the person's recourse to a congenial environment.

Counselling or clinical psychology perspectives frequently seem to describe experiences of depression or anxiety in politically neutral ways. These socially void accounts do not lend themselves to preventative approaches, and leave unanswered the challenge of how mental health workers can contribute to the development of social organisations and material conditions which enable people to feel psychologically and physically strong.

Traditionally, mental health services offer approaches that include several single-model orientations. These usually emphasise intrapsychic explanations of psychological distress. Such services tend to be developed as reactive to other NHS professionals like general practitioners via their judgements and individual clients' expressed needs or demands. Links are generally not made with unmet need, or with groups or communites seen to be at risk, or to potential service users directly. Services are directed towards individuals identified within a medical system and often provided in mental health or health service settings. Direct, professionally delivered, individual or group therapy are regarded as priorities.

What do people need?
People often give different reasons for their health problems to health professionals, favouring environmental factors rather than those which are individual and lifestyle related (Dun, 1989). When people describe what they need for their good health, they are likely to mention aspects of life such as clean air, the quality of their physical environment, employment and financial security (Research Unit in Health and Behavioural Change, 1989). In a local survey undertaken by professionals and local residents in the area we work in Nottingham, people commonly mentioned dogs' mess, dangerous traffic, rubbish on the streets, feeling unsafe to go out at night, dirt and pollution and fear of crime as affecting their health or causing them stress, (Bostock and Beck, 1993). A similar impression emerged from a Bradford community action project report where people described litter, pollution and traffic, poorly maintained, damp, and overcrowded housing as reasons for ill health (West Bowling Community Health Action Project, 1997).

Companionship and support from friends are also likely to be highly valued for emotional well-being. Occupational psychology findings (Warr, 1987) suggest that for enhanced psychological functioning people require: financial stability; a degree of control in their lives; some social status; an element of predictability and stability; physical safety; some diversity of interests; opportunities for the development of their talents, for socialising, and some publicly defined purposes.

There is also an impression from epidemiological studies that relative income distribution is linked with health (Wilkinson, 1996). For instance, Dahl (1994) recently reported that a representative group of employed Norwegians experienced more ill-health if they were from unskilled, low-paid occupations. There are inevitably psychological consequences to suffering physical health problems and a highly influential social and political context which pervades people's physical and psychological experiences. This realisation of the impact of social and economic phenomena is becoming more apparent in current government policies for a 'healthier nation'. The challenge is to ensure that funding is provided for integrated health, education, environmental, employment and economic interventions.

Those most at risk of psychological difficulties are widowed, divorced/separated, unemployed people, carers, people with physical disabilities, and people from lower social class groups (Hagan and Green, 1994). Given that people's needs are often material and social, how can we promote appropriate resources to meet these or to prevent them becoming incapacitating?

A number of us working in the Sneinton and St Ann's areas in inner-city Nottingham became concerned by the fact that many people's mental health problems were precipitated or prolonged by social and financial problems. Local enquiries (Corrie, 1992) indicated that many users of a GP practice wanted counselling, and accessible, practical help. Many seemed in circumstances that were too unstable to enable their use of formal referral routes, or they were keen not to be identified as psychiatric cases, and they were in danger of being recommended to voluntary agencies without ensuring that their expressed needs were actually met.

What can mental health professionals offer?

Mental health professionals can offer indirect and direct services to communities and individuals through: (1) Engagement with communities to develop strategies for the prevention of psychological distress; and (2) Information, support, and enabling the use of community and professional resources.

Engagement with communities to develop strategies for the prevention of psychological distress

Communities may be defined geographically, they may exist in relation to an institution (such as a school), a shared cause (such as lobbying for a playground), or a shared identity (such as age, race, culture or history). Local communities vary hugely, and the nature of a mental health professional's engagement will be influenced by their own strengths and definition of priorities, in interaction with the resources and needs of the people they meet.

For example, in Nottingham a community psychology role was encouraged for the clinical psychologist by an open and well-organised forum of local residents and professionals. They initiated an action research approach to ascertain what affected people's health or caused them stress. This provided a means of meeting local residents and collaborating with them and others such as community development workers, health visitors, GPs, a primary care health needs assessor, and a programme for promoting college courses. Different groups developed, some of which began by lobbying (e.g. for a playgroup and play area) and then provided accessible and direct voluntary support. This was backed up in varying degrees by health and community workers and their access to funds. Local people initiated a community survey about their priorities from their primary care services. This had constructive results in disseminating information about their impressions of local health services, in enabling them to experience their views being acted upon, and in helping to improve provision. For example, there is a now a nursery nurse based at a health centre who provides high quality childcare in a crèche as well as invaluable informal support. Support for mental health has become integral to other initiatives and close co-operation has had highly tangible and practical results.

As professionals based in a community we can become active participants, both contributing to, and learning from, the constituencies who support us and, ultimately, employ us. The Forum in the area we work has provided a quite informal structure outside of local government, statutory or professional organisations, which has been relatively free of bureaucracy and extraordinarily rich in good-will. It provides information about activities in the area which can be shared with people outside the Forum. It also alerts us to pertinent issues such as areas of particular kinds of crime and the policing response. This can have important repercussions in individual therapeutic work in building up an understanding of the strengths and difficulties in an area, and placing people's individual complaints into a context that may help them to feel less alone.

Engaging the continued involvement of more service users as well as providers in the work of the Forum remains a challenging task that needs ongoing imaginative efforts and active support. While a compromise, it is possible for mental health professionals to be advocates, to try to represent people's interests on the basis of the accounts they give of their lives. Thus private concerns can be validated in a public domain and may influence the actions and policies of service providers. For example, a woman seen for individual sessions of therapy described how ill at ease she felt because of the burnt out car left on the road near her house, which contributed to a sense of neglect and was an actual hazard to local children. The discussion of this at the Forum revealed a lack of communication between the police and the local authority which prompted an effective response.

Creating environments that are more conducive to people's psychological and physical functioning can be informed by our knowledge as mental health professionals, and by encouraging the participation of people we see in the course of our individual work. Recently the views of health service users as well as nearby residents and schools have been deliberately sought in consultations about the future use of a disused leisure centre. Thus a community regeneration project is attempting to recognise the importance of social aspects of the development of local facilities, in conjunction with proposed economic, employment and physical improvements.

Information, support, and enabling the use and development of community and professional resources

As mental health professionals we can work with users and providers of health and social services and voluntary agencies directly and indirectly. The community orientated work described above was instrumental in the development of ACTIONS which began as a pilot in 1994. ACTIONS is an example of direct support, advice and community counselling that aims to be informal, accessible, practical, educative, advice orientated, and local to the communities of Sneinton and St Ann's in Nottingham. It involves a part-time co-ordinator, three part-time welfare rights workers, and two part-time community counsellors. Most of the workers live or have lived in the area, and are highly committed to the people who live there. ACTIONS is directed by a steering group which includes representation from general practice, clinical psychology, social services, the Community Health Council, Community NHS Trust management and the staff themselves.

Both services (welfare rights and counselling) are well used and see high numbers of people. Welfare rights offered 975 consultations last year, and 70% of these people were disabled. Enquiries were mainly about disability benefits, housing benefits, housing conditions/transfers and income support. The counsellors saw 316 people usually for between one and three sessions, within one to three weeks of asking, and with diverse experiences such as assault, employment problems, breakdown in relationships, and histories of abuse. The majority of those seen were working part-time, unemployed or on long-term sickness benefit. Occasionally, referral to statutory services or the clinical psychology service is suggested. Usually self-help literature is provided and discussed, self-help or voluntary support/counselling organisations and other advice agencies are recommended. The counsellors always encourage people to ask for further clarification or to come back if they think it would be useful or if a particular recommendation or agency is not helpful. People are encouraged (often by their GP) to initiate their own first appointment with ACTIONS via health centre receptions and they may return if they wish to follow-up their appointment. There is an understanding that frequent, ongoing contact with ACTIONS is not available, and continuous demand for the service by the same people has not been a problem.

In their individual contacts with people, the community counsellors usually encourage people to talk to them about their prevailing resources and vulnerabilities. These may be physical, practical, psychological or social. They then consider these issues with the person they are seeing and offer advice and emotional support that might be helpful in the short-term. For example: recommendations for improved sleep; ideas about controlling anxious feelings; how to contact the housing department effectively; where to find employment advice if you have a criminal record; information about how bereavement can affect people; voluntary agencies that might be relevant (such as the victim support scheme, the Council for Voluntary Service); training or educational establishments and specific courses; statutory agencies (such as the alcohol and drugs team, the clinical psychology service); and contacts for many self-help groups (such as the hysterectomy self-help group, the deaf children's society parents' group, and the Nottingham tinnitus group). Close liaison with the person's GP may be required in advising on referral in some situations. Occasionally the counsellors help individuals by making contact with organisations on their behalf, by providing supportive letters, or by helping people to understand correspondence from statutory agencies.

Both counsellors have organised and facilitated support groups that have arisen from the identification of common needs among particular individuals. For example, one group was run with a trainee clinical psychologist and offered stress management to eight local people with a focus on providing information and helping them to support each other. Some highly supportive friendships were formed, and the group helped people to gain control over stressful situations, and to feel less isolated and worried about the idiosyncrasy of their experiences. In another locality the community counsellor suggested to five very reserved women she met through ACTIONS, that they might be interested in meeting each other to offer mutual support. Four of them met regularly with the counsellor for low-key support which they continued after she left the group to be self-sustaining. When the counsellor met them three months later, they had established strong friendships in two pairs.

The community counselling (Lewis and Lewis, 1989) in ACTIONS is linked closely with welfare rights, primary care health services, and clinical psychology. It aims to offer advice and support to people who may not wish to use more formal clinical psychology or psychiatric services or to disclose their concerns to their GP. Many of them are significantly troubled and ACTIONS offers a highly visible, directly accessible, source of advice and support, largely to people who currently do not have the capacity to search for other appropriate sources of help because of their challenging social circumstances. It is often available for people who are in crisis and request an appointment within a few days, but it does not operate an emergency service. People who seem at considerable risk of suicide or self-harm are aware that referral to statutory services will be made.

We make several assumptions:
• Services and therapeutic approaches need to strive to respond and adapt to different people's needs rather than select people to fit with what is on offer.
• People's distress is usually caused by a number of reasons, often social, past and/or present.

- The impact of social power is pervasive and potent and affects many aspects of life, such as opportunities for intimacy, access to practical help, self-confidence, education, physical stamina, stability of income, housing, and contact with institutions like the Department of Social Security.
- Talking or disclosure is not inevitably a cure and a person's responsiveness to counselling or mental health advice is contingent upon certain past and present conditions such as physical and sexual safety and supportive friendships.
- There are inevitable inequalities in power between providers and users of services and there are useful mutual support groups and resources which may be preferable to long-term counselling.
- Community counselling and mental health advice aims to be flexible, responsive, informal and to maximise people's actual control over their personal or wider circumstances.

Last year 45 people who used the ACTIONS counselling and welfare rights service over a two week period were asked their views of their services. They were consistently positive, particularly about being able to gain expert advice easily, and they mentioned the high quality of help they received. 37 referrers responded to questionnaires about their impressions of ACTIONS and described the benefits as: people were better informed with up-to-date expertise; services were quick and relatively easy to access; and ACTIONS eased their workloads.

In meeting different people who say they need counselling help, we have found that particular techniques or brand name therapeutic approaches are less relevant than a socially sensitive psychological approach. This sees facilitation of people's actual control of their physical health and their circumstances as central. We secured funding and credibility as a result of being located in NHS primary care, initially with a particularly responsive and innovative primary care team. This confers many organisational benefits and some disadvantages, but we have striven to listen as closely as we can to people's expressed wishes, in order to be accessible, flexible, useful and accountable for what we say. The work has been stimulating, varied and challenging, an enriching learning experience for us. It has felt particularly worthwhile to help marginalised people to gain access to attentive, careful counselling which is not so directly available in many conventional NHS services locally.

Conclusion

We maintain that an understanding of psychological well-being and distress is enlightened by a social and material analysis of peoples' situations and resources. Experiences of psychological suffering may often be meaningfully linked with situations of powerlessness. Exclusively psychiatric, narrowly psychological or psychotherapeutic approaches obscure the reality of peoples' needs and potentials. Socio-psychological thinking may influence the nature of psychological contributions with individuals, communities and wider society, so that mental health professionals and other services may work in socially relevant ways. The further development of such community resourcing should be entirely consistent with the philosophy and implementation of the present health agenda.

Acknowledgements

There are many lessons to learn from the resilience and experiences of the people who have used and helped to develop the services we discuss. We would like to thank them. Also we thank our ACTIONS colleagues Angela Tierney, Lisa Warren, Muna Zafar and Rebecca Blackman. Finally we would like to express our appreciation to the ACTIONS Steering group and to Michael Varnam for his indefatigable commitment and support.

References

Bostock, J. and Beck, D. (1993) Participating in Public Enquiry and Action, *Journal of Community and Applied Social Psycholgy, 3,* 213–24

Corrie, P.J. (1992) *People's views on health in their locality. G.P. Practice based health needs assessment, Nottingham*

Dahl, E. (1994) Social inequalities in ill-health: the significance of occupational status, education and income – results from a Norwegian survey. *Sociology of Health and Illness, 16,* 5, 644–67

Dalgard, O.S., Soensent, T., Sandanger, I. and Brevik, J. I. (1996) Psychiatric Interventions for Prevention of Mental Disorders: A psychosocial perspective. *International Journal of Technology Assessment in Healthcare, 12,* 604–17

Dun, R. (1989) *Pictures of Health? A report of a community health survey carried out in Clapham, South London.* London: West Lambeth Health Authority Community Unit

Hagan, T. and Green, J. (1994) *Mental Health Needs Assessment: The user perspective,* Wakefield: Dept. of Public Health

Hutchings, J., Midence, K. and Nash, S. (1997) Assessing Social Isolation Among Mothers of Conduct Problem Children: Preliminary findings from the Community Contacts Questionnaire. *Clinical Psychology Forum, 108,* 24–7

Lewis, J., and Lewis, M. (1989) *Community Counselling*, New York: Brooks/ Cole Publishing

Research Unit in Health and Behavioural Change (1989) *Changing the Public Health.* Chichester: Wiley

Sanford, L.T., and Donovan, M.E. (1993) *Women and Self-Esteem.* Harmondsworth: Penguin

Warr, P. (1987) *Work, Unemployment and Mental Health.* Oxford: Clarendon

West Bowling Community Health Action Project (1997) *Speaking Out.* Bradford: WBCHAP

Wilkinson, R.G. (1996) *Unhealthy Societies: The afflictions of inequality.* London: Routledge

CHAPTER 16

The role of education in the lives of people with mental health difficulties

TRACEY AUSTIN

Adult education provision exists throughout the continuum of mental health care and aftercare from psychiatric hospitals to community care settings – although often no direct reference is made to the word education. (Bee and Martin, 1997, p.129)

THIS CHAPTER HAS two main aims. Primarily it is a personal account of the role I believe education can play in a person's life, when mental health difficulties have been or are an issue. However, based upon my experience of working in a further education environment as a lecturer with special responsibility for learners with mental health difficulties, and as a member of national forums, (Skill Mental Health Working Party, Steering Committee National Institute of Adult and Continuing Education and Further Education Development Agency Research) it also gives a national overview of educational provision for learners with mental health difficulties. The following material will not be a comprehensive record, but it does pull together many of the strands which run through educational provision in Britain, with particular reference to the issues which underpin current thinking around good practice, curriculum design and partnerships.

My return to education

Like many of the students with whom I work, I returned to college after a long absence from education. I had been through a variety of life changes and felt I had very little that was of use to offer the world. I hesitated before I took what felt like an enormous step into the world of adult learning. It was not without turmoil. Internal and external pressures became seemingly insurmountable every time an essay was due in, or the money ran out, or a relationship ended, but it was also a time of change, confidence building, exploration and a sense of becoming 'myself'. For many of my fellow students, college had been a long held, unclaimed idea and having got there the pressures sometimes became too much. But we were lucky; the college offered support in the guise of counselling, sensitive tutors, student support groups and the chance to 'drop out' and resume the following year. The educational journey was made as easy as possible for us. For many reasons we had missed our first chance. Mental health difficulties (in their broadest, holistic sense) could have prevented the realisation of a second chance. I believed then, as I do now, that it was the college's approach to the student which enabled both myself and many of my colleagues to progress onto university, work or return to our homes, slightly different for holding a certificate and having completed a course. At college it felt absolutely OK to be apprehensive, anxious, under-confident, shy, angry and all of those other human conditions which afflict us, but which for many result in prevention from entering anything other than the mental health system.

After completing my course I got a job in a community mental health team. As a community mental health worker, prior to becoming a lecturer, I became increasingly committed to the idea that education could offer people who used mental health services a much more positive experience than sitting in a day centre five days a week. To support people in an environment which treated them as 'learner' not as a 'user' or 'patient' seemed to make perfect sense to me. Reflecting on my college experience, I could remember the overwhelming sense of achievement I felt on receipt of my first essay with affirmations of my ability to formulate an argument. I wanted other people to experience the same feeling, particularly those people with whom I worked, who were more than the sum of their psychiatric label. It is with hindsight that I can now see the errors I made in believing, at the time, that the curriculum of the local college would be accessible to people with mental health difficulties. The stigma relating to mental illness made it almost impossible for people to attend classes for fear of being 'found out'. As one student has written:

> Not only have I had to overcome my own personal barriers,
> but also those of people's attitudes and beliefs about

> *mental illness .... At times I have felt very isolated by my*
> *environment.* (Wertheimer, 1997, p.53)

This is not to lay blame entirely with the education system at the onset of community care the Department of Health also played a lead role in keeping education and mental health apart. A letter from the Department of Health in 1991 in response to The National Bureau of Students with Disabilities (Skill), stated the following:

> *Local health and family health service authorities are*
> *required from next April to produce community care plans*
> *addressing the needs for care services of the local*
> *population. These plans will not deal with further and adult*
> *education as this is not encompassed in the White Paper,*
> *Caring for people...... While I understand your view that*
> *further and adult education colleges could be said to*
> *provide some 'day services' in certain instances, the view*
> *that the DES and DH takes (is that it is) not appropriate to*
> *include them within the community care remit.* (Godding
> and Lavender, 1992, p.14)

This was a sad indication of the invisibility of many successful educational projects which were addressing the needs of people with mental health difficulties at the time. The idea that education could be inappropriate indicated an attitude that education was not, in fact, for all and certainly not for people who needed 'care'. Further, it assumed that people who go to college do not have mental health needs and those with mental health difficulties do not have educational needs. This attitude has been challenged. The work of both statutory and non-statutory mental health organisations, community education providers, education development agencies and individual commitment on the part of college staff has given rise to a much clearer understanding of 'the positive contribution which education can make to peoples mental health' (Wertheimer, 1997, p.10). To this end the Department of Health in its paper *Developing Partnerships in Mental Health* (1997) can now be given credit for the following statement:

> *Specialist mental health services...need to work closely*
> *with the agencies responsible for housing, income support,*
> *education, employment and training and leisure . . .*
> (Wertheimer, 1997, p.151)

In addition, recent Further Education Funding Council (FEFC)and Government reports (Tomlinson,1996; Kennedy 1997; Blunkett, 1998) have highlighted clearly the need for both inter-agency working and a greater effort on the part of further education and higher education colleges to become inclusive organisations: 'inclusion is about enhancing the capacity of all organisations and communities to include those at risk of marginalisation and exclusion and to thus affirm that everyone belongs' (Wertheimer, 1997, p.3). The organisations that I once thought might provide the chance for people to move from the status of 'patient' to 'student' now have a clear responsibility to do just that. It appears that now, some years after my own experience of college and my subsequent belief that education and mental health are natural partners, those of us in the field can truly begin to action the maxim 'education for all'.

Adult education: staying the course

Having begun to address the basic issue of education being a valid option for people with mental health difficulties, there remain the issues of getting in and staying in. The doors may be opening but the ramps that are in place in many institutions may be inadequate for people who need psychological, rather than physical, support to step over the threshold: 'The mere thought of entering a large or busy college environment can be simply too much for some students. I have seen one student in tears at the thought of entering our building' (Wertheimer, 1997, p.99). It is easy to forget that mental health difficulties may not relate to an inability to learn, but to difficulties in perceiving the self as being able to learn, or belonging to a learning environment. The latter may not be a college, it could be a class in a community centre, but the feelings around it may be the same. As one student remarked to me prior to entering a class, 'I thought college was only for normal people'.

It has been essential that those of us involved in creating accessible educational provision listen to the stories that students tell us about their experience of college. It is only then that we can begin to ensure that we are not simply attempting to 'fill up' a person's day, but we are working with them towards reaching their potential. It is not enough to simply place somebody in a classroom and expect them to 'get on with it': a number of factors have to be considered. If learning becomes a negative experience then education can easily be placed on a person's failure list. The beliefs that an individual holds about themselves might then be reinforced by the education system's failure to ensure appropriate guidance, advice, support and suitable environments. There must be opportunities which allow 'for the influence of learners on the learning process, both content and structure' (Austin, 1998a p.7). The process of inquiry which we are encouraged to undertake with students can itself be an empowering experience. Professor John Tomlinson, in his report to the Further Education Funding Council, recommended that:

> *We move away from labelling the student and towards*
> *an appropriate educational environment; concentrate on*
> *understanding better how people learn so that they can*
> *be better helped to learn.* (Tomlinson, 1996, p. 4)

It is important that education 'does not replicate or reinforce any of the messages experienced by people with mental health difficulties', mainly those which render the individual helpless, hopeless or without status. A key theme in current practice is that education treats a person as a learner not as a psychiatric label. It is my experience that once we begin to move people away from the self description imposed by psychiatry, the label or diagnosis becomes significant only to those who impose it. When a person becomes a student they are no longer a passive receiver of help, but are willing members of an environment designed, in the main, to encourage self expression, social skills and employability. To undergo a process of learning, however that may manifest itself, is to acknowledge an ability to change from where we are today. Unfortunately, for many people the experience of mental health difficulties and consequent treatment has taught them only that they cannot change their illness status:

> *Psychiatric hospitals are full of under achievers. Prolonged*
> *exposure to a culture where learning is not made possible,*
> *and frequently not believed to be possible makes people*
> *think they cannot learn.* (Bee and Martin, 1997, p.128)

People may also recall their previous education believing, for example, that their inability to achieve exam results renders them 'unintelligent'. It may be that a person has gone to university only to discover the stresses associated with higher education were too much. Whatever the level, a diagnosis of 'mental illness' should not render the person invalid or stupid: we should not be saying that a diagnosis of schizophrenia automatically disables learning. My work with students who have mental health needs constantly reaffirms my belief that psychiatry is a structure which serves only to contain people's self-doubt and dependent patient identity, both internally and externally, rather than enabling them to regain their identity as people who can lead full and valid lives. I watch people enter the classroom for the first time, seeing them doubt their reasons for being or belonging there. But, with time, the uncomfortable associations or feelings they may have about education are soon dissipated, as they realise that the psychiatric history with which they may have entered this environment can be allowed to fade into the background; their relationships with people can be built on different foundations, and their sense of being valuable can be nurtured.

It would, however, be folly to imagine that all students, can leave hospital or the day centre and immediately engage in educational pursuits. There are a number of factors which need to be addressed before this can happen. Some preparation for people prior to vocational education is consistently identified by students as being essential for their journey into mainstream education. It is vital that the passage taken is provided with escape routes, rest stops and ports of call for advice and guidance.

Removing the fear that people experience when they commence education can be achieved through the following methods. The most important is to allow time for people to become accustomed to the college environment. This can involve: tutors introducing themselves to the learner some time before the start of the course, for example whilst a person is still in hospital (continuity of a known tutor has been identified as one of the most important features in retention of students), inviting people in to the college during the summer break when it is quiet and uncrowded, exploring in an informal interview some of the fears the person has, particular issues include large numbers of people in a class, exams, time keeping, writing essays, being in a young person's environment, cost and transport. The tutor will be able to reassure a student that these are concerns most people have, not just those who experience mental health difficulties. Many colleges now run preparation courses, many of which are vocation based, and students are encouraged to attend these in order to re-establish skills and learn management techniques for attending college. In Lancashire a consortium approach has been developed to include link workers who support students during the initial stages of a course. They also offer advice and support to tutors whose own concerns about mental health difficulties create barriers for other people. Colleges also now recognise the need for adequate welfare support and there are increasing hours given to staff for supporting students with additional needs, including mental health difficulties.

Many of the classes which are designed to involve people with mental health difficulties focus on confidence building, assertiveness, anxiety management and other life management skills. Students are given the opportunity to develop study skills, such as note taking, organisation of information, using the library, information technology skills including use of the Internet, being involved with group projects, time management and literacy and numeracy skills. The current national focus on key skills (literacy, numeracy, I.T., communication skills and study skills) means many students now have access to extra tuition on a one-to-one or small group basis; for the student with mental health needs this is an added bonus. Students can also gain accreditation of these skills without being part of a mainstream class, taking away pressure encountered through examination whilst at the same time being able to gain recognition of the work they have done. Projects around the country, such as Dearne Valley College in South Yorkshire, have used creative writing classes to 'challenge the pattern of disempowerment which is rife amongst people with mental health difficulties' (Ruddock and Worrall, 1997 p. 1). In projects like these, learners are engaged with a creative medium which covers basic educational needs (literacy, structuring work, presenting information publicly, assessing personal work and making changes) whilst at the same time encouraging personal expression of opinion and group membership.

Education is now working towards becoming individually tailored. Following the Tomlinson report, and in common with community care, education now professes to meet individual needs. But unlike community care, many projects concerned with mental health within education deliver what they promise. Furthermore, within education, the person with mental health difficulties does not have to be just a silent participant; they are not part of a system which is designed to depress expression, but are actively encouraged to develop the ability to speak out. The identity of being a student gives people a new self description. It gives people a reason to believe that things can change. As one student explained: 'The whole experience of learning has keyed me up for the future . . . it's been like a personal revolution, it's been fantastic' (Wertheimer, 1997, p. xiii).

It appears that there are key themes which have to be in operation in order for participation in education to be successful. It is not enough to simply accommodate people with mental health difficulties in a college environment; there are far greater issues which need addressing. Education is not immune to the same problems which prevent full citizenship for people with mental health difficulties. Neither has it fully ironed out the difficulties around implementing the principles of full inclusivity and equal opportunities. The same things which affect people seeking employment following psychiatric admissions can be experienced within education – the full impact of which can result in exclusion on the grounds of other people's ignorance. Education does, however, address some of the more fundamental issues which affect people and their ability to determine the course of their life – issues which across the broad range of mental health services are often spoken about but not necessarily actioned. Empowerment is a word which has been over-used a great deal in the 'nineties. It is difficult to empower people within a structure designed to do just the opposite, but it is very easy to offer tokens which appear to be working towards that aim. The maintenance of a mental health day service rests entirely on the disempowerment of clients and their dependency on its free day trips, cheap meals and non-alcoholic pub type club culture. Education, it could be argued, offers an enormous threat to day services, since once involved in education, people's ability to question is awakened. The ability to 'focus on the oppressive aspects of their existence' (Ruddock and Worrall, 1997 p. 1) becomes possible through classes designed specifically to move people forward. Not necessarily to stop using those services, but to see them as only part of their lifestyle, rather than the whole of it. Projects, such as the Dearne Valley project, have at their hearts a fundamental belief in real empowerment, and work tirelessly towards that. Information is power. Qualifications are power. It is not in the interests of education to retain students for many years, since the whole aim is to learn in order to change. One of the keys to a successful course is the number of students who leave to do other things, not who come back the following term to repeat the same course. There is something exceptionally rewarding in knowing that a person who has spent several years sitting in a day centre, has enrolled onto a mainstream course following a 12 week confidence building course. It often occurs against the odds; against the belief of others.

Learning can offer real chances for empowerment and participation for people with mental health difficulties because the curriculum can offer the opportunity to take part in classes which really promote personal development. In the same way that mental health service users have been encouraged to participate in the design of statutory services, students are now invited to sit on advisory boards. They are encouraged to influence the design and delivery of the curriculum, and in some instances, deliver training to college staff. At Clarendon College in Nottingham, mental health awareness training is delivered by service users and providers working together. Users have also been involved in staff development sessions targeted at specific groups such as college reception staff. It is this type of work that illustrates the growing commitment of educationalists to the inclusion of students with mental health difficulties in further and higher education. Further, the reduction of stigma which can occur through such activities can permeate into the wider community, making other pathways possible. Whilst my personal experience as an adult learner may be shared only by those who attended the same college, the knowledge I gained from the approach of the organisation towards its students is now being shared with those people in charge of curriculum design. The curriculum, being the framework in which the essence of education is held, can make or break a person's educational pathway. It is the curriculum which holds the aims and objectives of the college, the plans and aspirations of its members and then, hidden beyond the pages of the prospectus, the attitudes and beliefs of that organisation which its members carry in their everyday life.

Conclusions
When I began to write this chapter I was reminded of my own experiences at college, the sense of confidence which grew day by day as I became more fully integrated into a system I had long before lost faith in. During my research for this chapter I realised that I was reading the same thing again and again, within the pages of each article and book: the need for people to be people. The argument for education to take on the role of another 'alternative' misses the point. I want to argue for education to be part of somebody's life, as it is mine, not because they have a mental health difficulty and therefore it will be 'meaningful' and fill their day, but because education appeals to them. Education is looking for solutions – implementing policies, naming the barriers and creating the ramps that will overcome exclusion.

For the moment we can concentrate our energies on education becoming a tool for empowerment and change and a means to people discovering that they can learn in spite of their mental health status. Students can find out that college is not just for those who were lucky in school and could sit exams, or did not have to work in the evening rather than do homework, or didn't get bullied. College is for everyone who wants to go there, and more and more it is for people who have been excluded on the grounds of requiring specific support. Without a doubt, education can prove to be a force in the struggle to end discrimination on the grounds of mental health difficulties. The doors are open and the ramps are down for people to enter.

People who are currently residing in psychiatric hospitals are enrolling on courses, no longer trapped in psychiatric ward classes. People who are using day centres are walking through college doors. Eventually those people will leave and become employees, employers, campaigners, trainers, teachers, shop assistants, parents, nurses, social workers and college staff. I feel part of a system that has the ability to see people not as bundles of symptoms, but as individuals who are able to move above and beyond the constraints of psychiatric diagnosis. A system that may still have a lot to learn about mental health, but which can offer much more than an outpatient appointment.

References

Austin, T. (1998a) The role of education in the lives of people with mental health difficulties. *A Life in the Day*, 2, 2, 6–10

Austin, T. (1998b) Creative writing and mental health – A positive partnership. *National Association of Writers in Education Journal*, June, p. 7

Bee, E. and Martin, I. (1997), The educational dimensions of mental health work. *Adults Learning*, 5, 128–31

Blunkett, D. (1998) *The Learning Age: A renaissance for a new Britain*. London: HMSO

Godding, B. and Lavender, P. (1992) Provision of education in the mental health sector. *Adults Learning*, 3, 6, 14

Kennedy, H. (1997) *Learning Works: Widening participation in further education* (The Kennedy Report). London: Further Education Funding Council

Tomlinson, J. (1996) Inclusive learning: Principles and recommendations. Learning Difficulties and/or Disabilities Committee. London:Further Education Funding Council

Ruddock, H. and Worral, I. (1997) *An outline of a current project in creative writing and literacy for people experiencing mental health difficulties*. Rotherham, Dearne Valley College

Wertheimer, A., (1997) *Images of Possibility: Creating learning opportunities for people with mental health difficulties*. Leicester: NIACE

CHAPTER 17

Green approaches to occupational and income needs in preventing chronic dependency

BRIAN DAVEY

WHAT IS A mental health crisis? Whereas the medical model emphasises things going wrong inside the individual (faulty brain chemistry as a result of a genetically caused vulnerability to stress) a holistic model approaches mental health crises as a crisis between a person and their pattern of living arrangements. In these living arrangements the specific way in which a person pursues their occupation, and gains their income, are quite crucial. Of course it is also true that these economic dimensions of existence cannot be taken in isolation; the occupational and income arrangements interpenetrate and overlap with habitat and emotional relationships. We get a better job with more pay and we can get a bigger place to live, perhaps. This may take the pressure out of our relationships because the other people we live with can have a room of their own. Our better living environments and relationships may make us happier, more relaxed and therefore more productive in our paid employment and so on. The quality of our life is therefore not made of a collection of isolated features. Our relationships are good and bad depending on our living environments, given the job and income we have. The job we have is good or bad depending on where we live, what our accommodation (and its costs) are, or with whom we are having relationships.

Adults are involved in the organisation of the pattern of their lives, co-ordinating the interwoven management of their relationships, their habitats and their economic arrangements. Day to day consciousness is pre-occupied with coping, reflection on, or planning about, this balancing act involving other people, the places we live in and visit and the things that we do in them to keep ourselves (our bodies) well. The pattern of responses available to the individual is dependent on his or her previous personal life history and what he or she has been able to learn from it to aid self-management. Typically a person will organise their life history into a story, or a set of ideas, of who they are or what they are like which will then help the person make their life management decisions. A psychological crisis occurs when an inadequate previously learned self management repertoire is confronted with a set of challenges or blocks on the normal pattern of growth and renewal for which that person has no prior learned responses. Within their previous experience, within the personal story or self-description (identity), it may be difficult or impossible to find a response to the new challenges and life tasks. They then cannot hold their mind together (including their identity) because they cannot hold the practicalities of their lives and their relationships together.

When relationships and practical arrangements break down

New tasks and challenges are inevitable to life and if they are not too large such situations may be experienced as exhilarating or exciting and as opportunities for new life (what humanist psychologists might call 'psychological growth'). If the individual is more overloaded the situation may be experienced as being unpleasantly stressful, frightening and or frustrating. If the challenge is too great and endures too long the person breaks down. The breakdown will then not only be a psychological process it will take the form of the inability of the person in crisis to continue to co-ordinate a pattern of habitat, relationships or economic arrangements. Practical arrangements for washing, eating, sleeping and relationships may break up as the mental state disintegrates. It is the structural disruption between the repertoire of learned (coping) responses and the environment together that creates the breakdown. Not surprisingly this will typically occur at points of major transition in life like separating from the parental home (Davey, 1997).

The medical response of drugs does not really help in the long term. The traditional psychotherapeutic response, which is to focus on reviewing identity through exploring the affected individual's life story is not without value. However the recovery of mental health is essentially the re-creation of a life style appropriate to age, consisting of satisfying emotional relationships, embedded in a comfortable habitat and satisfying and interesting work activities, which generate an adequate income.

The distorting effect of professional role boundaries on professional understanding

To make my point even more strongly a comparison with relativity might be useful. Einstein went beyond Newton's physics when he insisted that it did not make sense to separate space and time. They had to be taken as four dimensions that went together. In a similar way I wish to argue that the normal method of dividing up a psychological/medical brain process from a life process with economic, habitat and relationship dimensions is a convention that derives from professional specialist training and service boundaries but makes no sense if we want to understand psychiatric crises and if we want to respond helpfully to them. Precisely the problem for the individual is the creation of a unified habitat, economy and relationships pattern. Create this unified life style and one will have a unified day to day consciousness; one will be mentally well.

The professional perspective of psychiatry, their collective self interest and training create a joint point of view which is taken to be *the* reality of the situation rather than just a perspective on it from the outside formed by the role and training of the psychiatrists themselves. From the psychiatric viewpoint it appears that the person having a breakdown is in the midst of a mental crisis which is the primary and significant event that is occurring. The other things that are happening (disrupted relationships, disintegrating economic and habitat arrangements) are 'outside influences', 'further complications' or 'exacerbating circumstances' to the supposedly primary events of the mental breakdown process. This professional ideology obscures the interpenetrating and overlapping nature of the economic and habitat with the personal and psychic crisis.

A breakdown, understood as a crisis of transition in a life pattern, will be overcome when the person involved arrives at another life pattern that is satisfying for them and sustainable for them, i.e., one that they can manage for themselves. When they can hold their lives together (in a new way) they will be holding their minds together. However a life crisis may lead not to a new life but to a chronic state of helplessness and dependency with corresponding psychological features

The onset of chronic dependency

Part of the reason for the onset of chronic dependency lies in the way that the mental health services mislead people about their problems and seek solutions in medication which may remove the emotional energy from the change process. Another way in which the service creates dependency is by siding with the (more powerful) people in the person's work or personal network who are opposed to change for the person in crisis. Through these alliances, where the desire for change is described as pathological and unreasonable, the mental health services invalidate the person in crisis chronically. It is very typical for mental health professionals to pronounce that the broken down person 'will never work again'. It is likewise common to assume that they will never be able to live independently. These prophecies can have a terrible destructive effect unless the user reacts to them as a spur to prove the psychiatrists and other detractors wrong.

Partly however chronicity arises because, in a job market based on competition, a psychiatric record is just about the worst personal advertisement. Unemployment, and the poverty which tends to get associated with it, then intensifies a vicious circle for it also becomes difficult to mobilise the resources (purchasing power) to improve one's living environment (habitat) and one's impoverished personal relationships. The impoverished relationships are both because the person has not the purchasing power to get out and about, and also because real relationships are born of joint activities, but joint activities are usually very restricted without money or work.

The impoverished life style then leads to poverty of speech, flatness of affect and social isolation; the person has nothing to talk about and no one to talk to, lives in a grey limbo, suppressing hope (for fear of yet more disappointment). Fantasy satisfactions substitute for real ones. Occasionally the emotional fuel generated by the terror of dying before one has really lived breaks into bursts of crazy activity generated out of the powerful fatasies of the isolated and inactive person.

Users repeatedly say their main problem is one of income and employment

When users of the mental health services are asked what their main problems are they consistently refer to income and occupation. Their views are often discounted by mental health professionals – partly because of the medical model, partly because the professionals feel they cannot actually offer anything and do not want to listen in an area in which they themselves feel powerless. Instead the professionals offer treatment for symptoms rather than the underlying problem. But within the theoretical framework developed here, what the users have to say makes complete sense:

the absence of adequate income and occupation are strategic aspects of a general life style of systematised emotional, relationship and experiential deprivation. The mental health problems are the result of this.

What are called the 'symptoms' of psychosis do not have to be explained by reference to faulty genes and disordered brain chemistry. They are much more simply understood as the result of isolation, deprivation and inactivity which may arise when a person is unable to make a life transition and finds themselves without meaningful activities in purposeful human relationships. Anthony Storr (1994) explains how:

> *During waking hours, the brain only functions efficiently if perceptual stimuli from the external world is being received. Our relationship to the environment and our understanding of it depend on the information we gain through the senses. When asleep, our perceptions of the external world are greatly reduced, although significant sounds, like those of a child, may still arouse us. We enter the fantastic world of dreams; a hallucinatory, subjective world which is not dependent on memory in the here and now, but which is governed by our wishes, our fears and our hopes.* (Storr, 1994, p. 49–50)

Mental health workers need to listen again. When users say that a lack of income and work are their most important problems they are saying something very profound about their condition. The isolation, deprivation and the lack of purposeful activity, when combined with a lack of realistic hope that job searching or training will have positive outcomes, leads to a chronic lack of perceptual stimuli from the external world. Users are then tipped into a world of daydreams, as if they were in an endless sensory deprivation experiment and these daydreams are what the psychiatrist describes as their symptoms.

While never giving this area a high enough priority the mental health services have always recognised some importance in work for 'recovery' (in my system, a sustainable satisfying self managed life style) and an honourable few psychiatrists have given employment special attention in their thinking and practice (for example, Warner, 1985). Traditional approaches to dealing with such problems stress rehabilitative occupational therapy, training and eventually employment. Progress is measured against the ideal of a return into the competitive labour market. But not everyone can do this and in this chapter I want to make the case for another approach based on building up self supply activities and DIY, to a degree through recreation, or 're-creation'.

After a break-down people need meaningful activity in purposeful relationships. They need to re-create a life style which means to re-create a pattern of habitat, relationships, work income and body comfort. I use the hyphenated word re-create here deliberately for before one can take the stress and strain of work in a competitive labour market, with an earned income, one can re-create a life through recreation.

Trying to get into the competitive labour market

Unfortunately the results of decades of emphasising a return to the competitive labour market have not been particularly successful. In 1995 the OPCS published the results of a study carried out on the 'Economic Activity and Social Functioning of Adults with Psychiatric Disorder'. This study showed that in 1993 adults with a neurotic or psychotic disorder had a mean gross weekly income of £90 compared with the all adult mean of £150 per week. A very high proportion of users live on welfare benefits. Whereas 71% of adults with no psychiatric disorder are working, only 56% of those suffering from a neurotic disorder work and 39% of those with a psychotic disorder.

In competitive labour markets employers want workers who are able to take pressure. The competitive economy operates according to the performance principle because the undertakings that give a better product at a lower price outsell their rivals. Employers therefore put employees under pressure to meet deadlines, to reach quality standards, to attain production targets. The adverts for jobs in the newspaper say 'must be able to survive under pressure'. And the people who have had mental health problems are identified by employers as people who are liable to crumble under pressure, or even worse, start behaving unpredictably or uncontrollably when stressed. No matter how much propaganda work is done to overcome the stigma of mental health problems it looks as if users with a black mark on their employment record are bound to find it difficult to redeem themselves.

An alternative strategy to that of trying to win over existing employers is to set up work projects especially for people with mental health problems. Unfortunately and ironically this usually means operating in the most competitive fields. As a mental health development worker who previously trained as an economist I remember, a few years ago, being daunted by what would be entailed in developing an employment and training project because I would be starting without any capital. When I looked at information about the work schemes that existed elsewhere in the country their essential features seemed written in advance. Economists have a term called 'entry barriers' for the difficulties of setting up a business. If you start with little money it inevitably means that one has to go into those trades where entry barriers are very low, where it is relatively easy to start and the needed managerial talents and trade specific skills can be found generally in the population, e.g., gardening, making or retailing sandwiches, computer training and the like. In these fields market competition is usually intense. There is greater pressure from other undertakings, sales revenues are low and what one can pay, if anything will also be small.

DIY, self supply and recreation projects as an alternative

There are no ideal and complete answers in life but one approach is to organise work schemes based on self-supply. Before the competitive market economy developed in history most economic and work activity was organised around self-supply. As feminists have been pointing out for a long time not all work is paid work. Domestic labour is also work; washing up and cleaning at home, working in one's own garden, painting and decorating etc.

My colleagues and I arrived at this conclusion at the end of a process of searching. A few years ago I visited a project in Berlin called Atlantis that provided job training for young people who had had breakdowns (addiction problems) by training them in ecological fields of work. Atlantis trained people in wind energy techniques, solar energy technologies, ecological building to save energy and use non-toxic building materials, the greening of neighbourhoods through green gardening etc. I remember being very inspired by Atlantis and thinking what a huge range of job possibilities existed at all skill levels: manager, accountant, builder, gardener, engineer and designer, all in the same project. The idea inspired me too that the ecological theme must be a growing one, hence a growing market, and that it put users of the mental health services at the beginning of a process rather than at the end.

The example of Ecoworks

In Nottingham I hawked this idea around and discovered a group of people who wanted to form a Nottingham Alternative Technology Association. We joined forces and Ecoworks was born, as an alliance between some people in the user movement with our office resources and contacts and a small group of professionals with skills in architecture, building, ecological gardening, woodworking, engineering and design. At the beginning we very much saw ourselves as a smaller version of Atlantis. There were some quite high-powered people involved, however we were largely strangers to each other, the group was untried and untested and it had no substantial capital resources. The official mental health services did not understand the idea and did not support us. After some initially grandiose plans we realised we had to start very small and build up our activities step by step. We started working in a few allotment gardens and developed a protrusion window and woodworking activities with the idea of recycling wood and developing DIY approaches to saving energy and materials.

Ecoworks has now developed a long way in this organic fashion and as it developed we gradually adjusted the concept of what we were trying to achieve. Our first funding, from Social Services and Health 'joint finance', supported our ecological garden activities (permaculture) but it was stipulated that it be a leisure rather than a work project. In order to get people involved when we could not pay them what we did had to be fun. The remuneration had to be in the work satisfaction, in taking the products and crops home, in activities which reduce one's cost of living, rather than increasing one's income. Over time we began to think of this explicitly as a different kind of model. It is a model that matches the need to ecologically restructure the economy.

Ecological technologies and design principles are very much about saving energy and resources by modernising and updating self supply and DIY and through home improvement and re-using already used materials. In a host of books and magazines about the Green economy and the green future, recommendations are mostly very small-scale activities, projects and products that can be done at home, in a local community workshop and in community gardens or on one's own allotment. They are about improving life and work through improving habitat, e.g. insulation to bring fuel bills down, recycling fabrics with friends in a textile recycling club to make some wall hanging or new clothes out of old curtains. The improvement of habitat and the improvement of economic arrangements go together. Many of these activities are best done in leisure activities by a group who bounce ideas off each other and encourage others. Rather than recycling being a low-grade rag and bone activity it is one to integrate craft and art ideas: recycling is upcycling not downcycling. By making ecological renovation the theme we have attracted people into these activities who have had no previous contact with the mental health services but are interested in environmental things. Because these are all activities well within the scope of most mental health users there is no reason why mental health workers should be deeply involved. A degree in medicine or in psychology does not make one a better gardener nor give one any skills in recycling wood or running the office. Users can get involved at all levels, including taking leading roles. Relationships between users and non-users have developed without mental health workers intervening. In this way we have achieved a considerable degree of real social integration. People can feel they are not being regarded as 'cases'.

Combining community care and green community development
Rather than developing a workforce we are beginning to develop a community. We see ourselves as connecting community care and community development and are interested in the connection our projects have to their local neighbourhoods and communities. The development of a collective garden has proved a particularly positive way of bringing a diverse range of activities and very different people together. On our adjacent nine allotments we have built up step by step, shelter was needed so we re-built a hut and put a stove and sink in it for food and drink. Steps and paths followed and more huts for other activities. We needed a toilet, lighting (run first on pedal power and now on wind power), and a tree house and slides for the children. Later we needed flags, sculpture from scrap, structures from living willow. A forest garden has been planted and then supplemented. Each of these further developed the site and got more people involved so that it has become a focus not only for people with mental health problems.Community gardening is a flourishing response to urban degradation and poverty in the USA and we can understand why.

In conclusion, with Ecoworks and the related eco-sewing and crafts project we are trying to help people re-integrate their lives. We hope that through these activities people can re-create, in a relaxed and recreational way, new relationships in an evolving community of active people. We hope too that people can make some contribution to keeping living costs down, to learning skills that will help them run their habitats more cheaply and possibly pave the way to jobs later. It is a model that has enabled people to integrate on equal terms with many people from the green movement and gives participants a sense that they are part of a wider movement responding to the ecological crisis, as well as looking at what can be done in a broader search for new models of urban and community regeneration.

References

Davey, B. (1997) Meaning, madness and recovery. *Clinical Psychology Forum,* 103, 19–26

Storr, A. (1994) *Solitude.* London: Harper Collins

Warner, R. (1985) *Recovering from Schizophrenia: Psychiatry and political economy.* London: Routledge

CHAPTER 18

The future of mental health services

CRAIG NEWNES AND GUY HOLMES

T HERE IS AN extraordinary energy in and around psychiatry at the turn of the century. More money is being spent on developing and advertising new psychiatric drugs than ever before. There is a media campaign to stigmatise people with psychiatric histories as potential murderers whom the system has somehow failed. It is increasingly claimed that the genome project will reveal all that we need to know about the genetic basis for distress and disorder. The user voice is strong, both in advocating changes to services and in promoting user-led alternatives. Meanwhile there are more and more counselling and non-drug approaches to distress offered from outside the statutory services. In this chapter we explore some of the challenges facing psychiatry with particular emphasis on psychiatry's two key roles – as a state-run, drug oriented medium for social control, and as a way of helping people.

Modern psychiatry

Mainstream psychiatry once included a rich variety of psychotherapuetic as well as biochemical approaches to distress. Some of the greatest psychotherapeutic pioneers have been psychiatrists. Indeed, clinical psychology and other professions have drawn much from the work of people such as Aaron Beck, a psychiatrist, in the field of cognitive therapy. In the last twenty years, however, mainstream psychiatry has become increasingly dependent on physical interventions such as drugs and ECT. These interventions have several advantages in psychiatry's mixed role of controlling anti-social behaviour and offering what appears to be treatment for psychological distress. These include the expediency for staff of using fast acting tranquillizers on understaffed wards and the maintenance of an aura of unchallengable expertise in an area that is as obscure and confused as it is complex, i.e., the relationship between biochemistry, psychiatric treatments and personal conduct. The problem for vast numbers of individual psychiatrists and other mental health professions is, however, that they did not train in order to become agents of state control. It is a role that they find distressing, emotionally unrewarding and very demanding. (Notable critics of this coercive psychiatry include the 'Bradford Group' a collection of psychiatrists outspoken in their criticism of so-called assertive outreach programmes.)

In placing an emphasis on diagnosis and medical interventions, psychiatry opens itself up to philosophical and scientific scrutiny which it fails to adequately address. David Healy, a psychiatrist, points out some of the dangers for psychiatry in aligning itself with an exclusively biological model. He suggests that the vested interests of drug companies increase the likelihood that the intentions of stakeholders in modern neurosciences and psychopharmacology will be seen as 'duplicitous'. Furthermore, capitalism rather than altruism seems to be the dominant force in the shaping of modern psychiatry:

> *As with many other aspects of the modern marketplace, therapeutics (both psychotherapy and pharmacotherapy) at present seems to be leading to an atomization of distress. Just as the ideal market arrangements would have everyone living in a single's apartment, each complete with washing machine, dishwasher, and refrigerator, so also treatment development in practice has disconnected individuals from their social milieu.* (Healy, 1997)

Various writers in this volume have shown that the diagnostic system is fundamentally flawed (Boyle), that models of treatment practice combining drugs and psychotherapy are inconsistent (Johnstone), that the history of psychiatric treatment reveals haphazard experimentation rather than well-researched and safe treatment regimes (Newnes), and that the experiences of the recipients of services are ignored (Hudson). Causes of distress are revealed as social inequality (Williams) and oppression (Patel and Fatimilehin) rather than wayward brain biochemistry. Although these writers are not the first to make such claims, modern psychiatric textbooks rarely pay more than lip service to such issues, and regularly conclude with optimisic statements about the future of organically based psychiatry. Munro (1999), for example, confidently tells us that 'quasi-philosophical speculation will give way to objective observation' and that distress will become illness 'to be defined thereafter by psychophysiological criteria' (p.249).

Roy Porter (1997), in his monumental study of the history of medicine, is less optimistic about a scientific psychiatry's potential for helping people in distress:

> *The trump card of a new science of the brain has often enough been played, unsuccessfully, in the history of the discipline, and the claims of brain scientists to understand consciousness and its terrors have been shown to be shallow, indeed deluded. Whether civilization's treatment of the mentally ill has become more humane in a century which gassed to death tens of thousands of schizophrenics is a question which permits no comforting answers about rationality and sanity.* (Porter, 1997, p. 524)

Peter Breggin has argued that psychiatry is at the political centre of a 'multi-billion-dollar psycho-pharmaceutical complex that pushes biological and genetic theories, as well as drugs, on the society' and its powers should be dramatically curbed. The first step would be stripping the profession of its right to lock people up against their will and declare them insane. He urges a separation of the drug companies from both individual psychiatrists and the American Psychiatric Association. In addition:

> *Psychiatry and psychiatrists must not be allowed to make false claims about the genetic and biological origins of so-called mental illness. Such claims are unethical, if not fraudulent, and serve only to perpetuate the influence of the profession and individual practitioners. But if it rejected its biopsychiatric claims, the profession would admit to being something very difficult to justify or defend – a medical speciality that does not treat medical illnesses.* (Breggin, 1991, p. 408)

Alongside Breggin, several British commentators (e.g., Rogers and Pilgrim, 1996) have also highlighted the threat that the legal power of psychiatry poses to people's' rights. Psychiatry needs to separate its two key functions, so that the public is made aware that one objective of psychiatry is for the general protection of society and one is to help individuals in distress. On some occasions the two functions might coincide but more often the social control function would be distinguished from a stance of profferring individual help. Mainstream psychiatry and its control functions, typified by coercive assertive outreach schemes, the Mental Health Act, risk assessments, locked wards, involuntary treatment and the monitoring and drugging of worrying individuals would thus be differentiated from true mental health services which offered informed consent, user friendly therapies, comfort, care and practical support. This would liberate mental health services and allow the recommendations made in each chapter of this book to come to fruition. Such a separation would also remove the irony noted by some commentators (e.g., Fennel, 1996) whereby people detained under the Act are not then given treatments of proven effectiveness. They are protected from a prison term only to find themselves exposed to an indefinite period of psychiatric experimentation. The most extreme examples of this are to be found in the special hospitals, one of which, Ashworth, has faced two public enquiries in ten years. The second of these (Fallon, et al, 1999) called for its closure, a sorry advertisement for the ability of psychiatry to combine its control and helping functions.

The future of mental health sevices

In a system where the helping and social control functions of psychiatry were separate, mental health workers trying to help people would be released from feelings of being responsible for what those deemed to be mentally ill might do to themselves or others. The terror of this destroys innovative practice and always leads to back-covering caution; to recommend someone does not take or stops taking medication, or even be given full information about the harmful effects of medication, becomes frightening to a professional who fears they will be made to be responsible if the person later harms themself or another person. Most of our resources are now being spent assessing, categorising and monitoring rather than helping people. Separation of control and helping functions would make the task of mental health professionals much easier. Their role would be to create services which people wanted to use rather than do their best to manage and control a system which many people have been forced into.

Over the past two years there has been a clamour for 'evidence-based practice'. In many instances this has become a euphemism for giving everybody a mix of psychotropic medication and cognitive-behaviour therapy. It is difficult to overstate the caution with which this type of evidence should be viewed. Drug company sponsored research is published more often than independent research in professional journals which are also heavily biased towards reporting successful rather than failed treatment trials. For every positive finding of any given drug treatment there are likely to be many more unpublished examples of drug or therapy failure. Further, the complexity of the modern mental health system, featuring as it does a mixture of health professionals, relatives of the patient, general practitioner and assorted others offering advice and assistance, means that the chances are slim indeed of following any systematic treatment regime.

The evidence cited in this book suggests that we need to do more to combat the origins of mental distress. We need to address the problems of poverty, powerlessness, alienation and racism. We need to reduce the levels of physical, sexual and psychological abuse perpetrated on children and adults. We need to increase peoples' sense of physical and psychological safety, hope, self-worth, and control over their lives. People who are safe are more likely to feel safe, and do not tend to suffer from 'stress', 'agoraphobia', 'anxiety' or 'paranoia'; people who have had lives free from oppression, have had some degree of control over what happens to them and some means of escaping the hardships of life (including their own internalised oppression) do not tend to find themselves diagnosed depressed.

This requires action at all levels of society. It is not possible to outline here all the ways in which this could be achieved, and some would argue that what is needed is fundamental and revolutionary changes in our society, however some suggestions are outlined below.

Government and community action
At national and local level the Department of Health and Health Authorities would be made responsible for mental health as conceptualised by psychological well-being rather than mental illness. The people in charge of these departments would lobby for and fund changes that would improve people's quality of life, from ensuring that people live in decent accomodation to the setting a minimum wage that reduces rather than induces poverty. They would argue against changes that worsened people's mental health. For example, they would try and prevent changes that reduced the

level of protection for workers from bullying and oppression at work, on the basis that such changes increase peoples' levels of psychological insecurity and lead to anxiety related problems, psychosomatic illnesses, time off work, etc. They would argue against economic policies that did not lead to meaningful and rewarding jobs, on the basis that the only thing worse for someone's mental health than no job is a meaningless job or an oppressive workplace. At present there is no-one taking an holistic view of the underlying causes of distress. The Department of Health has no funds or remit to tackle the real causes of mental distress (e.g., poverty) and therefore spends its money on wasted searches for the medical underpinnings of experiences that have been labelled as illnesses. Under the influence of powerful lobbyists – the British Medical Association and the psychopharmaceutical industry – its officials and ministers get caught up in debates about the rights of people to have the most expensive drugs rather than the ways in which people might live lives that are less characterised by abuse, misery and fear. These lobbyists have good reason to be vocal and persistent; the pharmaceutical industry is an extraordinarily wealthy concern. Drug sales are calculated in billions of pounds while profits for psychotropic medication (half of which is not used by those to whom it is prescribed) are now calculated in hundreds of millions of pounds for many manufacturers. The influence of drug companies also extends deep into professional scientific bodies: at the 1998 Toronto convention of the American Psychiatric Association no less than 46 symposia were supported by drug companies.

Under the auspices of a Minister for psychological well-being issues such as domestic violence would be given a higher priority (you only need common sense to realise that women and children terrorised in their own homes by violent men are likely to experience 'depression' as a consequence of their oppression, and 'anxiety', 'panic disorder' and 'paranoia' due to being consistently terrified). Common sense would lead to legislation and the funding of services that would help women and children escape such violence and services that would help those men who want to change the ways in which they behave to others. At present, these services tend to be non-existent or precariously funded as these are not seen as health issues.

Individual help

In terms of how individuals seeking help are to be assisted and supported, the clear conclusion from this book is that we need to abandon the disease model. This will be incredibly difficult. When people think of the future they tend to think in terms of sci-fi: pills, machines and other techno-fixes. Although psychiatric treatments are crude (pills are not magic bullets but affect the whole of the brain and many other organs; ECT and lobotomy 'work' by creating brain damage), they are easily sold by drug companies and practitioners as high-tech and thus meet recipients' wishes for the most modern approach available. (The marketing of most psyco-active drugs features this idea of high specificity. In reality, however, drugs like so-called anti-psychotics are simply powerful tranquillisers, some of which are commonly used to suppress domestic and other animals, but marketed in a quite different way if the recipient is non-human.) People tend to think in binary, either-or, terms and tend to project discomforting feelings onto others (for centuries people have drawn comfort from locating madness in others). It is time for us to abandon this way of thinking and to see human experiences and feelings such as despair, hopelessness, terror, paranoia, confusion and the hearing of voices as on continua. These are experiences that all of us have to a greater or lesser extent, and are dependent on factors such as our current and past life experiences and ways of seeing the world. They are not illnesses. Nor are they necessarily treatable. As David Smail (1992) has remarked, this message is hard to bear for many people whose lives feel hopeless. Collective struggle, standing up to and overcoming or escaping oppression and abuse, trying to being honest and straightforward in our everyday ways of communicating with each other, enrolling on a college course, community action, making sense of our lives and experiences and all the other suggestions in this book require hard and often painful effort.

Service users

The future of mental health services envisaged by the chapter writers of this book, whatever their background, is one where current and ex-users of services have a greater role. Rather than just providing feedback and information about existing services, users should be able to pass on their expertise about how services need to be changed, and this ought to be seen as a valid role for users by the people in power in Health Authorities, NHS Trusts and Social Services. Current and ex-users of services should be paid for their work, whether that be as consultants, members of interview panels interviewing prospective employees, members of steering groups, or people providing training for existing workers. They also need to be allowed and encouraged to provide their own services, with funding agencies handing over money and control in the knowledge that users may well operate differently to professionals (e.g., have more democratic and consequently chaotic ways of making decisions). The existing track record of current providers is not good enough to have earned the right to dictate to others the best ways of helping people in psychological distress. Mental health professionals need to let go of their need to be needed, curb their instincts for colonisation, and allow users to provide services in their own way. There is plenty of evidence to suggest that crisis houses, drop-ins, housing schemes, works collectives, support groups and advocacy projects that are user controlled are very effective. Given proper funding, innovative ways of helping people are more likely to come from user groups than aged bureaucracies like the NHS and Social Services.

Social control

In terms of the social control aspect of psychiatry, there is a need for a strong national user voice to represent all those who come into this system. At present, representatives and relatives of people who have been killed by people who have been given a psychiatric diagnosis are, with media and government support, clamouring for things to be done to others that they would never countenance being done to themselves. Our society is in the grip of a movement towards everyone having either an official or moral duty to monitor people deemed to be deviant (e.g. paedophiles, illegal immigrants, benefits recipients, school truants, as well as people diagnosed as mentally ill). As part of a system that is funded to improve mental health, it seems ironic that the increasing emphasis on monitoring people diagnosed as mentally ill increases rather than reduces peoples' paranoia.

A powerful voice is needed to represent the rights of people psychiatry is monitoring, locking up without prosecution for a criminal offence, and planning to forcibly medicate. Rather than increase the powers of the Mental Health Act, we would argue for its abolition. Not guilty due to insanity would no longer be a defence: some people would have to give up their get out of jail free card. People committing crimes would enter the justice system, with their mental health being considered during sentencing, rather than be kept out of the system but face being locked up in a psychiatric institution for an indeterminate length of time without trial. Thomas Szasz has described the arguments for this in greater detail than is possible here (see Szasz, 1994). In this country we need a far-reaching public debate, not just about whether people should be locked up and treated or medicated against their will 'for their own good', but also whether people should be locked up and treated or medicated when they have not committed a crime but others do not like their anti-social behaviour or self-defined experts predict that they may commit a crime. We are very close to regarding people with a diagnosis of personality disorder as legitimate targets for coercive treatment even if they only threaten an anti-social act. In the United States such practice is already commonplace.

An equally powerful lobby is needed to protect children. Hundreds of thousands of children world-wide have now been diagnosed with Attention Deficit Hyperactivity Disorder (ADHD) and prescribed Ritalin. Indeed some parent groups demand this treatment as their 'right'. Advertisements directly appeal to teachers to consider referral of unruly children to ensure a diagnosis and treatment. The general acceptance of such practices places already vulnerable young people in a particularly precarious situation; urged not to take drugs by the state and then prescibed drugs by their doctors.

Talking therapies
Although many of the chapter writers have remarked upon some of the dangers and limits of talking therapies, particularly those that solely individualise a person's distress in terms of something that they lack or are doing wrong, there is also an acknowledgment that talking and reflecting upon one's life can be very helpful. Many therapies try to get people to see the world and their problems in the same way as the therapist, not withstanding the fact that every therapist's view of the world and mental health is different. At its worst this can lead to people being crow-barred into the therapist's model. The authors in this book emphasise the need for what Peter Hulme (chapter ten) calls collaborative conversation, where both therapist and the person seeking help meet together, as far as possible with open minds, in attempts to understand each other and work together on the person's goals. There is an emphasis on making sense of the person's difficulties, which can be therapeutic in itself but can also free the person up to make changes in their life in order to escape some of the causes of distress and get some of the things that protect people from breaking down and being overwhelmed. The therapeutic space would be one where problems, although experienced individually, could be contextualized;

internalised oppression from parents, school, work, peers or wider society could be spoken about, witnessed, thought about and put into context. Given our history of appallingly narrow ways of describing and understanding feelings and experiences traditionally labelled as mad, an open mind and commitment not to silence people's attempts to verbalise their distress and come up with their own solutions seems a good place to start.

As there is no evidence to show one type of talking treatment is any more effective than another and it is the relationship between the therapist and client which is of paramount importance, we would favour a system where choice is possible, where people seeking help are encouraged to think about what they want and people offering help are honest with themselves and their clients about what might be achieved. Clients' rights would be explicit in such a system. Therapists could make good use of the guidelines issued by organizations like the Minneapolis Walk-In Counselling Centre (Newnes, 1993). We would also echo Barker and Baldwin's (1991) demand that all those approaching a therapist should have access to an independent advocate. In such a system services would employ people on the basis of their skills in helping people (e.g., their abilities to empathise and be calm and thoughtful with people who may be agitated, distressed and confused) rather than on the basis of them having a professional qualification. People who have used services are as likely to have these skills as professionals. On top of this, they are more likely to have insights and to be able to empathise with the false hope of receiving a diagnosis, the stigma of having been in a psychiatric hospital, the crushing effects of being sectioned under the Mental Health Act, and so on. Empathy through personal disclosure has been trained out of many professionals but is a powerful way of relating to and helping people; members of the user movement seem much more aware of this.

Informed consent
Whatever the type of help being offered, enshrined within that offer should be the principle of informed consent. In terms of psychotropic medication and ECT, these issues have been discussed earlier in this book (chapters five and six). The principle should apply to all forms of help. People should be encouraged to ask the kinds of questions that have in the past made professionals uncomfortable: 'How likely is it that this type of therapy will help me? What might be the unwanted effects of accepting this type of help? What are my other options?' People should have a right to honest answers,

including, 'I don't know'.

Regarding the future of mental health services, we feel it would be a mistake to invest much hope in gene replacement therapy, smart drugs, laser lobotomy or any of the other techno-fixes that undoubtedly will be hyped and become fashionable before fading only to be replaced by another equally dramatic sci-fi style cure. Psychological distress is a fact of life due to us living in a far from perfect world. If one technology, however, is going to make a difference it could be information technology. Access to information is getting easier and easier. Professional groups will not be able to continue to pretend that they have the answers whilst everyone else is portrayed as, and made to feel, ignorant. Debate about many things in society, including mental illness, will be great. The internet may make it an open debate. The ways of understanding the world that gain ascendancy will not be in the control of those who control access to information. People will have to live with a multitude of ideas about descriptions, causes and ways of alleviating distress. It will become obvious to everyone that professionals do not know everything, and many of them know very little. Already web-sites are available giving a wealth of information about new drugs, their effects, the likely bias of researchers, the success or otherwise of particular psychiatrists and psychologists, the availability of alternative therapeutic approaches in any given location and so on. From this a healthy debate may lead to less mad ways of responding to madness. All we can hope is that the information and ideas in this book play some part in this process.

References

Barker, P.J. and Baldwin, S. (1991) In search of ethical parameters. In: P.J. Barker and S. Baldwin (eds) *Ethical Issues in Mental Health*. London: Chapman and Hall

Breggin, P. (1991) *Toxic Psychiatry*. New York: St. Martins Press

Fallon, P., Bluglass, R., Edwards, B. and Daniels, G. (1999) *Report of the Committee of Inquiry into the Personality Disorder Unit, Ashworth Special Hospital*. London: The Stationary Office

Fennell, P. (1996) *Treatment Without Consent: Law, psychiatry and the treatment of mentally disordered people since 1845*. London: Routledge

Healy, D. (1997) *The Anti-depressant Era*. Cambridge, Ma.: Harvard University Press

Munro, D. (1999) *Delusional Disorder: Paranoia and related illnesses*. Cambridge: The University Press

Newnes, C. (1993) Editorial. *Clinical Psychology Forum, 54*, 2

Porter, R. (1997) *The Greatest Benefit to Mankind – A medical history of* humanity from antiquity to the present. London: Harper Collins

Rogers, A. and Pilgrim, D. (1996) Mental Health Policy in Britain. Basingstoke: Macmillan Press

Smail, D. (1992) Psychotherapeutic theory and wishful thinking. Changes: An International Journal of Psychology and Psychotherapy, 10, 4, 274–81

Szasz, T.S. (1994) Cruel Compassion: Psychiatric control of society's unwanted. Chichester: Wiley

CONTRIBUTORS

Katy Arscott is a clinical psychologist working in learning disabilities, based part-time at the Tizard Centre, University of Kent. Her previous work in adult mental health settings has influenced her current thinking and practice and she has a particular interest in the uses and abuses of medication and ECT. Her published research is in the area of informed consent.

Tracey Austin is a lecturer working specifically with students who have identified mental health difficulties. She has worked both within further education and a social and health services setting. Her work in education has led to her participation in numerous national conferences as a workshop leader and she is currently a member of the *Life in the Day* editorial board. She is particularly committed to developing educational opportunities for long term mental health service users and survivors of psychiatry.

Janet Bostock worked as a community clinical psychologist in Nottingham for nine years with local communities, health and community workers. She has recently published work in the areas of women's experiences and community psychology, and is now based in Northumberland.

Mary Boyle is professor and head of the doctoral degree in clinical psychology at the University of East London. She has published widely on social and cultural influences on psychiatric and psychological theory and is the author of *Schizophrenia: A scientific delusion?* (Routledge, 1993).

Peter Campbell is a mental health system survivor. He worked for many years with pre-school children. He is a founder member of Survivors Speak Out and of Survivors' Poetry and has been involved in action to change the mental health system since the early 1980s. He now works as a freelance writer and trainer and as a performing poet. He has contributed chapters to *Mental Health Care in Crisis* (Pluto Press) and *Speaking Our Minds* (OUP).

Ron Coleman is an ex-user of services and has been running interactive workshops, principally about hearing voices, for three years. He is also founder of the Hearing Voices Network and a Director of Handsell Publishing.

David Crepaz-Keay received a range of psychiatric treatment for over ten years and has also received six diagnoses including schizophrenia and personality disorder. He is currently Deputy Director of Mental Health Media, Specialist User Consultant to the Centre for Mental Health Services Development and an Associate of the Mental Health Foundation.

Brian Davey trained as an economist and has worked for several years in the mental health services user movement. Growing disillusioned with how little is achieved talking with the mental health services he has for the last few years been developing a project called Ecoworks where users of the mental health services are working on community economic and environment issues.

Cailzie Dunn is a clinical psychologist working in a Community Mental Health Team in Shrewsbury. She has interests in working with people who hear voices, and in finding alternatives to psychiatry.

Iyabo Fatimilehin is a clinical psychologist working with children and families in Liverpool. She has a specific remit to facilitate the development of services for families from ethnic minority groups. She has research and practice interests in service delivery as well as the racial and ethnic identities of adolescents.

Lesley Hitchman is presently in New Zealand working for Auckland Healthcare Services Ltd. as a clinical psychologist in a CMHT. As part of her work she is involved in a treatment programme for people diagnosed with borderline personality disorder using the model of dialectical behaviour therapy developed by Marsha Linehan.

Guy Holmes is a clinical psychologist working in Telford. He has published articles on users' views of services, patients' councils, the medicalisation of human distress, sexual abuse, and psychotropic medication. He has an interest in dogs, people and justice.

Marese Hudson is an ex-user of the mental health system. She had previously been an assistant psychiatric nurse and was married to a psychiatric nurse. She supports self-advocacy through Shelton Patients' Council and is a trainer for various professional groups.

Peter Hulme is a clinical psychologist working collaboratively with very distressed clients who hear voices.

Pam Jenkinson has worked for more than twenty years in voluntary mental health organisations. She has run support groups and training programmes for the National Schizophrenia Fellowship and has served on its National Council. All her involvement with mental health has been personal, either through her own or family experience. Pam describes herself as a 'radical separatist' and holds the philosophy that just as a musical person can compose and play music and thus be a musician without seeking qualifications or membership of any institution, so can the person who is interested in mental health promote and provide for mental health without seeking professional status.

Lucy Johnstone trained as a clinical psychologist and spent 11 years working in the NHS before moving to her present post as senior lecturer in clinical psychology and counselling at the University of the West of England, Bristol. She is the author of *Users and Abusers of Psychiatry* (Routledge, 1989, 2nd edition 2000) and a number of articles taking a critical view of traditional psychiatric practice. She has recently researched into psychological trauma after ECT.

Viv Lindow is a survivor of the psychiatric system who is interested in the psychiatric survivors' liberation movement in all its forms including the provision of survivor-run projects of many kinds. She works as a freelance researcher, trainer and consultant on mental health issues. She is author of *Self Help Alternatives to Mental Health Service* (MIND).

Val Noble was born and brought up in St Ann's in Nottingham, worked with the Probation Service from 1984, and as a Community Counsellor for ACTIONS for three years. She now works for the Probation Service in Torquay addressing issues such as homelessness, unemployment and poverty.

Craig Newnes is a dad and gardener. He is Psychological Therapies Director in Shropshire's Community and Mental Health Services NHS Trust and editor of *Changes: An International Journal of Psychology and Psychotherapy*.

Nimisha Patel is clinical director on the doctoral clinical psychology course at the University of East London. She also works as a clinical psychologist at the Medical Foundation Caring for Victims of Torture. She has research and practice interests in developing appropriate services for black and minority ethnic people including working with refugee people and survivors of political violence.

David Pilgrim is a consultant clinical psychologist at Communicare NHS Trust, Blackburn and Visiting Professor of Mental Health at the Department of Sociology, University of Liverpool. His books include: *Clinical*

Psychology Observed (with Andy Treacher, Routledge, 1992); *Experiencing Psychiatry: Users' views of services* (with Anne Rogers and Ron Lacey, Macmillan, 1993); *A Sociology of Mental Health and Illness* (with Anne Rogers, OUP, 1993); *Mental Health Policy in Britain* (with Anne Rogers, Macmillan, 1996); and *Psychotherapy and Society* (Sage, 1997).

Jennie Williams is a clinical psychologist working at the Tizard Centre at the University of Kent. She is concerned about the effects of social inequalities on mental health and on mental health services, and about ways in which these issues continue to be disregarded within services. She has published numerous articles about gender issues in mental health services.

Rachel Winter has worked with ACTIONS as a Community Counsellor for three years. She has wide and long-standing experience of work in primary care, mental health and voluntary settings, particularly in areas of disadvantage.

NAME INDEX

SUBJECT INDEX

Implausible Professions
Arguments for Pluralism and Autonomy in Psychotherapy and Counselling

edited by Richard House and Nick Totton
1997 ISBN 1 898059 17 9   148x210   pp348   £16.00

Twenty-eight papers, with contributions from Val Blomfield, Cal Cannon, Jill Davies, Michael Eales, Colin Feltham, Guy Gladstone, Marion Hall, Sue Hatfield, Catherine Hayes, John Heron, Richard House, Juliet Lamont, Peter Lomas, Michael McMillan, Katharine Mair, Richard Mowbray, Denis Postle, Andrew Samuels, Robin Shohet, David Smail, Annie Spencer, Brian Thorne, Nick Totton and David Wasdell.

> 'Implausible Professions stimulates, educates and challenges the reader at every turn, and could easily become a core text in any psychotherapy training... This is not some smooth political offering but a very human, very rich compendium of research, thought, feeling and experience. The many quotes and references mean that probably a hundred or more voices are all singing the same song: a powerful chorus. This book makes it easy for us to develop our own response by delivering hundreds of hours of the preliminary hard work... Buy it now.'
>   Christopher J. Coulson Self & Society March 1998

> 'House and Totton bring together many voices against the regulation of a kind of work that surely should have as one of its foundational aims the provision of a space for varieties of experience that escape the constraints of our administered world. the arguments collected here are invaluable for the development of that kind of work... A careful reading of this book would serve to open up questions about registration and help therapists and clients register their dissent and find some better ways forward.'
>   Ian Parker The European Journal of Psychotherapy, Counselling and Health, Vol. 1 No.3 Dec 1998

> 'I sometimes found this book uncomfortable, for it challenged some of my own beliefs and consistently made me reflect on what I am doing and my own transferential attitudes to these matters. I believe anyone involved in any psychotherapy or counselling regulating body, in training, accreditation, supervision, research or practice would benefit from reading this book...'
>   Whizz Collis International Journal of Psychotherapy, Vol.3 No.2 1998

> 'At last a book on counselling and psychotherapy that demands to be read. What you get here is a lot of what Virginia Satir once called 'levelling' — telling the honest truth ... Together they [the authors] demonstrate the persistence in many humanistic practitioners of a deep tenacity and groundedness that resist the creeping 'McDonaldisation' of the treatment of contemporary woe that the professionalisation process has ushered in.'
>   David Kalisch Self & Society March 1998

First Steps in Counselling 2nd edition
A Students' Companion for Basic Introductory Courses

Pete Sanders
1996 ISBN 1 898059 14 4 200x200 pp138+vi £11.00

This bestselling book is used as the standard course text on hunderds of basic courses in colleges and independent training institutes throughout the UK. Now in its second edition it comprehensively covers the theory, skills and contextual issues of counselling in the 1990s for all those wanting an introduction to counselling. Each year some 5000 volunteers, social workers, carers, teachers, nurses, community workers, managers, beginning counsellors and their trainers use *First Steps in Counselling* as their starting point for learning.

'This is the second edition of a remarkable book. Its title suggests that it is for beginners only but this is far too modest a claim. . .

The reader is swept into companionship with a trainer and practitioner who knows his subject from top to bottom and who is keenly alert to the whole range of tensions that arise as counselling 'comes of age' in our society. Pete makes no apology for confronting his beginners with some of the harsh realities of what it means to be a counsellor as the twentieth century draws to a close.

At no point, however, does he assume an authoritarian or prescriptive stance. He imparts information — some of it complex and detailed — with lightness of touch . . .

For beginners and their tutors this book will be a resource without price but for the seasoned practitioner, too, it offers much more than an elegant revision course.'

Professor Brian Thorne

'. . . highly accessible with good use of text, diagrams, discussion points and exercises. Sanders' writing style and his creative and appropriate use of poems and popular song lyrics is engaging and adds to the accessible quality and tone of this impressive series*. With suggestions on reading, personal exploration and development, the books parallel — and truly accompany — the learning process.'

Keith Tudor *Person Centred Practice, Vol.5 No.1*

* Series includes *Next Steps in Counselling* by Alan Frankland and Pete Sanders, and *Step in to Study Counselling* by Pete Sanders. All Available from bookshops or direct from PCCS Books by calling 01989 770 707 for discounts or emailing sales@pccsbks.globalnet.co.uk.